S.F.B.J.
Captivating Character Children

by Ann Marie and Jacques Porot
and Francois Theimer

Published by   HOBBY HOUSE PRESS, INC.

Cumberland, Maryland 21502

Additional copies of this book may be purchased at $25.00
from
HOBBY HOUSE PRESS, INC.
900 Frederick Street
Cumberland, Maryland 21502
or from your favorite bookstore or dealer.
Please add $2.75 per copy postage.

Printed in the United States of America
ISBN: 0-87588-279-X

Acknowledgments

We thank all the collectors and friends who have been so willing to help us with information and documents, particularly: Mesdames Azou, Bellancourt, Borel, Brisou, Broust, Chauveau, Chovet, Du Buisson, Dulac, Fichter, Flé, Girard, Godard, Hocq, Jacquier, Lauroua, Mantel, Ogino, Pesche, Petrement, Robert, Sambat, Simon, Strawczynski, Wothe and Messieurs, Bailly, Bazin, Bossi, Cheval, Malafosse, Peigne, Plancke, Griffith, as well as:

Le Musée des Arts Décoratifs: Mmes Burckhardt and Spadaccini

Les Éditions Gautier-Languereau: Mme Canlorbe

La Revue du Jouet: Mr and Mme Chapelon

La Galerie de Chartres: Mes J. and J.P. Lelièvre Commissaires-Priseurs

La Salle des Ventes de Bourges: Me Darmancier

La Salle des Ventes Drouot: Me Gilles Néret-Minet

Le Tribunal de Commerce de al Seine: Mr Rogeron

L'Institut National de la Propriété Industrielle: Mmes Verderosa and Monka, Mr Colette and staff

le Conservatoire National des Arts et Métiers: the staff of the Bibliothèque

Les Archives Départementales de la Seine

Maîtres Philippot et Berthon

Mr and Mme Moynot

The color photographs are by: Mesdames and Messieurs Azou, Doumic, Fichter and Simon from the collections of Mesdames Azou, Chovet, Fichter, R.B. and Sambat. All the photographs, black and white or color, not otherwise attributed, are by Jacques Porot.

Translation by Abigail DeSoto in collaboration with Didier Don, Barbara Grafe, Dafna Ben-Nath, Sarah Stewart, and Yen Smith.

Table of Contents

Preface
by Jacques Porot

In 1899, several French doll makers and one German toy maker combined forces to create a syndicate entitled *Société Français Fabrication Bébés et Jouets* (the French Society for the Fabrication of Dolls and Toys), better known to collectors as S.F.B.J.

The creation of the S.F.B.J. provides an interesting example of the evolution which took place in the European toy industry at the end of the 19th century. Such industrial consolidation was not unique. In Paris during the same period, other toy manufacturers combined to organize the *Jouet de Paris*. What is most remarkable in the case of the S.F.B.J. is the fact that this merger brought together toy and doll making which at that time in Paris were normally separate industries. Further, it also brought together German and French manufacturers at a period when the competition between them was reputed to be merciless and sometimes unfair.

Since the 1880s, the sale of manufactured toys and dolls had increased appreciably in Europe; the middle classes were a little richer, industrialization had brought about lower prices, and German sales methods had mastered the technique of creating demand. This was true to so great a degree that there was room for all manufacturers. French and German manufacturers could, for a considerable length of time, each turn out their products according to the standards that best suited them. The French were credited with inventiveness and high quality, but were encumbered by the high prices which remained for their products. The Germans had the advantage of moderate prices for their goods, and were able to maintain a generally satisfactory level of quality. Furthermore, there were specific characteristics of a technical order. The French were better at dressing dolls, but the Germans made extremely fine heads at competitive prices. It is not surprising, then, that even before the creation of the "cartel," close relations had been established among manufacturers and between dealers and customers on both sides of the Rhine. From such commercial trade-offs to associating in business was an easy step to take. Jumeau and Fleischmann took it without difficulty and painlessly.

It is true that Salomon Fleischmann, by the end of the century, had already been established in Paris for some time, first as an importer, then as an "assembler." He was married to a French woman, and his descendants have always occupied important posts in the S.F.B.J., to the point that one may consider that the S.F.B.J. was for a very long time a family affair. (This is true also for the Girard and Gaultier families.) There was only one relatively brief break in this continuity: the 1914-1918 war. Fleischmann had become a Frenchman by adoption, but had neglected to become naturalized. It became necessary for him to leave France at the declaration of this war which he had certainly wanted. But it was only he personally who had to get out of the country; his French family retained all of their rights in the S.F.B.J. Their holdings were sequestered, but were restored to them in 1919. Unfortunately, Fleischmann had died in exile at San Sebastian in Spain before the end of the hostilities.

Fleischmann, as an importer, had a toy agency in Paris. Dolls were included in his business, but as *article d'appel* or "loss leaders" or "come-ons." His dolls were very inexpensive, sold perhaps at even less than their real value. He was thus assured of the loyalty of his clients: commissioned agents, bazaars, department stores and retailers. For these dolls, he acquired some parts in France and others in Germany and had them assembled in Paris. He also manufactured some parts in a factory which he had set up in the rue Montempoivre. Since the dolls were no more than a loss leader item, he did not take great care to fall into line with the high quality, high priced products that the French doll manufacturers were turning out.

There were only a few French doll makers left by the end of the century. Jumeau had taken such a leading role in the mass production of dolls that his competition had run out of breath, then collapsed. There was little left except for the house of Bru, now run by the Girard family. Steiner had greatly cut back. Danel, who with his *Paris Bébé* had given Jumeau some competition for a time, had been once and for all put out of the running after the trial of 1892. There still remained one important firm, that of the Gaultier Brothers. But they made only porcelain heads which they supplied to other manufacturers. Pintel, who also became a part of the S.F.B.J., like Fleischmann furnished the market with inexpensive dolls.

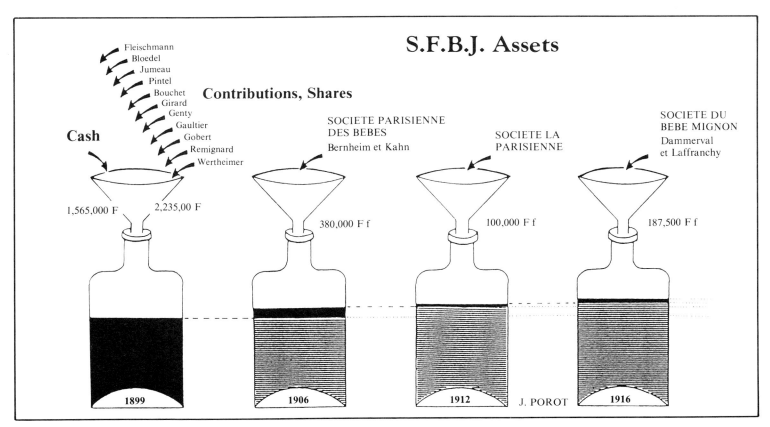

S.F.B.J. Assets

Fleischmann
Bloedel
Jumeau
Pintel
Bouchet
Girard
Genty
Gaultier
Gobert
Remignard
Wertheimer

Cash

Contributions, Shares

SOCIETE PARISIENNE DES BEBES
Bernheim et Kahn

SOCIETE LA PARISIENNE

SOCIETE DU BEBE MIGNON
Dammerval et Laffranchy

1,565,000 F   2,235,00 F   380,000 F f   100,000 F f   187,500 F f

1899   1906   1912   J. POROT   1916

As for Jumeau, we have good reason to believe that for some years he had been losing interest in the manufacture of dolls. There were, moreover, financial difficulties. He was having to borrow money in order to assure the survival of his enterprise. Why were there difficulties, since his dolls were highly valued and were selling well? It was just that to manufacture dolls exclusively was no longer profitable. Like the Germans, one had to make dolls and toys. Jumeau, then 56 years old, was not disposed towards this new orientation. Associating with Fleischmann offered him an opportunity. Nothing justifies our saying today that Jumeau was crushed under or dominated or cheated by Fleischmann.

It is scarcely probable, either, that Jumeau, through his prestige or his political connections, thought that he could draw Fleischmann into an association which would end up being a trap. It seems to us much more sensible to conclude that the Fleischmann-Jumeau merger was an *alliance de raison*, a mutually beneficial association. If we speak only of Fleischmann and Jumeau it is because the other partners had only a very small share in the affair. The Fleischmann-Jumeau union seemed surprising to us for quite a time, almost inexplicable when judging it through the works of Leo Claretie where the French-German rivalry was presented in a terrifying guise. In point of fact, on the practical plane, relations were both realistic and very carefully delineated. There was rivalry, certainly and competitiveness, of course, but who would have been so foolish as to turn his back on an arrangement which was both necessary and profitable? We think that it was in this sort of climate that the S.F.B.J. was created.

The two attached tables will make clear the part played by each of the partners in the joint venture of the S.F.B.J. If the Society was created through Fleischmann's initiative, Jumeau was the major stockholder. Bloedel was no more than a financial associate for Fleischmann; he was not a toy maker, nor even a merchant. The tables also show that the contributions added after 1899 scarcely made any difference in the makeup or even in the capitol volume of the firm.

In the S.F.B.J. merger came the marriage of dolls and toys. Fleischmann contributed toys to the company, Jumeau contributed dolls. This explains why the S.F.B.J. dolls continued to be referred to as "Jumeau dolls" for many years.

And, further, it is thus that a source of toy multi-national, a "toy-Europe" came into being. Perhaps it was because the pressures of American competition were already beginning to be felt.

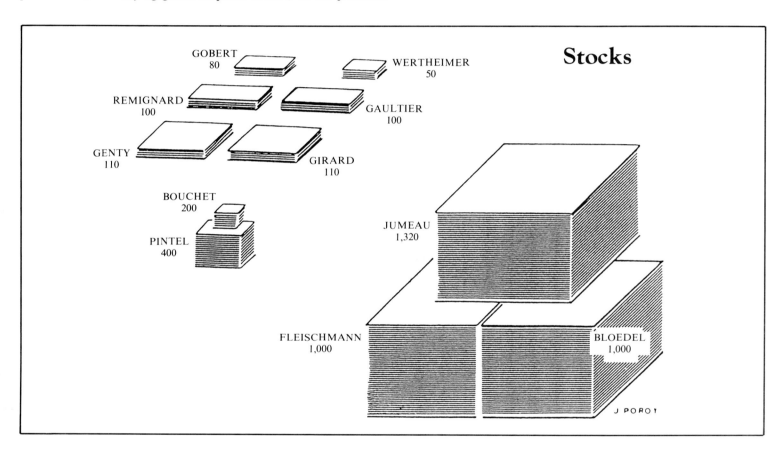

I

L'Histoire
History

by François Theimer

Post card showing "Jumeau" bébés at the Exposition of 1900. *A.M. Porot Collection.*

LES BÉBÉS JUMEAU A L'EXPOSITION DE 1900 - HORS CONCOURS

Post card of "Les Bébés Jumeau" at the 1900 Exposition. *A.M. Porot Collection.*

Les apporteurs dans la S.F.B.J.
S.F.B.J. Contributors

Société Fleischmann & Bloedel

Société Fleischmann and Bloedel contributed the factory at 2-4-6 rue Montempoivre in Paris, which made the S.F.B.J. "cheaper" baby dolls. They also contributed the store at 160 rue Picpus, right in front of the Vincennes Wood, called the "*Villa de la Porte Dorée*" (the Golden Door Villa). The factory was rented in 1893 with an 18 year lease. The structure at number 2 was an enlargement of the initial building and rented in 1896 for 15 years. Sale pledges gave purchase deadlines of 1911 for all three buildings.

Fleischmann and Bloedel did not contribute their show room in the Temple quarter, 51 rue de Turbigo or their business office in Fürth in Bavaria.

The *Eden-Bébé* brand, as well as the registered trademarks of the company went to the new company. On the other hand, the *Bébé Triomphe* brand was retained even though it was registered one year before the creation of the S.F.B.J.

The Fleischmann and Bloedel company was accorded the maximum number of shares, about 2,000, which represented 27.63 percent of S.F.B.J.

47355. — M. p. désigner des articles de bimbeloterie et de bazars, jouets de toutes sortes, etc., déposée le 1er juin 1895, à 1 h. 20, au greffe du tribunal de commerce de la Seine, pour la *Société Fleischmann et Bloedel*, manufacturiers à Paris.

Cette marque est de dimensions et de couleurs variables. Elle s'appose sur les produits et sur leurs emballages.

Trademark registered in 1890 by Fleischmann & Bloedel in *Bulletin Officiel de la Propriete Industrielle*.

CL. XLIV — JEUX ET JOUETS.

EDEN-BÉBÉ

33072. — M. p. désigner des bébés-jouets, déposée le 31 mars 1890, à 2 h. 40, au greffe du tribunal de commerce de la Seine, par la *Société Fleischmann et Bloedel*, fabricants de jouets à Paris.

A 1895 trademark registered by Fleischmann & Bloedel.

799.2. — M. p. désigner des jouets de tous genres, déposée le 5 juin 1903, à 1 h., au greffe du tribunal de commerce de la Seine, par la *Société Fleischmann et Bloedel*, fabricants à Paris.

Cette marque s'appose par tous moyens appropriés et en toutes couleurs sur les produits, ainsi que sur les boîtes, étuis et emballages les renfermant, etc.

A trademark registered in 1898 by Fleischmann & Bloedel.

Trademarks registered by the Société Fleischmann & Bloedel before the creation of the S.F.B.J.:

204 739	4/1/1890	Attachment system
204 800	4/1/1890	Attachment system
210 529	12/30/1890	New kind of articulated doll
221 685	5/17/1892	Unbreakable clay for doll production
236 162	2/9/1894	Eye mechanism
236 639	2/28/1894	Walking baby doll
239 230	6/11/1894	Walking mechanism
239 738	7/2/1894	Walking mechanism
241 365	9/12/1894	"Kiss-throwing" mechanism
243 005	11/20/1894	Auto-walking baby doll
263 708	2/3/1897	Combined movement baby doll

Société Pintel & Godchaux

This was Fleischmann & Bloedel's chief competitor in making "cheap articles." Henri Pintel and Ernest Godchaux had created the partnership Pintel & Godchaux June 28, 1890. They used the initials P.G. for their doll heads. The headquarters was at 4 avenue du Trône.

This factory made dolls and toys in papier-mâché, porcelain, rubber and other materials. But bisque heads were made by the porcelain-works Gaultier Frères.

The name and the factory mark *Bébé Charmant* was brought to the S.F.B.J. but never used. There was no registration of this brand. A study of the patent registered by Henri Pintel on January 1, 1890, with the addendum certificate, is confusing because it is entitled "Production procedures for articulated clay baby dolls." In fact, it is a catch system of elastic attachments for the limbs of clay dolls.

This establishment produced other toys and odds and ends which it continued to produce and sell.

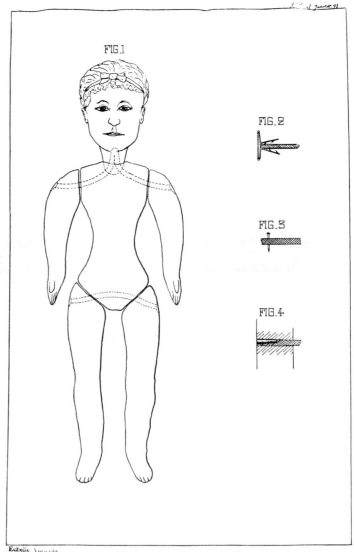

ABOVE and BELOW: Drawings from patents registered by Henri Pintel.

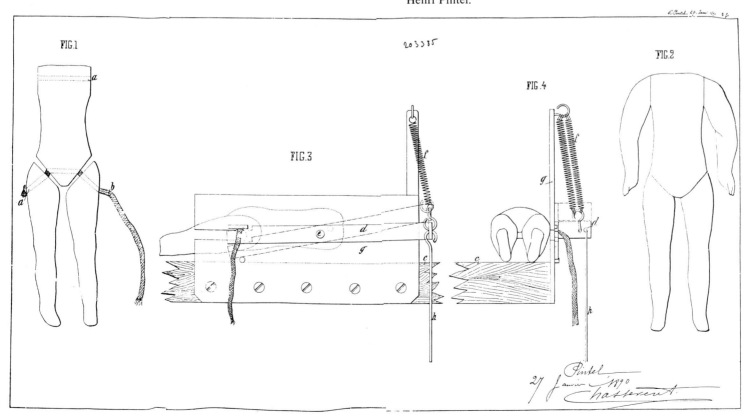

Monsieur Bouchet

Monsieur Adolphe-Henri Bouchet had a small factory for medium quality dolls which was situated at 24-26 rue de Cauchy, overlooking the Seine, at the limit of the old Grenelle and Vaugirard "communes." His show room was at 169 rue du Temple, close to that of Fleischmann and Bloedel (rue de Turbigo).

In 1890, he appeared for the first time in the *Almanach du Commerce*, the commercial almanac. Whatever the case, it was June 6, 1894, that he registered his first patent for a doll made in his factory. He called it *l'Indestructible* (the Indestructable); it was made with rubber head and hands, paperweight eyes, and a cardboard body.

A few months later on August 22, 1894, another patent was added. It was for another doll head attachment, which he called *Bébé a tête mobile* (doll with movable head) because the head was removable.

Finally, on June 4, 1898, the last patent was registered for a procedure for making dolls and doll heads of paper, cardboard and clay.

No drawings accompany the patents to allow recognition of his products. None of the trade names of his dolls, such as *Bébé geant, Gentil Bébé, l'Indestructible, Bébé à tête mobile* or *Bébé musique* were registered as a factory make. Monsieur Bouchet received 200 shares of S.F.B.J.

Monsieur Genty

Emile Louis Genty owned a show room in Paris, 63 rue des Archives, and a factory in Limeil. Information on Genty is hardly plentiful — there is no record of patent or factory make registration. A name used, however, was that of *Bébé de Paris*. The percentage of 110 shares he received indicates it was a very small firm.

Monsieur Paul Girard

Paul Eugène Frederic Girard, was the successor to the Casimir Bru house which was founded in 1867 and which appeared in the *Almanach du Commerce* in 1868.

The firm made *poupées* as well as *bébés*. Its very special doll with a kid body was unique in the world of dolls at this period. The body, patented March 18, 1879, was improved by Henri Chevrot's patent of November 23, 1883, which added clever articulation.

Henri Chevrot took over from Casimir Bru, Junior, in 1883. He directed the house until 1890, when he passed it on to Paul Girard.

Because it specialized in high quality dolls, the Bru firm was jolted during the last hard ten years of the 19th century. Its rich and foreign clientele diminished as did that of the Jumeau house.

Paul Girard encountered more and more problems, and was obliged to make more and more commercial concessions. In the 1892 catalog supplement to the paper *la Mode Illustrée*, the recognizable kid doll was no longer advertised; all the dolls had articulated wooden or composition bodies. The *Modèle Extra* (extra model) had a hollow wooden body at the Girard period. Paul Girard only sold dolls under the name of *Bébé Bru*. He registered the factory make on July 4, 1891.

Despite all the innovations and improvements to the dolls, the face of the old, prestigious firm completely changed. In the battle of patents, it was once Bru who could best produce the most complex doll. Girard, like the other French firms, lost momentum and once ruined, he yielded the vestiges of his business to the S.F.B.J. He received 110 shares, the same as a small establishment.

Trademarks registered by Mr. Girard of Maison Bru in 1891 in the *Bulletin Officiel de la Propriete Industrielle*.

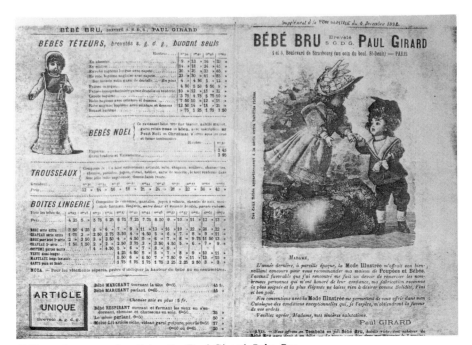

1892 catalog page advertising the Paul Girard *Bebe Bru*.

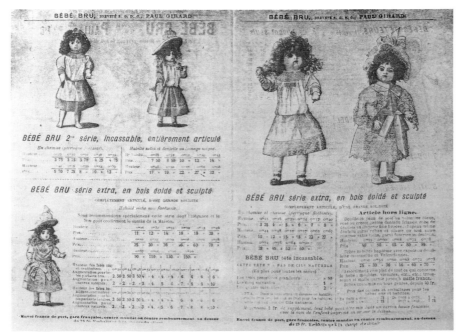

Advertisement of the Paul Girard *Bébé Bru*.

Brevets déposés par Paul Girard
Trademarks registered by Paul Girard

214 359	6/22/1891	System for movable eyes and eyelids.
216 294	9/23/1891	Walking, talking doll called *Bébé petit pas*. Additional certificate registered on 2/25/1892.
220 001	3/9/1892	Breathing, talking, sleeping doll. Additional certificate registered on 8/12/1895.
247 060	5/1/1897	Kissing doll.
264 955	3/13/1897	Doll with complex movements.

Like a number of other manufacturers, Paul Girard was very interested in perfecting the doll's mechanics. Towards the end of the century these dolls became more and more like automatons, as the "Pygmalion" manufacturers sacrificed aesthetics to animation.

A trademark registered by Remingard in 1888.

Monsieur Frédéric Remignard

Frédéric Remignard owned a shop in the Temple area, located at 14 bis, rue des Minimes. He could hardly be called a manufacturer, since he produced and sold only one doll model exclusive to him. On November 9, 1888, he registered this *Petit Chérubim* as a trademark.

He obtained 100 shares of the invested capital of S.F.B.J., which is *a priori* a large transaction for a small merchant as compared to a formerly great company such as Monsieur Girard's.

La Société Gaultier Frères
The Gaultier Brothers Company

This partnership was comprised of Emile-Jules and Eugène Gaultier, sons of François, founder of the Gaultier company. The registered offices were at St. Maur. The company was founded in 1888, and manufactured porcelain objects, including doll heads. This company supplied a great number of doll assemblers since there were few factories as complete as Jumeau's and Steiner's. Pintel and Godchaux, for example, were customers. The Gaultier Brothers Company signed many heads using the initials F.G. (Frères Gaultier) of their factory, a practice demanded by their customers. Pintel and Godchaux signed their products P.G., and the Falck-Roussel Co. used the letters F.R. and so on.

Going by the evidence of their 1884 catalog, the Gaultier Company seems to have been set up in 1860. It has been known since the Second World Congress of Old Doll Collectors[1] that François Gualtier brought a suit against the government because his name was misspelled, as "Gauthier" instead of "Gaultier," after his birth certificates were lost in a fire in the Paris Town Hall. This error caused him great injury and even today there is still confusion. This is why the 1872 patent must be attributed with certainty to the founder of the Gaultier firm, even if the name *is* misprinted, since this was before the lawsuit took place. This company which supplied so many doll heads, received only 100 shares, the same amount as Monsieur Remignard. It should not be forgotten, however, that the company did not own the factory in the rue des Epinettes, and so their only contribution to S.F.B.J. was to supply materials and products.

The only existing patent which François Gaultier took out, on February 21, 1873 (first registered on December 2, 1872), was for the perfecting of doll heads. The S.F.B.J. could not take advantage of this patent, since it fell into public domain.

Monsieur Gobert

Alphonse-Benoît Gobert owned a small factory which, like those of his colleagues, was on the outskirts of Paris, at 186 bis, rue de l'Alisia. Most of the doll factories lay within the Octroi Gate (the customs limit of Paris) because the raw materials were taxed on entry into the city.

Monsieur Gobert's doll was called *Bébé Colosse* but was never registered as a trademark. He received 80 shares of S.F.B.J. Here again, there was no building contribution.

---

[1] A conference in Paris in 1982 given by Madame Poison, curator of the Roybe-Fould Museum at Courbevoie and President of the C.E.R.P.

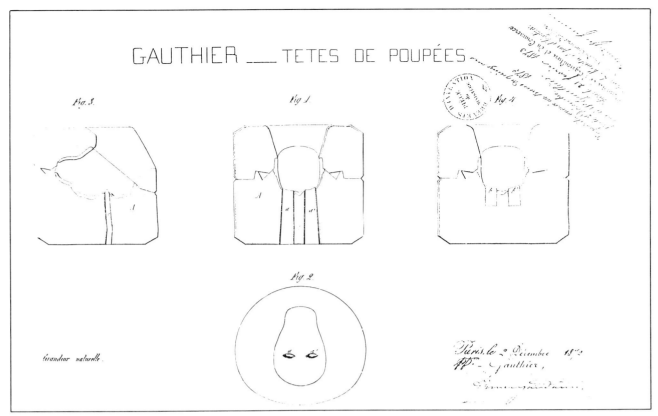

Drawings from doll head patent registered by Gauthier in 1873.

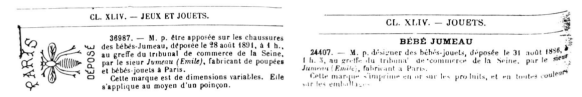

Trademarks registered in the *Bulletin Officiel de la Propriete Industrielle* by Société Jumeau & Co. in 1896.

Monsieur Wertheimer

Arthur Wertheimer's commercial base was in the rue Pastourelle, at number 21, not far from Jumeau's factory. It would become the social seat of S.F.B.J. The name *Le Baby* was not registered, and was used by the Wertheimer firm. He was the S.F.B.J.'s smallest contributor and received 50 shares.

Emile Jumeau

The Jumeau company, formed around 1842 by Pierre-Francois Jumeau and directed with a master's touch by his second son Emile after 1872, ran into serious difficulties towards the end of the 19th century.

Emile Jumeau followed the trend by changing his production, and creating new categories of average quality dolls in addition to luxury dolls. But it was a severe blow to his exports (which comprised 30 percent of his trade) when heavy taxes were imposed on the exportation of goods to the United States. Although French competition was stiff, he was never in conflict with the Maison Bru, which was far too small to pose any kind of threat. The many small doll assemblers who surrounded him from 1876 onwards were the menace. They adapted, copied and plagiarized his *Bébé articule* (articulated doll). The Danel case in 1891 showed Jumeau that his empire was in danger. He was obliged from this point onwards, as were his colleagues, to turn his interest towards novelty goods and the dolls made in his factories after 1892 were of lower quality.

In 1893, the idea of the *Lioregraph Jumeau* inspired by Edison's talking doll, showed how he had changed direction. It was evident to Emile Jumeau that if his doll was talking, its mouth must be open. This head model was officially continued by Jumeau's factory. He realized that by aiming at the novelty market, he would bring himself into the highest strata of the world of articulated dolls. Looking at the doll production at the end of the century, it can be seen that the doll was becoming further and further removed from its original aspect. It could do many things: it talked, threw kisses, nursed, opened and shut its eyes, shouted, cried and walked. But where was the *real* doll, which charmed children in 1876? Simply articulated, aesthetically perfect, the bébés, perfection cast its aura over French manufacturers in 1899 at the Universal Exhibition and was crowned by an unprecedented victory: golden medals for all of them. Jumeau's *bébé* was named as being above competition. What had happened to this magnificent doll? This is a question which Emile Jumeau must surely have asked himself. This industrial genius who, unlike Salomon Fleischmann, prized quality above quantity.

The patent war continued to be waged, and Emile Jumeau clutched at one last straw: dolls with character faces. This fabulous series of impressive and varied faces did not have the success anticipated. It is, however, an entrancing series of studies, from mold number 200 to number 220 (excepting number 213). These numbers were all listed in the inventory made for the founding of the S.F.B.J. The numbers 221-225 have not been found.

Emile Jumeau, having played his last card, was crushed in the path of all these changes. He was a forerunner of what was to come. The factories at Montreuil, 64, rue François Arago and 152 rue de Paris which had removed themselves from each other to prevent any communication of ideas, became the S.F.B.J.'s industrial base. The dress-pattern shop at 8, rue Pastourelle, whose windows were so ably dressed by Ernestine-Stephanie Ducruix, wife of Emile Jumeau, was the S.F.B.J.'s registered office. The cost of the lease was doubled by a promise of sale which would be effected in 1909. Surprisingly, this was to coincide with the sale of Fleischmann & Bloedel's premises.

The *Bébé Jumeau* trademark was registered on August 31, 1886, after the incident at Anvers, when the *Bébé Jumeau* was shamelessly copied, right down to the mark. This mark would, of course, become the property of the S.F.B.J., as would those of *Bébé Prodige* and *Bébé Français*.

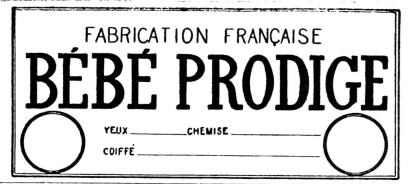

51420. — M. p. être apposée sur des boîtes, caisses et autres emballages renfermant des poupées ou bébés, déposée le 17 octobre 1896, à 1 h. 10, au greffe du tribunal de commerce de la Seine, par la *Société E. Jumeau et C*ie, à Paris.

Cette marque a 0.053 de haut sur 0.117 de large. Elle est imprimée en noir sur fond blanc.

51421. — M. p. être apposée sur des boîtes, caisses et autres emballages renfermant des poupées ou bébés, déposée le 17 octobre 1896, à 1 h. 10, au greffe du tribunal de commerce de la Seine, par la *Société E. Jumeau et C*ie, à Paris.

Cette marque a 0.070 de haut sur 0.122 de large. Le fond est or, l'encadrement blanc bordé de noir, de même que la bande portant les mots *chemise... yeux... coiffé*, et le cartouche recouvrant en partie cette bande or; les mots *Jouet national*, *Bébé Jumeau* sont en lettres blanches entourées de noir; les autres mentions sont imprimées en noir.

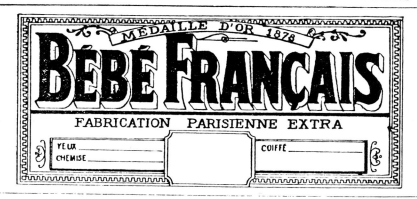

51422. — M. p. être apposée sur des boîtes, caisses et autres emballages renfermant des poupées ou bébés, déposée le 17 octobre 1896, à 1 h. 10, au greffe du tribunal de commerce de la Seine, par la *Société E. Jumeau et C*ie, à Paris.

Cette marque a 0.054 de haut sur 0.117 de large. Elle est imprimée en deux couleurs (or et noir) sur fond rougeâtre.

51423. — M. p. être apposée sur des boîtes, caisses et autres emballages renfermant des poupées ou bébés, déposée le 17 octobre 1896, à 1 h. 10, au greffe du tribunal de commerce de la Seine, par la *Société E. Jumeau et C*ie, à Paris.

Cette marque a 0.014 de haut sur 0.088 de large. Le fond est or, la banderole bleu, blanc et rouge, l'inscription en lettres or et noir.

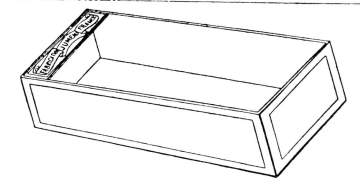

51424. — M. p. désigner des poupées et bébés, déposée le 17 octobre 1896, à 1 h. 10, au greffe du tribunal de commerce de la Seine, par la *Société E. Jumeau et C*ie, à Paris.

Cette marque est caractérisée par une petite languette située à l'intérieur de la boîte contenant le produit, et sur laquelle on peut coller une étiquette.

Trademarks registered in the *Bulletin Officiel de la Propriete Industrielle* by Societe Jumeau & Co. in 1896.

In 1890 the Société Jumeau was founded by Emile Jumeau and Emile Douillet who never signed any dolls' heads. Jumeau and Company, was dissolved just before the founding of the S.F.B.J. Jumeau handed over, in his own name and that of his wife, his factories, patents, trademarks, and his reputation. Monsieur and Madame Jumeau received 1,320 shares of the company.

Patents registered by:
Emile Jumeau

166 885	2/7/1885	For the perfecting of sleeping eyes[2]
177 127	7/1/1886	For the perfecting of the mechanism of sleeping eyes.
182 307	3/21/1887	For the perfecting of movable eyes

Societe Jumeau & Cie

| 260 167 | 10/3/1896 | For the method of mounting movable eyes. |
| 260 168 | 10/3/1896 | For packaging boxes with advertisements inside. |

In examining these patents it is interesting to note that the Maison Jumeau's research centered exclusively on eye movement.

La S.F.B.J. après sa création et avant 1914
The S.F.B.J. between its foundation and 1914

The *Bébé Jumeau*, whose production had been continued by the S.F.B.J. won the highest prize at the Universal Exhibition in 1900. In fact, all the S.F.B.J. products won prizes, since Monsieur Lefevre, one of their adminstrators, was on the jury panel.

The French people thought that an enormous trust was being set up to counteract the invasion of German toys onto the market. Fleischmann forced the S.F.B.J. onto a commercial and economic scheme, and the turnover doubled within fifteen years, but his main policy towards production was one of modification of structures.

A series of business operations took place before 1914, starting with the purchase of *La Villa de la Porte Dorée* which was used by Fleischmann and Bloedel's soceity before being amalgamated into the S.F.B.J., at a price of 22,000 francs with no increase in the original investment on April 25, 1904.

---

[2]This patent is defined as being for the perfecting of the construction of *poupées* and *bébés*. To accept this statement without examining the patent leads to confusion, because in reality it is a question of studying the sleeping eyes, or, more precisely, the movable eyelids.

1906 — Absorption de la Société Bernheim & Kahn
1906 — Absorption of Bernheim & Kahn's company

The absorption of the *Société Parisienne des Bébés*, still known as the *Société Bernheim et Kahn* took place on August 27, 1906. Marcel Bernheim joined forces with Achille Kahn in order to form the company just before its retrocession. The offices were in the Temple area of Paris at 20, rue des Quatrefils. Their capital amounted to about 280,000 francs. This, together with the office building and the Impasse du Bureau factory (still within the Paris city boundary) at numbers 7, 9 and 11, and the sum of their materials, gave them an income of 380,000 francs in the S.F.B.J. bringing their invested capital from 3,800,000 to 4,180,000 francs. The trademark *Etoile Bébé* was registered as a proper name in itself and *Bébé Mondain*, registered as part of the company's name were added to the S.F.B.J.'s assets. Many heads of German origin are to be found in this company's contribution to the S.F.B.J., for example, those signed 1902, BK, 1894, and Simon & Halbig mold number 1078. These supplies would be "reconditioned" by the S.F.B.J., and, like the rest of the objects taken up by the S.F.B.J. from a variety of companies at the beginning of the century, present real problems for those trying to research these artifacts.

ETOILE BÉBÉ

85556. — M. p. désigner des bébés, poupées, jeux et jouets, déposée le 22 juin 1904, à 3 h., au greffe du tribunal de commerce de la Seine, par MM. *Bernheim et Kahn*, demeurant à Paris.

CL. XLIV. — JEUX ET JOUETS

BÉBÉ MONDAIN

95901. — M. p. désigner des bébés et poupées, déposée le 30 mai 1906, à 10 h. 30, au greffe du tribunal de commerce de la Seine, par la *Société Bernheim et Kahn*, manufacturiers à Paris.

Etoile Bébé and *Bébé Mondain* were names trademarked by Bernheim and Kahn and later acquired by the S.F.B.J.

1909 — Opérations immobilieres
1909 — Real estate operations

In January 1909 the S.F.B.J. brought to fruition the pledges of sales set out in the statutes of May 1899. These concerned Monsieur and Madame Jumeau for the Montreuil factories (at 152, rue de Paris; 109, rue Etienne Marcel; 64, rue François Arago and 18, rue Raspail). Henceforth, the S.F.B.J. owned these properties. They also bought a piece of land, still in the old area of *Villa de la Porte Dorée* which was rented to Fleischmann and Bloedel (160 rue de Picpus).

Advertising postcard published by S.F.B.J. for 1900's exhibition.

Color 1. Bébé SFBJ No. 226. Bisque head, Left, incised 226 (only); tinted hair. Right, incised SFBJ 226, Paris; painted hair.

Couleur 1. Bébés S.F.B.J. 226. À tête en biscuit. A gauche, tête marquée en creux seulement 226, cheveux peints à petits traits. A droite, tête marquée en creux; S.F.B.J. 226, Paris. Cheveux peints. Langue plus détachée.

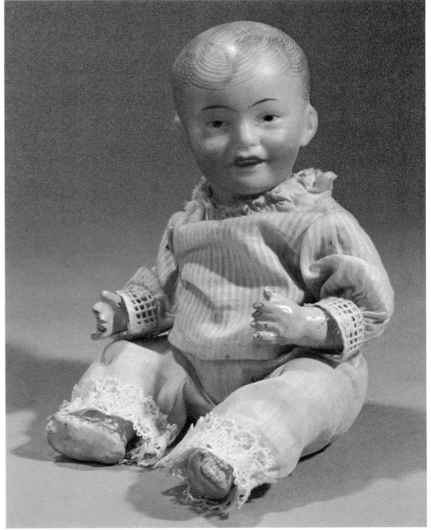

Color 2. Bébé SFBJ No. 227. Bisque head incised 227 (only). Height 7 inches.

Couleur 2. Bébé S.F.B.J. No. 227. Tête en biscuit marquée seulement 227 en creux. Hauteur 17 cm.

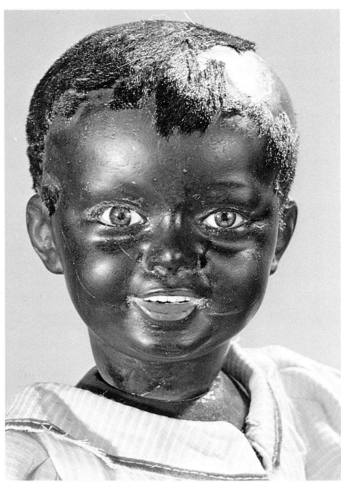

Color 3. Bébé SFBJ No. 227. Black version. Bisque head painted in black. Incised 227. Height 20 inches.

Couleur 3. Bébé S.F.B.J. No. 227. Version noire. Tête en biscuit teinteé de noir, marquée SFBJ 227. Hauteur 50 cm.

Color 4. Bébé SFBJ No. 230. Bisque head incised SFBJ 230. Height 12.5 inches. Molded eyebrows, fixed eyes. Open mouth with four teeth.

Couleur 4. Bébé S.F.B.J. No. 230. Tête biscuit marquée SFBJ 230. Hauteur 31 cm. Sourcils moulés en relief et peints. Yeux fixes. Bouche ouverte 4 dents.

Color 6. Bébé SFBJ No. 235. Bisque head incised SFBJ 235. Height 19 inches. Original French military dress from the first World War (1914-18).

Couleur 6. Bébé S.F.B.J. No. 235. Tête biscuit marquée en creux SFBJ 235. Hauteur 47 cm. Habillé d'origine d'un costume militaire français de la guerre 1914-18.

Color 5. Bébé SFBJ No. 234. Bisque head incised SFBJ 234. Height 12.5 inches. Sleeping eyes.

Couleur 5. Bébé S.F.B.J. No. 234. Tête biscuit marquée SFBJ 234. Hauteur 31 cm. Yeux dormeurs.

Color 7. Bébé SFBJ 235. Bisque head incised SFBJ 235. Height 13.5 inches. Dress not original. Wears a wig on a bald head.

Couleur 7. Bébé S.F.B.J. No. 235. Hauteur 34 cm. Habits non d'origine. Il porte une perruque sur sa tête pleine.

Color 8. Two Bébés SFBJ No. 235. Left, bisque head incised 235 (only). Tinted hair. Two teeth jointed. Right, bisque head incised SFBJ 235. Molded hair. Two separate teeth.

Couleur 8. Bébés S.F.B.J. No. 235. A gauche, tête biscuit marquée 235 seulement. Cheveux peints à petits traits. Les deux sont jointes.
A droite, tête biscuit marquée SFBJ 235. Les cheveux sont legerement moulés en relief. Les deux dents sont separees.

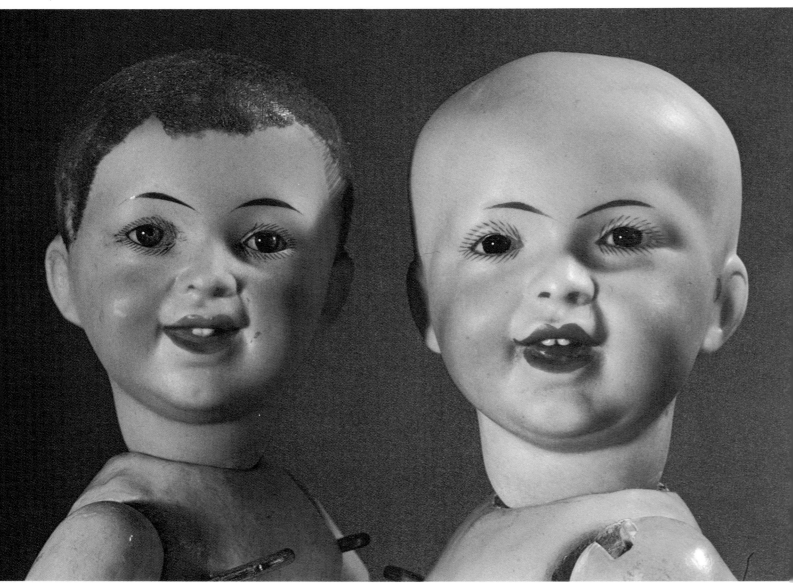

Color 9. Bébé SFBJ No. 236. The most well-known of character babies by the SFBJ. Bisque head incised SFBJ 236. Height 16.5 inches.

Couleur 9. Bébé S.F.B.J. No. 236. Le plus connu des bébés caractères de la SFBJ. Tête biscuit marquée SFBJ 236. Hauteur 41 cm.

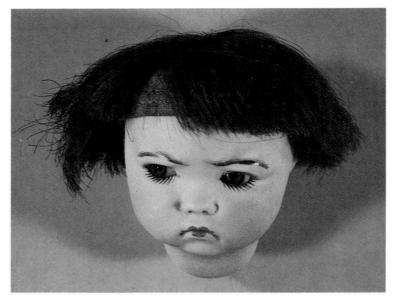

Color 10. Bébé SFBJ No. 248. Bisque head incised 248. Very rare.

Couleur 10. Bébé S.F.B.J. No. 248. Tête en biscuit marquée SFBJ 248. Très rare.

Color 11. Little Bébé SFBJ. Bisque head incised 235 (only). Height 9.5 inches. Brown tinted hair.

Couleur 11. Petit Bébé S.F.B.J. Tête marquée seulement 235. Hauteur 19 cm. Cheveux peints à petits traits marrons.

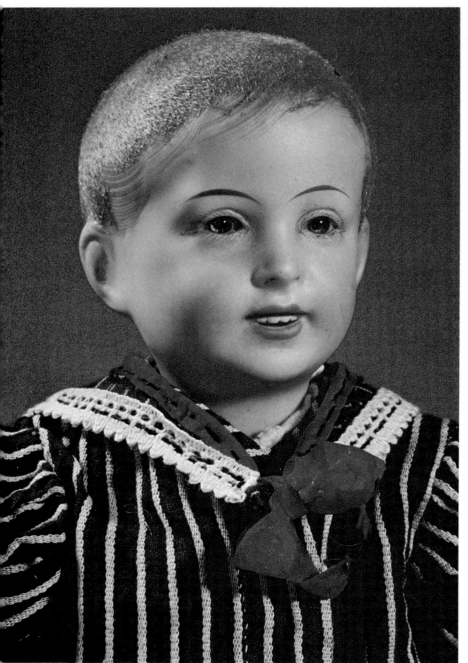

Color 12. Bébé SFBJ No. 237. Bisque head incised 237 (only). Height 14 inches. Tinted hair.

Couleur 12. Bébé S.F.B.J. No. 237. Tête en biscuit marquée seulement 237. Hauteur 35 cm. Cheveux peints à petits traits.

Color 13. Bébé SFBJ No. 237. Bisque head incised 237. Height 15 inches. Molded hair.

Couleur 13. Bébé S.F.B.J. No. 237. Tête biscuit marquée SFBJ 237. Hauteur 38 cm. Cheveux moulés en relief.

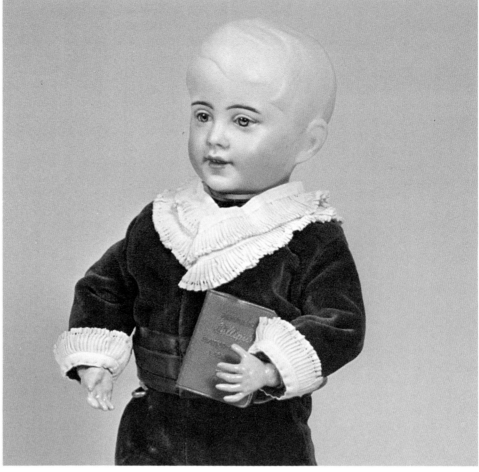

Color 14. Bébé SFBJ No. 238. Bisque head incised SFBJ 238. Height 19 inches.

Couleur 14. Bébé S.F.B.J. No. 238. Tête en biscuit marquée SFBJ 238. Hauteur 47 cm.

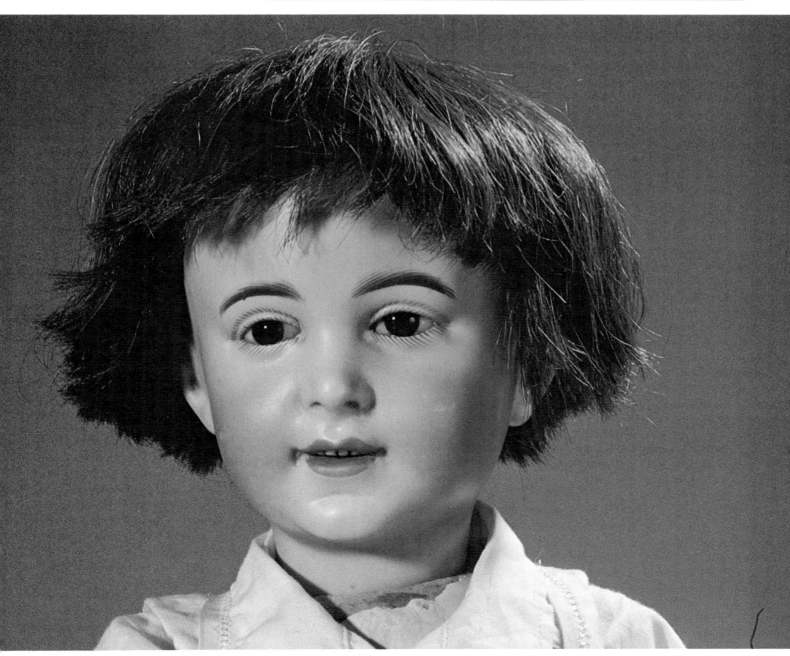

Color 15. Bébé SFBJ No. 239. Bisque head incised SFBJ 239 and with signature POULBOT. Original clothes.

Couleur 15. Bébé S.F.B.J. No. 239. Tête en biscuit marquée SFBJ 239 et signée POULBOT. Vêtement d'origine.

Color 16. Bébé SFBJ No. 239. Girl version. Original wig.

Couleur 16. Bébé S.F.B.J. No. 239. Version fille. Perruque d'origine.

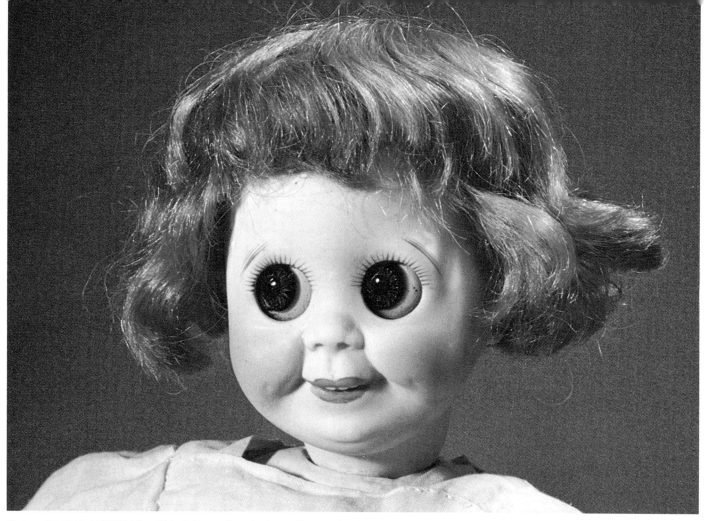

Color 17. Bébé SFBJ No. 245. Bisque head. Googlie. Incised SFBJ 245. Height 11 inches.

Couleur 17. Bébé S.F.B.J. No. 245. Tête en biscuit. Modèle Googlie. Marquée SFBJ No. 245. Hauteur 27 cm.

Color 18. Bébé SFBJ No. 247. Bisque head incised 247. Height 10 inches.

Couleur 18. Bébé S.F.B.J. No. 247. Tête en biscuit marquée 247. Hauteur 24 cm.

Color 19. Bébé SFBJ No 252. Bisque head incised SFBJ 252. Height 20 inches.

Couleur 19. Bébé S.F.B.J. No. 252. Tête en biscuit marquée SFBJ 252. Hauteur 50 cm.

Color 20. Bébé SFBJ No. 252. Bisque head incised 22-SFBJ 252. The number represents the date of the mold (1922).

Couleur 20. Bébé S.F.B.J. No. 252. Tête en biscuit marquée 22-SFBJ. Le 22 représente la date (1922).

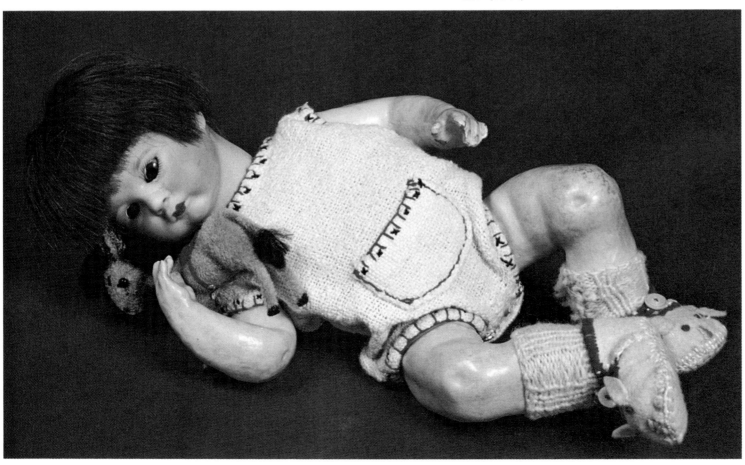

Color 21. Bébé SFBJ No. 255. Bisque head incised SFBJ 255.

Couleur 21. Bébé S.F.B.J. No. 255. Tête en biscuit marquée SFBJ 255.

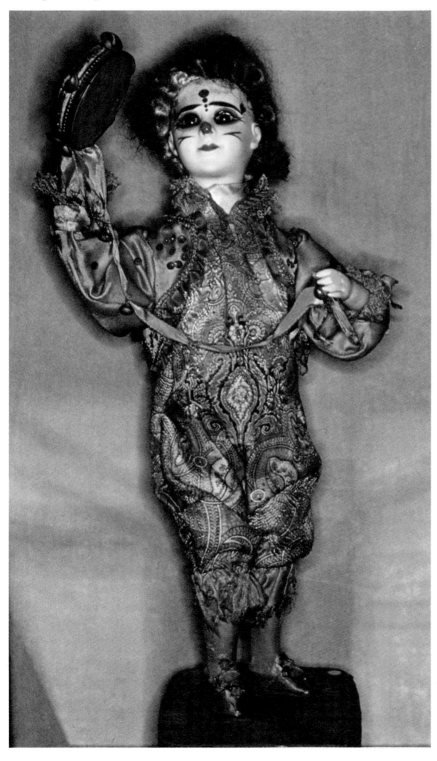

Color 22. Bébé SFBJ No. 301. Brown bisque head incised SFBJ 301.

Couleur 22. Bébé S.F.B.J. No. 301. Tête en biscuit mulâtre marquée SFBJ 301.

Color 23. BAMBINO by the SFBJ. Bisque head with a 3 incised.

Couleur 23. BAMBINO de la S.F.B.J. Tête biscuit marquée uniquement du chiffre 3.

Color 24. BLEUETTE by the SFBJ (dated 1920). Bisque head incised SFBJ 60 8/0. Trunk and original clothes.

Couleur 24. BLEUETTE de la S.F.B.J. (datée de 1920). Tête en biscuit marquée SFBJ 60 8/0. Hauteur 27 cm. Malle et trousseau d'origine.

Color 25. Other Bébé SFBJ with interchangeable head incised 233-237-227.

Couleur 25. Autre Bébé S.F.B.J. à têtes interchangeables marquées S.F.B.J. No. 233-237-227.

Color 26. ROSETTE by the SFBJ (1957). Bisque head incised SFBJ 301, size 3. Height 14 inches. Trunk and original clothes.

Couleur 26. ROSETTE de la S.F.B.J. (1957). Tête en biscuit marquée SFBJ 301 taille 3. Hauteur 35 cm. Malle et trousseau d'origine.

Color 27. Bébé JUMEAU by the SFBJ. Bisque head incised SFBJ 6. Height 17.2 inches.

Couleur 27. Bébé JUMEAU fabriqué par la S.F.B.J. Tête en biscuit marquée SFBJ 6. Hauteur 43 cm.

Color 28. Bébé SFBJ No. 272. Bisque head incised UNIS-FRANCE 272. Height 8.5 inches.

Couleur 28. Bébé S.F.B.J. No. 272. Tête en biscuit marquée UNIS-FRANCE 272. Hauteur 21 cm.

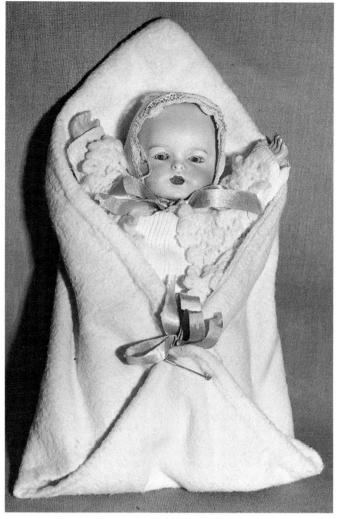

Color 29. Bébé SFBJ No. 306. Bisque head incised UNIS-FRANCE 306, JUMEAU 1938, Paris.

Couleur 29. Bébé S.F.B.J. No. 306. Tête en biscuit marquée UNIS-FRANCE 306, JUMEAU 1938. Paris.

Color 30. Bébé SFBJ No. 250.
Bisque head. Details of the face.

Couleur 30. Bébé S.F.B.J. No. 250. Tête en biscuit. Détails du visage.

Color 31. Bébé SFBJ No. 251. Details of the face.

Couleur 31. Bébé S.F.B.J. No. 251. Détails du visage.

1912 — Absorption de la Société "La Parisienne"

1912 — Absorption of the La Parisienne company

For several reasons, this transaction is of great interest. First, it consisted of a toy factory, but one which also made ordinary dolls. This company was founded by Monsieur Kratz-Boussac and was a subsidiary of the Kratz-Boussac society founded in 1884. It was oriented towards bulk business and importation of toys, knick-knacks and Parisian articles. In 1888 this company took out an American patent license for the manufacture of the *Eureka* pneumatic dart which was manufactured at Eu in the Seine Maritime, and from 1898 onwards, at Pont-Saint-Pierre in the Eure.

Another asset was the revival of the *diabolo*, formerly called the *diable*. In 1892, Monsieur Henri-Othan Kratz-Boussac registered a patent for the manufacture of one-piece, celluloid dolls' heads. (No 221.627). The doll section of this company was responsible for the creation of *La Parisienne* whose name was registered in 1910.

The first patent (227,054) was taken out on July 15, 1910, a short time after the creation of the company, concerned the mounting of movable eyes. The second was for "clay for the manufacture of heads, limbs, and bodies of dolls and other toys,"

CL. 44. — JEUX ET JOUETS

LA PARISIENNE

120914. — M. p. désigner des poupées, déposée le 10 mai 1910, à 1 h. 15, au greffe du tribunal de commerce de la Seine, par M. Kratz-Boussac Henri-Othon, 15, rue Martel, à Paris.

A trademark registered by Mr. Kratz-Boussac in 1910 in the *Bulletin Officiel de la Propriete Industrielle*.

221.627

Drawings for a doll head patent registered by Kratz-Boussac in 1892.

and was of interest to the S.F.B.J. after the transfer. (Patent number 423,842 was taken out on February 25, 1911.)

The La Parisienne company was quite prolific in 1911, but the company was liquidated the following year. The two patents which were registered by La Parisienne were:

437,611   2/22/1911   Concerned the perfecting of the manufacture of molded dolls
431,066   6/14/1911   Concerned a method of mounting movable dolls' eyes

Judging by their descriptions, these two patents were taken out for the manufacture of cheap dolls which were this company's main preoccupation. A simpler, cheaper clay had preceded this one, and was the reason why the company bought Lorentz's patent. On September 6, 1911, three marks were registered: *Bébé Euréka*, which seems to have been the company's pet-name; *Bébé le Rêve* and *Bébé Luxe*.

The S.F.B.J. took over these patents which were under license for the trademarks. Monsieur Kratz-Boussac continued to make games and brought out the first pedal-car in 1921. From this time on, the company was called New Inventions and was still in business in 1980.

Another interesting factor in this policy of absorption was the patent war which was waged at the end of the 19th century. The S.F.B.J., always well-managed, effected a strategy by which they were able to dominate the market, absorbing not only their rival's companies, but their patents as well, thus preventing any possible suit being brought against them. The control of La Parisienne's assets was a great gain for the S.F.B.J. creating 200 new shares at 500 francs each, and brought an increase in the social capital, bringing it from 418,000 to 428,000 on July 23, 1912.

The S.F.B.J. *had* power, in terms of capital, property and reputation. Fleischmann was still the Director General. The dream had been realized, but a threat was waiting in the wings.

The page from the *Bulletin Municipal Officiel de la Ville de Paris* of September 10, 1912, which announced the liquidation of la Parisienne Société and lists the doll trademarks of Krantz-Boussac which were turned over to the S.F.B.J.

A September 1911 listing of dolls by *la Société La Parisienne*.

Map of Montreuil area where several doll makers were located.

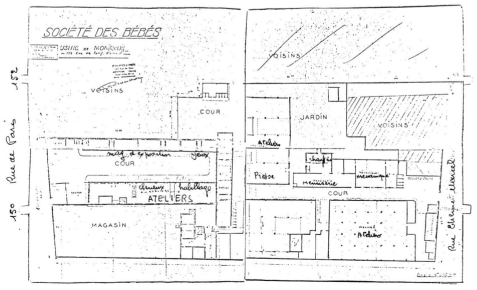

Plan of the S.F.B.J. factory.

1917 — Absorption de la Société du Bébé Mignon
1917 — The Bébé Mignon Company Takeover

From the time Salomon Fleischmann left until 1930, Paul Girard administered the S.F.B.J. During the war, and long after, France was swept by a sort of witch-hunt: German toys, no matter what kind were banned. In the midst of this war-like context, the *Bébé Mignon* spent a decade fighting for its survival. It was one of the first to join the post-war vogue of new doll faces, but soon had to abandon this venture in view of the war's consequences.

The Bébé Mignon Company was founded October 24, 1909, by Jules and Charles Damerval and François Laffranchy; its headquarters were established at 81 avenue Victor Hugo in Montreuil sous Bois, the homeland of doll producers. The Bébé Mignon Company belonged to the old Falck-Roussel firm, which had filed the F.R. trademark in 1885, as well as the *Bébé Mignon* trademark; the heads of *Bébé Mignon* dolls bore the signature D.L.

The company was dissolved January 1, 1917, and its capital was transferred to 375 shares at 500 francs each, thereby increasing the S.F.B.J.'s capital from 4,280,000 to 4,467,500 francs. The property was taken over with a lease guaranteeing a sales agreement. The take over did not change the spirit with which Salomon Fleischmann had directed the business, but at this point the toy industry became rather inactive.

During the war and long after, artisan workshops sprung up everywhere, completely changing the face of the doll industry. The war of the giants, which had greatly dominated the end of the 19th century, was buried in the past. The last colossus managed to resist, from one world war to another, but without much bustle or stir.

BÉBÉ NOUVEAU ARTICULÉ

22285. — M. p. désigner un jouet, déposée le 30 juillet 1885, au greffe du tribunal de commerce de la Seine, par le sieur *(Adolphe)*, négociant à Paris.

CL. XXXVI. — JOUETS.

22465. — M. p. être apposée sur des poupées et sur les cartons les renfermant, déposée le 3 septembre 1885, à 1 h. 25, au greffe du tribunal de commerce de la Seine, par le sieur *Falck (Adolphe)*, négociant à Paris, et y faisant le commerce sous le nom de *Falck-Roussel*. Cette marque est de dimensions variables. Elle s'applique en toutes couleurs.

Fabrication Française
Bébé MIGNON Articulé
Modèles déposés
Douz^{ne}........N°......

22466. — M. p. être apposée sur des cartons renfermant des bébés articulés, déposée le 3 septembre 1885, à 1 h. 25, au greffe du tribunal de commerce de la Seine, par le sieur *Falck (Adolphe)*, négociant à Paris, et y faisant le commerce sous le nom de *Falck-Roussel*. Cette marque est de dimensions variables. Elle s'imprime en toutes couleurs.

Trademarks registered in 1885 by Mr. Falck-Roussel in the *Bulletin Officiel de la Propriete Industrielle*.

L'entre deux guerres — 1918-1939
Between Two World Wars 1918-1939

The S.F.B.J. fell into a dismal and doleful era, characterized by a monotonous routine, which eventually gave way to what is known as the post-war boom. Assets from the Fleischmann era enabled the S.F.B.J. to build an empire, which succeeded in resisting the trials and tribulations of war.

By 1922 the S.F.B.J. owned four factories, one in Montempoivre, one on the rue de Paris, one on the rue de Picpus, and finally, one in Champagneuilles (Meurthe and Moselle). Headquarters still stood at 8 rue Pastourelle in the Temple quarter.

In 1923, the S.F.B.J. acquired the Lang and Gillemaud Company, a business with a factory in Sannois. 1925 marked the year of *l'Exposition des Arts Décoratifs* (the Decorative Arts Exposition). The S.F.B.J. exhibited its productions in the Toy Village, and won the Decorative Arts grand prize. Among the neighboring stands was one representing the Gautier-Languereau publishing house. It was enthroned with the distinguished presence of *Bleuette*, which the S.F.B.J. especially created for the magazine *La Semaine de Suzette*. *Bleuette* had been quite popular and her presence signaled a comeback after a prolonged disappearance during the war. To the enchantment of many, *Bleuette* was rediscovered, and her little brother was not long in joining her.

In 1931, the S.F.B.J. won yet another prize, this time at *l'Exposition Coloniale* (the Colonial Exposition) in Paris. Its collection was accented by several exotic creations, among which were colored dolls, notably *Bamboula*, the little black brother of the already familiar *Bambino*. The same year, at Anvers, the S.F.B.J. proved itself in a class of its own — a feat that repeated the 1900 World Exposition.

From one exposition to another, creativity touched the natural course of development, transformation and diversification. Character dolls followed a distinct evolutionary path, moving closer to the number 300. Some enjoyed considerable success, others did not.

The S.F.B.J. followed the initiative of *l'Union Inter-Syndicale* (the Manufacturers Trade Union), and began to place the abbreviation Unis France on all their new models. The ones not bearing this mark, were nonetheless, labeled.

In 1938 The Queen of England visited France. This visit gave the S.F.B.J., the largest French doll producer, an opportunity to distinguish itself. For the special occassion, it created the number 306 mold, producing two dolls: *France* and *Marianne*. They were characterized by a stiff, tight-lipped smile, which became the French *pandores* (pandoras). Accompanied by their wardrobes, they crossed the Channel, just as the fashion dolls had done in the old days.

Drawings by J. Vazquez, from a book published in 1927 by Henry Renè D'Allemagne, of the Le Village du Jouet. Le Village du Jouet was the section of French toys at the Exposition Internationale des Arts Decoratifs et Industriels Modernes in Paris in 1925.

Drawings by J. Vazquez of le Village du Jouet. The village was built by the Peltier brothers and had 34 cottages, five pavillons, a town hall, a central mill and greens. It was described as being "itself a great toy of 1,300 square meters."

La fin d'un empire
The End of an Empire

On May 7, 1940, the S.F.B.J. moved its headquarters to 160 rue de Picpus. In the interim, Paul Girard and Jean Arnaud (Fleischmann's son-in-law) finally gained control.

The post-war years were marked with a barrage of change. Society changed rapidly, shedding its old face, preparing to take another. American influence rode high; the new world, having come to the rescue of the old, left indelible traces. Construction succeeded destruction. The birth rate rose, and though encouraged by the government, surpassed all predictions.

Aesthetic values changed. Their roots had been previously planted during the post-war era, but the sprouting only took place now, taking on a definite shape. The success of the *Barbie* doll, first in America, then in France, was the result of the newly emerging plastics industry: rhodoid, then PVL.

Surprisingly enough, children warmly received these new products. Softer than bisque, more solid than celluloid, more resistant than rubber, this new material proved to respond quite well to the changing needs, thus the plastic doll embarked upon a new era. These social transformations, with all of their implications, went unheeded by the S.F.B.J. directors. When they finally decided to act, it was too late. Using these new materials would have required necessary changes that were too time-consuming and too costly. Furthermore, market studies showed that the S.F.B.J. was too weak and too far behind others, who had taken the lead. Moreover, foreign competition, especially American, proved too aggressive and powerful. The era of articulated dolls had thus met its end. In 1957 doll activity came to a halt; this coincided with the trend for *Bleuette*, which only survived three more years.

In 1963 M. Arnaud was President of the Board of Directors. In 1955 the S.F.B.J. had left its headquarters at 160 rue de Picpus to establish itself at 152 rue de Paris, and in 1963 the S.F.B.J. completely modified its factory for the manufacture of ball-point pens. Today the company still exists, but under the name it took May 16, 1963: Sobitu, manufacturing company of balls, tubes and plastics.

Corporate Bylaws of the S.F.B.J.

BÉBÉS ET JOUETS

SOCIÉTÉ ANONYME

au capital de 3.500.000 francs.

Siège social à Paris, 8, rue Pastourelle.

I.

D'un acte reçu par Mᵉ Georges Bertrand et Mᵉ Edmond Leroy, son collègue, notaires à Paris, le 6 mars 1899, portant cette mention :

« Enregistré à Paris, sixième bureau, le 10 mars 1899, vol. 598 bis, nº 120. Reçu trois francs, décimes soixante-quinze centimes.

« Signé : DOPPELD. »

aux termes duquel M. Salomon Fleischmann, négociant, demeurant à Paris, rue de Turbigo, nº 55, ayant agi tant en son nom personnel qu'au nom et comme mandataire de M. Jean Bloedel, a établi les statuts de la Société anonyme que son mandant et lui avaient l'intention de former,

Il a été extrait littéralement ce qui suit :

STATUTS

TITRE PREMIER

FORMATION. — DÉNOMINATION. — SIÈGE. DURÉE ET OBJET DE LA SOCIÉTÉ.

Article premier.

Il est formé, entre les propriétaires des actions ci-après créées et de celles qui pourront l'être ultérieurement, en la forme ci-après indiquée, une Société anonyme régie par les lois des vingt-quatre juillet mil huit cent soixante-sept et premier soit mil huit cent quatre-vingt-treize, ainsi que par les présents statuts.

Art. 2.

Cette Société prend la dénomination de *Société française de fabrication de bébés et jouets.*

Art. 3.

Le siège de la Société est à Paris, au domicile sont établis à Paris, rue Pastourelle, nº 8.

Art. 4.

La durée de la Société est fixée à soixante-quinze années, à partir du jour de sa constitution définitive, sauf les cas de prorogation ou de dissolution anticipée, dont il sera parlé plus loin, sous divers articles des statuts.

Art. 5.

La Société a pour objet :

1º L'exploitation en France et à l'étranger de la fabrication de bébés et jouets;

2º L'acquisition, par voie d'apport ou autrement, de toutes maisons de même genre ou de tous autres genres, y compris leurs marques,

brevets, dépôts, titres, ainsi que le matériel et les articles jouets d'enfants et même de tous articles généralement quelconques ;

3º La fabrication, achat et vente de tous les articles jouets d'enfants et même de tous articles généralement quelconques ;

4º L'acquisition ou la location, avec ou sans promesse de vente, de tous immeubles nécessaires à la Société, tant pour la fabrication que pour la vente en France et à l'étranger ; ; ; ;

5º L'exécution des travaux nécessaires pour l'aménagement de ces immeubles ;

6º La vente des immeubles qui seront apportés ou acquis ;

7º La création de toutes succursales ou dépôts, tant en France qu'à l'étranger, et l'acquisition ou la location des immeubles et locaux nécessaires à l'installation desdits succursales et dépôts ;

8º L'absorption, par voie de fusion, de toutes sociétés similaires;

9º Et généralement toutes opérations commerciales pouvant se rattacher directement ou indirectement aux opérations sociales.

TITRE II.

CAPITAL SOCIAL. — ACTIONS.

Art. 6.

Le capital social est fixé à la somme de trois millions huit cent mille francs, représenté par sept mille cinq cents actions de cinq cents francs chacune.

Quatre mille quatre cent soixante-dix de ces actions, entièrement libérées, seront attribuées ci-après à divers apporteurs, dans les proportions qui seront indiquées, en représentation de leurs apports 4.470

Il reste, par suite, trois mille cent trente actions à souscrire contre espèces 3.130

Le capital social pourra être augmenté en une ou plusieurs fois, par décision de l'Assemblée générale des actionnaires, prise sur la proposition du Conseil d'administration, soit par l'émission d'actions nouvelles, soit au moyen de l'introduction, dans le capital social, de tout ou partie des actions autres émises, soit au moyen d'augmentation du capital social, soit par tout autre mode d'augmentation du capital social.

Art. 7.

Les appels de fonds seront portés à la connaissance des actionnaires, tant par lettres recommandées adressées aux domiciles par eux, que par l'insertion dans un journal d'annonces légales du département de la Seine, et ce, un mois avant l'époque fixée pour le versement.

Art. 8.

À défaut de versement dans les délais par le Conseil d'administration, l'intérêt de plein droit et à la charge de l'actionnaire en retard, sur le pied de cinq pour cent l'an, à compter du jour de l'exigibilité.

Le retardataire est mis en demeure par simple avis publié dans un journal d'annonces légales de Paris.

Faute par les retardataires de se conformer dans le délai d'un mois, à partir dudit jour à l'exigibilité, la Société aura le droit, sans qu'il soit besoin de recourir à aucune formalité judiciaire et d'ajouter audit délai aucun délai de distance, de faire vendre aux enchères publiques, par le ministère d'un agent de change près la Bourse de Paris, si d'agent de change sont cotées, et au ministère d'un notaire, dans le cas contraire, aux risques et périls des retardataires, le tout, sans préjudice du droit que la Société conserve de suivre, par les voies ordinaires, l'action en défaut.

Cette vente pourra être faite en masse ou par partie, sous quelque prétexte que ce soit, et valeurs de la licitation, ni s'immiscer en aucune manière dans son administration ; ils doivent, pour l'exercice de leurs droits, s'en rapporter aux inventaires sociaux et aux délibérations de l'assemblée générale ou du conseil d'administration.

TITRE III.

ADMINISTRATION DE LA SOCIÉTÉ.

Art. 18.

La Société est administrée par un Conseil composé de cinq membres au moins et de huit au plus pris parmi les actionnaires et nommés par l'Assemblée générale pour six ans. Ils sont indéfiniment rééligibles.

Par exception, les premiers administrateurs de la Société sont :

1º M. Salomon Fleischmann, négociant, demeurant à Paris, rue de Turbigo, 55, comparant ;

2º M. Eugène-Louis Gaultier, négociant, demeurant à Saint-Maurice (Seine), avenue de l'Asile, 4 bis ;

3º M. Émile-Louis Jumeau, négociant, chevalier de la Légion d'honneur, demeurant à Paris, boulevard Beaumarchais, 67 ;

4º M. Edmond Lefèvre, propriétaire, demeurant à Paris, avenue de la République, 44 ;

5º M. Adolphe Scherb, négociant, demeurant à Paris, rue Tiquetonne, 15.

Leurs fonctions dureront trois ans.

En conséquence et conformément au paragraphe troisième de l'article vingt-cinq de la loi du 24 juillet mil huit cent soixante-sept, il est stipulé que leur nomination ne sera pas soumise à l'approbation de l'Assemblée générale.

Le Conseil pourra se compléter lui-même par la nomination de un, deux ou trois membres jusqu'au maximum ci-dessus fixé.

Lorsque les fonctions des premiers administrateurs auront cessé, le Conseil sera renouvelé par cinquième de cette époque, il se renouvellera par roulement établi d'après le nombre des administrateurs en fonction, tous les ans, d'abord par voie de tirage au sort et ensuite par ancienneté ; les membres sortants sont rééligibles.

En cas de décès, retraite ou empêchement d'un ou plusieurs administrateurs dans l'intervalle qui s'écoule entre deux assemblées générales, les membres restant en fonction ont le droit de pourvoir au remplacement provisoire jusqu'à la première réunion de l'Assemblée générale ; toutefois, le Conseil d'administration serait tenu de pourvoir à la fixation des administrateurs membres, si le nombre des administrateurs en fonction était descendu au-dessous de quatre.

Les administrateurs ainsi nommés ne demeurent en fonction que pendant le temps d'exercice qui restait à leur prédécesseur.

Art. 16.

Chaque administrateur doit être propriétaire de cinquante actions qui seront inaliénables pendant la durée de ses fonctions et affectées, conformément à la loi, à la garantie des actes de sa gestion.

Les titres de ces actions sont revêtus d'un timbre indiquant l'inaliénabilité et déposés dans la caisse sociale.

Art. 20.

Le Conseil d'administration est investi des pouvoirs les plus étendus pour l'administration et la gestion des affaires de la Société.

Il notamment les pouvoirs suivants :

Il nomme et révoque tous directeurs, agents ou employés de la Société ; il fixe leurs salaires et leurs émoluments.

Il décide la création ou transformation des usines ou comptoirs de vente et agences, en nomme les directeurs et détermine leurs pouvoirs et attributions.

Il règle et arrête toutes les dépenses générales de l'administration et pourvoit à l'emploi des fonds restés disponibles.

Il propose à l'Assemblée générale toutes modifications aux statuts.

Il fixe l'époque et règle le mode de versement, des actions, en cas d'augmentation du capital social.

Il autorise, dans tous les cas où la loi le permet, toutes actions judiciaires, soit en demandant, soit en défendant.

Il transige et compromet sur tous les intérêts de la Société.

Il donne mainlevée, avec tous désistements nécessaires, de toutes inscriptions de privilège et hypothèque, de toutes saisies, oppositions et autres empêchements, le tout avant comme après paiement.

Il accepte tous baux, détermine le placement des fonds disponibles, soit en décommandant, soit en défendant.

Il autorise tous achats, ventes, échanges ou partages d'immeubles, il donne à bail tout locaux et donne dans les immeubles pouvant appartenir à la Société.

Il autorise toutes constructions et tous travaux, et statue sur les études, plans et devis proposés pour leur exécution.

Il consent tous traités, marchés ou entreprises et fournit ou autrement, relativement à l'objet social, demande et accepte toutes concession et contrat, à l'occasion de toutes ses opérations, tous engagements et obligations.

Il prend tous brevets et licences en France et à l'étranger.

Il conclut tous prêts et emprunts ou ouvertures de crédit, avec ou sans hypothèques ou autres garanties.

Il peut émettre des obligations, sans l'autorisation de l'Assemblée générale, jusqu'à concurrence du quart du capital et, avec l'autorisation de l'Assemblée générale pour la somme quelle aura fixée, mais il devra réserver un droit de préemption de ces obligations en faveur des actionnaires.

Il donne toutes quittances et décharges.

Il arrête les comptes qui seront soumis à l'Assemblée générale, fait un rapport sur ces comptes et sur la situation des affaires sociales, il propose la fixation des dividendes à répartir, il désigne l'emploi des sommes dues appartenant à la Société.

Il encaisse toutes sommes dues à la Société.

Il délègue un de ses membres auquel il peut répartir, il élit domicile partout où besoin sera.

The original statutes of the S.F.B.J. are in the April 15, 1899 *Bulletin Municipal Officiel.*

gestion et l'administration des affaires de la Société, ce membre prend la part à la délibération, etc.

Art. 21.

Le Conseil peut se faire assister d'un conseil spécial chargé de donner son avis sur les affaires sociales, il détermine ses attributions et ses émoluments.

Il peut aussi constituer pour mandataires spéciaux telles personnes que bon lui semblera pour un objet déterminé.

Art. 22.

Tous marchés, traités, billets à ordre, lettres de change, chèques et engagements quelconques concernant la Société, tous les actes généralement quelconques se rapportant à des immeubles, tels que cessions, ventes, achats, baux, actes conférant hypothèque contre la Société, mainlevées d'inscriptions hypothécaires, avant comme après paiement, devront être signés, soit par l'administrateur délégué ou deux administrateurs, soit par le président.

Art. 23.

Il est interdit aux administrateurs de prendre ou de conserver un intérêt direct ou indirect dans une entreprise ou un marché fait avec la Société ou pour son compte à moins qu'ils n'y soient autorisés par l'Assemblée générale; il sera chaque année rendu à l'Assemblée générale un compte spécial de l'exécution pour chaque séance, celui de les autorisés aux termes de la disposition qui précède.

Art. 24.

Chaque année, sous le siège social où elle aura autre endroit, aussi souvent que l'intérêt social l'exige et au moins une fois par mois, par convocation signée par le vice-président et, à défaut du président, qui pourra, ou bien encore par deux administrateurs.

Pour la validité des délibérations du Conseil, il faudra la présence de la majorité en exercice de ses membres.

Les délibérations sont prises à la majorité des voix des membres présents.

En cas de partage égal de voix, celle du président est prépondérante.

Nul ne peut voter par procuration dans le sein du Conseil.

Art. 26.

Les délibérations du Conseil sont constatées par des procès-verbaux transcrits sur un registre spécial tenu au siège de la Société et, signés par les administrateurs qui ont pris part à la séance.

Les copies et extraits de ces délibérations à produire en justice et ailleurs sont certifiées par le président et un membre quelconque du Conseil, ou, à défaut, par deux membres quelconques du Conseil.

Les mineurs et interdits peu présentés aux assemblées par leurs nus-propriétaires membres par les usufruitiers par leurs mandataires, et à la société par leurs administrateurs...

Conformément à l'art. 32 du Code de commerce, les membres du Conseil d'administration ne contractant, à raison de leur gestion, aucune obligation personnelle, ils n'encourent d'autre responsabilité que celle imposée par la loi.

TITRE IV.

DES COMMISSAIRES.

Art. 29.

Il est nommé chaque année, en assemblée générale, ou dans tout autre lieu, conformément à l'article trente-deux et de la loi du vingt-quatre juillet mil huit cent soixante-sept.

Le ou les premiers commissaires sont nommés par l'assemblée constitutive de la Société.

Ce ou ces commissaires exercent la mission de vérification et de surveillance et ont les attributions que confère la loi précitée.

Les commissaires auront droit à une indemnité dont l'importance est fixée par l'Assemblée générale.

En cas de refus, d'empêchement, de décès, de démission de l'un des commissaires, l'autre ou les autres commissaires en exercice rempliront seuls leur fonction.

S'il est nommé plusieurs commissaires, ils peuvent agir ensemble ou séparément.

Lorsqu'un seul commissaire sera désigné, l'Assemblée pourra nommer un commissaire adjoint qui ne remplira ses fonctions qu'en cas d'impossibilité du premier.

TITRE V.

DES ASSEMBLÉES GÉNÉRALES.

Art. 30.

L'Assemblée générale représente l'universalité des actionnaires, ses décisions sont obligatoires pour tous, pour les absents comme pour les incapables ou dissidents.

Art. 31.

L'assemblée générale se compose de tous les actionnaires propriétaires au moins de vingt-cinq actions; exception est faite pour tout actionnaire à droit de prendre part aux délibérations et aux votes, avec voix d'un moins ou d'au plus.

Chaque actionnaire a droit à une voix par vingt-cinq actions; dans aucun cas il n'aura droit à plus de cinquante voix.

Tout actionnaire peut être représenté par un mandataire, actionnaire lui-même, qui ne pourra pas disposer comme mandataire d'un nombre de voix supérieur à celui qu'il aura comme actionnaire, et sans qu'en aucun cas le mandataire puisse disposer de plus de cinquante voix, non compris celles auxquelles il a droit personnellement.

Tous propriétaires d'un nombre d'actions inférieur à vingt-cinq pourront se réunir en former l'un d'eux, conformément et se faire représenter par l'un d'eux, conformément à l'article trente-deux...

TITRE VI.

INVENTAIRES. — BÉNÉFICES.

Art. 37.

L'année sociale commence le premier janvier et finit le trente-et-un décembre.

Par exception, le premier exercice comprendra le temps écoulé depuis la constitution définitive jusqu'au trente-et-un décembre mil huit cent quatre-vingt-dix-neuf.

Art. 38.

Il sera dressé, chaque semestre, un état sommaire de la situation active et passive de la Société et, au trente-et-un décembre, un inventaire général de l'actif et du passif.

L'état semestriel, l'inventaire, le bilan et le compte des profits et pertes seront mis à la disposition du commissaire, quarante jours au moins avant la réunion de l'Assemblée générale annuelle.

Quinze jours au moins avant la réunion de l'Assemblée générale, tout actionnaire peut prendre au siège social, communication de l'inventaire, de la liste des actionnaires et se faire délivrer copie du bilan résumant l'inventaire et le rapport du commissaire.

Art. 39.

Sur les produits nets annuels, déduction faite de toute charge sociale, il est prélevé :

1° Cinq pour cent pour constituer le fonds de réserve prescrit par la loi ;

2° Dix pour cent par le Conseil d'administration, qui en fera la répartition entre ses membres comme il le jugera convenable ;

3° Le reste, soit quatre-vingt-cinq pour cent, sera partagé entre toutes les actions, par parts égales, à moins que l'Assemblée générale, sur la proposition du Conseil d'administration, ne décide de constituer une réserve spéciale. Le prélèvement y afférent ne pourra, dans aucun cas, dépasser dix pour cent.

Lorsque le fonds de réserve aura atteint le dixième du capital social, le Conseil d'administration pourra proposer à l'Assemblée générale de suspendre le prélèvement affecté à sa formation ; s'il venait à être entamé, ce prélèvement reprendrait son cours.

Art. 40.

Le paiement des dividendes a lieu aux époques fixées par le Conseil d'administration.

Aucun dividende ou acompte ne pourra être distribué, s'il n'est entièrement disponible.

Tout dividende qui n'est pas réclamé dans les cinq ans de son exigibilité est prescrit au profit de la Société.

TITRE VII.

MODIFICATIONS AUX STATUTS. — DISSOLUTION. — LIQUIDATION.

Art. 41.

L'Assemblée générale extraordinaire délibérant, comme il est dit sous le paragraphe trois de l'article trente-cinq qui précède, peut, sur l'initiative du Conseil d'administration, apporter aux présents statuts toutes les modifications qui lui paraîtront utiles.

Elle peut décider notamment :

L'augmentation du capital social ou sa diminution en une ou plusieurs fois, de telle manière et suivant telle forme qu'elle déterminera ;

La prorogation ou la dissolution anticipée de la Société ou sa fusion avec une autre société ou compagnie ;

Art. 42.

Le transfert ou la vente à tous tiers, ainsi que l'apport à toute société de tout ou partie des biens, droits et obligations, tant actifs que passifs, de la Société ; les modifications pourront porter même sur l'objet de la Société.

Elle peut statuer sur toute question de prorogation ou déliquidation, pour quelque cause que ce soit, et sur toutes causes prévues ou non prévues aux présents statuts.

En cas de perte de moitié du capital social, constaté par un inventaire, le Conseil d'administration est tenu de convoquer l'assemblée générale, pour statuer sur la question de savoir s'il y a lieu de prononcer la dissolution.

Art. 43.

À défaut, par les administrateurs et le commissaire, de réunir l'Assemblée générale, comme dans le cas ci-dessus, tout actionnaire peut demander régulièrement, tout actionnaire peut demander la dissolution de la Société devant les tribunaux.

À la fin de la Société, soit par l'expiration de sa durée, soit par sa dissolution anticipée, pour quelque cause que ce soit, l'Assemblée générale règle...

...ou plusieurs liquidateurs.

La nomination du ou des liquidateurs met fin aux pouvoirs du Conseil d'administration.

L'Assemblée générale extraordinaire remplissant les conditions prévues par les troisième article trente-cinq, constituée par la délibération qui prononce la mise en liquidation de la Société, conférer aux liquidateurs les pouvoirs les plus étendus pour mener à bien cette liquidation notamment ceux de vendre en tout ou en partie, par lots ou autrement, les biens meubles et immeubles appartenant encore à la Société et d'en recevoir le prix en principal et accessoires.

L'actif provenant de la liquidation sera employé, avant toute répartition, au paiement du passif.

Le solde servira d'abord à rembourser aux actionnaires le capital versé sur leurs actions et le surplus, s'il y en a, constituera des bénéfices et sera réparti entre toutes les actions, par parts égales.

Pendant la durée de la liquidation, les pouvoirs de l'assemblée générale continuent comme pendant l'existence de la Société. Elle conserve, notamment, la Société conservant, pendant toute la durée de la liquidation, son caractère d'être moral. Elle a notamment le droit d'approuver les comptes et de donner décharge.

Les copies des délibérations sont délivrées par le ou les liquidateurs.

TITRE VIII.

CONTESTATIONS.

Art. 44.

Tout actionnaire est tenu de faire élection de domicile à Paris et toutes convocations ainsi que toutes modifications faites à ce domicile élu, seront valablement faites à ce domicile réel.

À défaut d'élection de domicile, les notifications et assignations judiciaires lui seront valablement faites au parquet de M. le procureur de la République près le Tribunal civil de première instance de la Seine.

Le domicile étant formellement et implicitement attributif de juridiction aux tribunaux compétents du département de la Seine, tant en demandant qu'en défendant.

Aucune action en justice introduite par un ou plusieurs actionnaires contre la Société ne pourra être déférée aux tribunaux qu'un mois après avoir été soumise à l'examen de l'assemblée générale des actionnaires, dont l'avis sera soumis aux magistrats, en même temps que la demande elle-même, le tout à peine de non-recevabilité, etc.

PUBLICATIONS LÉGALES.

Art. 47.

Tous pouvoirs sont donnés au porteur d'une expédition ou d'un extrait des présentes pour faire les publications légales.

APPORTS.

Par ces mêmes présentes, M. Fleischmann déclare apporter à la Société française de fabrication de bébés et jouets dont les statuts précèdent, tant en son nom personnel qu'en sadite qualité de mandataire de M. Bloedel :

§ 1er. — Le fonds de commerce de bébés et jouets qu'ils exploitent à Paris, tant dans leurs...

usines et fabriques, sises rue Montempoivre, nos 2, 4 et 6, que dans leurs magasins sis rue de Picpus, n° 160 ; ledit fonds de commerce comprenant :

1ent La clientèle et l'achalandage qui y sont attachés, la dénomination de « Eden Bébé » et toutes autres sous lesquelles la maison est connue, toutes les marques de commerce et de fabrique et tous brevets et dépôts de modèles qui peuvent en dépendre, et le bénéfice de tous traités et marchés qui ont pu être conclus par les apporteurs relativement audit fonds de commerce.

2ent Les matériel, machines, outils, agencements et objets mobiliers servant à la fabrique, à l'exploitation et à la vente, tels qu'ils sont décrits et estimés en un état qui est demeuré ci-joint et annexé, après avoir été certifié sincère et véritable par M. Fleischmann et revêtu d'une mention constatant le tout par les notaires soussignés.

3ent Le droit au bail avec promesse de vente d'un immeuble sis à Paris, rue Montempoivre, nos 4 et 6, d'une superficie d'environ trois mille cent mètres comprenant terrain, cours, bâtiments d'habitation, ateliers, magasins, hangars et bureaux, consenti à MM. Fleischmann et Bloedel par M. Charles-Eugène Bénard, propriétaire, demeurant à Paris, rue Michel-Bizot, n° 131, suivant acte sous signatures privées en date à Paris du 23 février 1893, dont l'un des originaux a été enregistré à Paris, le 12 mai 1893, folio 98, case 5, par le receveur du 12e bureau qui a perçu 95 fr. 25 c. pour trois ans.

Ce bail a été fait pour dix-huit années, qui ont pris cours le 1er avril 1893, et moyennant le loyer annuel de douze mille francs payables en quatre termes égaux, les 1er janvier, avril, juillet et octobre de chaque année.

Il a eu lieu sous les conditions suivantes, etc....

4ent Le droit au bail d'un immeuble contigu aux précédents, sis à Paris, rue Montempoivre n° 2, d'une superficie de 575 mètres environ, comprenant construction légère, bâtiment, cour pavée, aisances et dépendances, consenti à MM. Fleischmann et Bloedel, par M. Bénard, susnommé, suivant acte sous signatures privées en date à Paris du 31 mars 1896, dont l'un des originaux a été enregistré à Paris, le 15 avril 1896, folio 7, case 12, par le receveur du 12e bureau qui a perçu 18 fr. 75 c. pour 3 ans.

Ce bail a été fait pour quinze années, à compter du 1er avril 1896, et moyennant le loyer annuel de 2,500 francs payables en 4 termes égaux aux époques ordinaires de l'année.

Il a eu lieu sous les conditions suivantes, etc.

§ 2e. — Les constructions, reconstructions, améliorations, aménagements et installations qui ont été faits par MM. Fleischmann et Bloedel sur les immeubles loués et plus spécialement sur celui sis à Paris, rue Montempoivre, n° 6, lesquels pour ce dernier immeuble sont les suivants :

1° Un bâtiment sur rue et sur cour à usage d'habitation sur le devant et d'ateliers pour le surplus, élevé sur terre-plein d'un rez-de-chaussée et d'un étage, ayant 8 mètres 50 centimètres de façade et 22 mètres de longueur ;

2° Une étuve en briques au fond et à gauche de l'avenue centrale de l'usine, mesurant 12 mètres sur 5 mètres, élevée d'un rez-de-chaussée sur terre-plein ;

3° Une autre étuve sur le devant de la précédente, ayant 5 mètres sur 5 mètres, même [illegible]

3° Un bâtiment annexe en construction légère, situé entre la grande étuve et le grand bâtiment du fond, avec installation du moteur des trois générateurs et accessoires.

Explication étant faite ici que le bâtiment article 1er a été élevé en remplacement des locaux qui étaient occupés par les époux Sabatier, ainsi qu'il a été expliqué sous l'article troisième, paragraphe premier, du présent apport.

M. Fleischmann, tant en son nom personnel qu'au nom de M. Bloedel, déclare ne comprendre dans leur apport que le fonds de commerce s'exploitant dans les lieux susdésignés et les droits y rattachés, et non la maison de commerce qu'ils exploitent à Fürth (Bavière) avec comptoir d'échantillons à Paris, rue de Turbigo, n° 51.

Aux présentes sont intervenus :

I. — M. Henri Pintel, négociant, demeurant à Paris, avenue du Trône, 6,

Et M. Ernest Godchaux, négociant, demeurant à Enghien (Seine-et-Oise), Grande-Rue, n° 68 ;

MM. Pintel et Godchaux agissant au nom et comme seuls membres de la société en nom collectif formée entre eux sous la raison sociale « Pintel et Godchaux » avec siège social à Paris, avenue du Trône, n° 4, aux termes d'un acte reçu par Mes Chatelain et Galin, notaires à Paris, le 28 juin 1890.

Laquelle société a été publiée conformément à la loi ainsi qu'ils le déclarent.

Lesquels déclarent apporter à la société dont les statuts précèdent :

Le fonds de commerce s'appliquant à la fabrication et à la vente des bébés et jouets en pâte, porcelaine, caoutchouc et autre matière que la Société Pintel et Godchaux exploite en ses usines et magasins sis à Paris, avenue du Trône, n° 4, et à Montreuil-sous-Bois, rue Voltaire, n° 12, ledit fonds de commerce comprenant :

1ent La clientèle et l'achalandage qui y sont attachés, la dénomination de « Bébé Charmant » et toutes autres sous lesquelles la maison est connue, toutes les marques de commerce et de fabrique et tous brevets et dépôts de modèles qui peuvent en dépendre.

2ent. Les matériel, machines, outils, agencement et objets mobiliers servant à la fabrique, à l'exploitation et à la vente, tels qu'ils sont décrits et estimés en un état qui est demeuré ci-joint et annexé, après avoir été certifié sincère et véritable par MM. Pintel et Godchaux et revêtu d'une mention constatant le tout par les notaires soussignés.

Ne sont pas compris dans le présent apport la fabrication et la vente des objets autres que ceux susindiqués, fabriqués et vendus par la Société Pintel et Godchaux, qui continuera à pouvoir les fabriquer et les vendre.

II. — M. Adolphe-Henri Bouchet, négociant, demeurant à Paris, rue Cauchy, nos 24 et 26.

Lequel déclare apporter à la Société dont les statuts précèdent :

Le fonds de commerce de bébés et jouets qu'il exploite à Paris, rue Cauchy, nos 24 et 26 et rue du Temple, n° 169, comprenant :

1ent. La clientèle et l'achalandage qui y sont attachés, la dénomination de « Bébé Géant » et toutes autres sous lesquelles la maison est connue, toutes les marques de commerce et de fabrique et tous brevets et dépôts de modèles qui peuvent en dépendre.

2ent. Les matériel, machines, outils, agencements et objets mobiliers servant à la fabrique, à l'exploitation et à la vente, tels qu'ils sont décrits et estimés en un état qui

certifié sincère et véritable par M. Bouchet et revêtu d'une mention constatant le tout par les notaires soussignés.

III. — M. Emile-Louis Genty, négociant, demeurant à Paris, rue des Archives, n° 3.

Lequel a déclaré apporter à la Société :

Le fonds de commerce de bébés, jouets, articles en porcelaine, qu'il exploite en ses usines et magasins, sis à Paris, rue des Archives, n° 63, et à Limeil (Seine-et-Oise), rue de Toulouse, le dit fonds de commerce comprenant :

1ent. La clientèle et l'achalandage qui y sont attachés, la dénomination de « B[illegible] Paris » et toutes autres sous lesquelles la maison est connue, toutes les marques de commerce et de fabrique et tous brevets et dépôts de modèles qui peuvent en dépendre.

2ent. Les matériel, machines, outils, agencements et objets mobiliers servant à la fabrique, à l'exploitation et à la vente, tels qu'ils sont décrits et estimés en un état qui est demeuré ci-joint et annexé, après avoir été certifié sincère et véritable par M. Genty et revêtu d'une mention constatant le tout par les notaires soussignés.

IV. — M. Paul Girard, négociant, demeurant à Paris, boulevard Saint-Denis, n° 9.

Lequel a déclaré apporter à la Société :

Le fonds de commerce de bébés et jouets qu'il exploite en ses usines et magasins sis à Paris, boulevard Saint-Denis, n° 9, rue Pelleport, nos 89 et 91, comprenant :

1ent. La clientèle et l'achalandage qui y sont attachés, la dénomination de « Bébé Bru » et toutes autres sous lesquelles la maison est connue, toutes les marques de commerce et de fabrique et tous brevets et dépôts de modèles qui peuvent en dépendre.

2ent. Les matériel, outils, agencements et objets mobiliers servant à la fabrique, à l'exploitation et à la vente, tels qu'ils sont décrits et estimés en un état qui est demeuré ci-joint et annexé, après avoir été certifié sincère et véritable par M. Girard et revêtu d'une mention constatant le tout par les notaires soussignés.

V. — M. Frédéric Remignard, négociant, demeurant à Paris, rue des Minimes, n° 4 bis.

Lequel a déclaré apporter à la Société :

Le fonds de commerce de bébés qu'il exploite à Paris, rue des Minimes, n° 4 bis, comprenant :

1ent La clientèle et l'achalandage qui y sont attachés, la dénomination de « le Petit Chérubin » et toutes autres sous lesquelles la maison est connue, toutes les marques de commerce et de fabrique et tous brevets et dépôts de modèles qui peuvent en dépendre ;

2ent Les matériel, machines, outils, agencements et objets mobiliers servant à la fabrique, à l'exploitation et à la vente, tels qu'ils sont décrits et estimés en un état qui est demeuré ci-joint et annexé, après avoir été certifié sincère et véritable par M. Remignard et revêtu d'une mention constatant le tout par les notaires soussignés.

VI. — M. Emile-Jules Gaultier, négociant, demeurant à Saint-Maurice (Seine), rue du Plateau, n° 44,

Et M. Eugène-Louis Gaultier, négociant, demeurant à Saint-Maurice (Seine), avenue de l'Asile, n° 4 bis ;

MM. Emile-Jules Gaultier et Eugène-Louis Gaultier agissant au nom et comme seuls membres de la société en nom collectif formée entre eux sous la raison sociale « [illegible] Gaultier

rue des Epinettes, n° 25, aux termes d'un acte reçu par Me Leclerc, notaire, à Charenton (Seine), le 25 janvier 1888,

Laquelle Société a été publiée conformément à la loi, ainsi qu'ils le déclarent ;

Lesquels ont déclaré apporter à la Société dont les statuts précèdent :

Le fonds de commerce d'articles en porcelaine que la Société Gaultier frères exploite à Saint-Maurice (Seine), rue des Epinettes, n° 25, comprenant :

1ent La clientèle et l'achalandage qui y sont attachés, toutes dénominations sous lesquelles la maison est connue, toutes les marques de commerce et de fabrique et tous brevets et dépôts de modèles qui peuvent en dépendre ;

2ent Les matériel, outils, agencements et objets mobiliers servant à la fabrique, à l'exploitation et à la vente, tels qu'ils sont décrits et estimés en un état qui est demeuré ci-joint et annexé, après avoir été certifié sincère et véritable par MM. Gaultier et revêtu d'une mention constatant le tout par les notaires soussignés.

VII. — M. Alphonse-Benoît Gobert, négociant, demeurant à Paris, rue d'Alésia, n° 186 bis.

Lequel a déclaré apporter à la Société :

Le fonds de commerce s'appliquant à la fabrication et à la vente des bébés et jouets en pâte, porcelaine, caoutchouc et autres matières qu'il exploite en son usine sise à Paris, rue d'Alésia, nos 186 bis et 188, et comprenant :

1ent La clientèle et l'achalandage qui y sont attachés, la dénomination de « Bébé Colosse » et toutes autres sous lesquelles sa maison est connue, toutes les marques de commerce et de fabrique et tous brevets et dépôts de modèles qui peuvent en dépendre ;

2ent Les matériel, machines, outils, agencements et objets mobiliers servant à la fabrique, à l'exploitation et à la vente, tels qu'ils sont décrits et estimés en un état qui est demeuré ci-joint et annexé, après avoir été certifié sincère et véritable par M. Gobert et revêtu d'une mention constatant le tout par les notaires soussignés.

Ne sont pas compris dans le présent apport la fabrication et la vente des objets, autres que ceux ci-dessus indiqués, fabriqués et vendus par M. Gobert, qui en restera propriétaire et continuera à pouvoir les fabriquer et les vendre.

VIII. — M. Arthur Wertheimer, négociant, demeurant à Paris, rue Pastourelle, n° 27.

Lequel a déclaré apporter à la Société :

Le fonds de commerce de bébés qu'il exploite à Paris, rue Pastourelle, n° 27, comprenant :

1ent La clientèle et l'achalandage qui y sont attachés, la dénomination de « le Baby » et toutes autres sous lesquelles la maison est connue, toutes les marques de commerce et de fabrique et tous brevets et dépôts de modèles qui peuvent en dépendre ;

2ent Les matériel, outils, agencements et objets mobiliers servant à la fabrique, à l'exploitation et à la vente, tels qu'ils sont décrits et estimés en un état qui est demeuré ci-joint et annexé, après avoir été certifié sincère et véritable par M. Wertheimer et revêtu d'une mention constatant le tout par les notaires soussignés.

IX. — Et M. Émile-Louis Jumeau, négociant, chevalier de la Légion d'honneur, et Mme Ernestine-Stéphanie Ducruix, son épouse, qu'il autorise, demeurant ensemble à Paris, boulevard Beaumarchais, n° 67.

Lesquels ont déclaré apporter à la Société :

Le fonds de commerce de fabrication et de vente de bébés par eux exploité à Paris, rue Pastourelle, n° 8, comprenant :

La clientèle et l'achalandage ;

Le matériel et le mobilier industriel servant à son exploitation et se trouvant dans les locaux de la rue Pastourelle, n° 8, et dans les deux usines ci-après indiquées ;

La propriété des marques de fabrique et notamment de la marque « Bébé Jumeau » ;

Pour la somme de 360,000 francs les marchandises et matières premières se trouvant rue Pastourelle, n° 8, et dans les deux usines de Montreuil-sous-Bois, telles qu'elles sont décrites et estimées en un état qui est demeuré ci-annexé, après avoir été certifié sincère et véritable par M. et Mme Jumeau et revêtu d'une mention constatant le tout par les notaires soussignés.

Le droit au bail consenti à M. et Mme Jumeau des locaux à Paris, rue Pastourelle, n° 8, par Mme Marie-Victorine Moreau, veuve de M. Saint-Charles Cosson, propriétaire, demeurant à Paris, rue de La Boétie, n° 7, M. Albert Durand, propriétaire et Mme Caroline Cosson, son épouse, demeurant ensemble à Paris, mêmes rue et numéro, et M. Paul-Henri-Charles Cosson, propriétaire, demeurant à Paris, avenue de Friedland, n° 9, suivant acte reçu par Mes Blanchet et Naret, notaires à Paris (ledit Me Naret ayant substitué Me Leroy), le 11 avril 1890, pour 3, 6, ou 9 années consécutives, qui ont commencé à courir le 1er avril 1890, pour finir à pareille époque des années 1896 ou 1899, à la volonté des preneurs et moyennant divers loyers s'élevant à 8,800 francs.

Et le droit à un nouveau bail consenti à M. et Mme Jumeau, et à la société Jumeau et compagnie, par M. Cosson, pour prendre cours le 1er avril 1893, et expirer le 1er octobre de l'une des années 1899, 1902, 1905 ou 1908, à la volonté des preneurs seuls, aux termes d'un acte reçu par Mes Blanchet et Leroy, notaires à Paris, le 31 janvier 1893.

Ce bail comprenant divers locaux à Paris, rue Pastourelle, n° 8, a été fait moyennant un loyer annuel de 9,200 francs sur lequel il a été versé 4,600 francs pour 6 mois d'avance.

Le bénéfice des opérations de commerce depuis le 1er mars 1899.

Néanmoins le loyer du bail susénoncé restera à la charge personnelle de M. et Mme Jumeau, jusqu'au 1er juillet prochain, quoique la Société ait le droit de se servir des locaux à partir de la constitution définitive.

En outre, M. et Mme Jumeau font bail et donnent à loyer à la Société pour 10 années à partir du 1er juillet prochain :

De deux usines dont M. et Mme Jumeau sont propriétaires, situées à Montreuil-sous-Bois.

L'une, rue de Paris, n° 152, comprenant diverses constructions et terrains, le tout d'une contenance de 4,314 mètres environ.

Et l'autre, rue François-Arago, n° 64 et rue Raspail, n° 18, comprenant diverses constructions et terrains, le tout d'une contenance de 2,463 mètres environ.

La Société prendra les deux usines avec tous les immeubles par destination qui en dépendent et toutes leurs dépendances sans exception ni réserve.

Elle aura droit jusqu'au 1er juillet prochain à la jouissance gratuite des immeubles en question et à partir du jour de sa constitution définitive sans payer aucun loyer.

Le loyer est fixé à 15,000 francs par an, payable par quart aux termes d'usage.

La Société pourra faire, pendant la durée du bail, tels aménagements et changements de distribution qu'il lui conviendra, elle pourra faire telles constructions nouvelles qu'il lui plaira et même démolir les constructions existantes, mais à la condition de les remplacer par d'autres constructions de valeur au moins égale à celles détruites et qui appartiendront aux propriétaires.

La Société entretiendra lesdits immeubles en bon état de toutes espèces de grosses et menues réparations et en supportera toutes les contributions foncières et primes d'assurances et autres charges de toute nature, le loyer ci-dessus fixé étant expressément net de toutes espèces de charges.

En outre, M. et Mme Jumeau confèrent à la Société la faculté d'acquérir ou de faire acquérir si bon lui semble, pendant le cours du bail ci-dessus, c'est-à-dire avant le 1er juillet 1909, les deux usines ci-dessus avec leurs dépendances, telles qu'elles existeront à l'époque de l'acquisition, à la charge par ladite Société de prévenir M. et Mme Jumeau, six mois d'avance.

En cas de réalisation, le prix de la vente serait de 300,000 francs.

Ce prix serait payable après les formalités à remplir sur le contrat de vente.

Les intérêts à 5 % de ce prix courraient à partir du jour de l'acte de vente, date à partir de laquelle cesserait de courir le loyer ci-dessus stipulé.

La vente serait réalisée sous les conditions ordinaires et de droit et aux frais de la Société.

M. et Mme Jumeau s'obligent solidairement à établir par acte en suite des présentes l'origine de propriété régulière desdits immeubles.

ATTRIBUTION EN REPRÉSENTATION DES APPORTS.

En représentation des apports ci-dessus faits, il est attribué, savoir :

1° A MM. Fleischmann et Bloedel, à raison de chacun moitié, 2.000 actions entièrement libérées de la Société, faisant partie de celles créées sous l'article six ci-dessus, soit 1,000 actions pour chacun d'eux,

	actions	francs
lesdites actions représentant 1,000,000 de francs, ci	2.000	1.000.000
2° A la Société Pintel et Godchaux, 400 des mêmes actions, représentant 200,000 francs, ci	400	200.000
3° A M. Bouchet, 200 des mêmes actions, représentant 100,000 fr., ci	200	100.000
4° A M. Genty, 110 actions représentant 55,000 francs, ci......	110	55.000
5° A M. Girard, 110 actions représentant 55,000 francs, ci......	110	55.000
6° A M. Remignard, 100 actions représentant 50,000 francs, ci.	100	50.000
7° A la Société Gaultier frères, 100 actions représentant 50,000 fr., ci	100	50.000
A reporter.....	3.020	1.510.000

(Page contenant des statuts et procès-verbaux d'assemblées d'une société, reproduits en colonnes d'orientation tournée et en très mauvais état de lisibilité.)

actions	francs
Report..... 3.020	1.510.000
8° A M. Gobert, 80 actions représentant 40.000 francs, ci.... 80	40.000
9° A M. Wertheimer, 50 actions représentant 25.000 francs, ci. 50	25.000
10° Et à M. et Mme Jumeau, 1.320 des mêmes actions, représentant 660,000 francs, ci. 1.320	660.000
Totaux..... 4.470	2.235.000

Ces actions devront demeurer à la souche pour n'en être détachées et ne demeurer négociables que deux ans après la date où l'assemblée générale qui aura vérifié et approuvé les apports ci-dessus.

Elles porteront les numéros suivants :

1° Celles de M. Fleischmann, de 1 à 1.000.
2° Celles de M. Bloedel, de 1.001 à 2.000.
3° Celles de la Société Pintel et Godchaux, de 2.001 à 2.400.
4° Celles de M. Bouchet, de 2.401 à 2.500.
5° Celles de M. Genty, de 2.001 à 2.710.
6° Celles de M. Girard, de 2.711 à 2.820.
7° Celles de M. Remignard, de 2.821 à 2.920.
8° Celles de la Société Gaultier frères, de 2.921 à 3.020.
9° Celles de M. Gobert, de 3.021 à 3.100.
10° Celles de M. Wertheimer, de 3.101 à 3.150.
11° Et celles de M. et Mme Jumeau, de 3.151 à 4.470.

(Le reste du texte, fortement dégradé, comprend : Conditions des apports — II — III — Première résolution, Deuxième résolution, Troisième résolution — Quatrième résolution, Cinquième résolution, Septième résolution — et la signature du Président du Conseil d'administration, E. Lefèvre.)

Quelques Considérations Economiques
Some Economic Considerations

At the end of the 19th century and beginning of the 20th, the following points sum up the characteristics of French trade and industry: fear of taking risks, restraint in desires, conservatism and lack of combativity.

German industry found its force in the opposing tendencies pushed sometimes to excess. The general French spirit, which with rare exceptions like Emile Jumeau, was more preoccupied with maintaining savings or slowly increasing them by being economical, than by multiplying them with sometimes risky speculation.

At this turning-point in the century, social clashes brought, on a purely social level, an amelioration in labor prices. This should be a phenomenon to celebrate, and yet from a purely economic point of view it was a snag, because this rise preceded a lowering in the birth rate. The lack of man-power was a cause of low production which brought on a supplemental charge in terms of international competition. Machinism or industrialization allowed, in increasing each person's productivity, to buy more expensive labor, and to sell the resulting products at a better price. In Paris, life was expensive and the worker wanted to be paid in accordance. In Germany, life was inexpensive and workers' salaries were cheap.

In France, a small number of toy industries, those who did not produce "novelties," were established in the provinces. For the others, the Paris air was as necessary as it was to artists and writers. They needed to know what was going on, the fashion of the day, to feel around them the shiver of Parisian life which passed into their creations, and which gave them that particular stamp, so appreciated the world over.

In France, speculators preferred to subscribe small state loans, or to private company or bank securities, those of mines, ports, railroads and other distant speculations. These same speculators, so adventurous, refused to invest even a few thousand francs in French trade or industry, which made some native owners borrow at the usurious rate of thirty percent.

In Germany, numerous advantages existed for industries, especially for those, like the toy manufacturers, which exported their products. For the Germans, the toy problem was seriously considered. This field was particularly advantageous: one handled a lot of business with little money.

Nevertheless, what in France was considered a heavy capital based company was nothing compared to the factories of Nüremberg, Sonneberg, and Fürth which started with enormous capital. Germany possessed a gigantic credit structure. Everything functioned by reciprocal confidence on the part of industrialists and bankers. For example, if a toy producer without capital received orders for 300,000 francs at the Leipzig fair, his banker, after familiarizing himself with the clients, would advance 25% of the amount of the orders, and later, the rest — in other words, a discount policy.

France found this "cavalry" of bank bills undignified. The French producers ran up against banks which were haunted by the fear of immobilization and too conservative to take risks with this seasonal industry, the toy market. France had money, but did not have the courage to risk it.

The Germans were great workers; they did not fear creating new machinery. The French were more apathetic and said it was too difficult. They were also disorganized. However there was no lack of ideas and there was no need of a production school in France although one was created in Thuringia.

Another economic phenomenon was the unjust cost of transportation. An extract from the speech of Mr. Chauvin, President of the *Chambre Syndicale du Jouet*, on February 20, 1897, gives a clear view of this inequity. "In Germany, 1000 kilos of toys sent from Fürth to Petit-Croix (the French border) costs 68 francs for 490 kilometers, while in France, for the same distance, same weight, you pay 111 francs or 42 francs more. Another example: 100 kilos of toys sent from Paris to Nancy costs, for a distance of 349 kilometers, 8 francs 09; the same weight and same articles leaving Lichtenfelds for Nancy, costs 5 francs 30 to cover 550 kilometers, or 2 francs 79 less to do 207 kilometers more."

Germany understood before the French and the British, that across the world, there existed a clientele that only a low price could reach and win over. Society was renewing itself at the turn of the century and the middle class was expanding. Germany was going to conquer this clientele in the two hemispheres by supplying it what it wanted: inexpensive articles. The models were simplified; the cost of production was brought down and then an all-out-effort was made to sell it. It was the intensive production circle creating the inexpensive, which in turn created the enormous output.

German commercial methods were full of discoveries, tricks and inventions. What the French put into the product and its quality, the Germans put into distribution and promotion. Discounts, possibilities of prolonged payments by drafts, thanks to German credit, the "placing in consignment" or deposit-sale, were strong and effective arguments in this economic joust.

If advertisements had been used in France by French producers, direct contact with the client would have been easier. The Germans not only had numerous specialized papers, but also illustrated catalogues from each producer and unionized group. These were sent all over the world in preparation for the salesmen's visits. France sent only few salesmen and the foreign buyer was obliged to come to France to order.

The situation before World War I can be summarized: the German doll reigned everywhere. This success was the result of a methodic and patient struggle. The Germans had acted on this market as on others, in offering the buyer articles at a greatly reduced price. Was this a lure? Almost. Everything was combined to obtain orders: facility of payment, speed of delivery and duty-free handling. In Paris, the display rooms multiplied, and their directors imagined and anticipated the client's desires. Provided with specific information, Germany transformed, invented, or imitated. Her incessant activity always corresponded to a need of the moment. This rivalry was impossible to overcome and in a few years it ruined the French doll industry.

Several houses, such as Rabery, Bru, Pintel and Godchaux, gave up the fight and let themselves be absorbed, before 1900 by the S.F.B.J. From then on this company exerted a true monopoly. Its autonomous set up — the only one in France — allowed it to produce complete baby dolls. Other companies, dependent on Germany for porcelain heads[3] and glass eyes, painfully kept body and soul together.

After 1900, Fleischmann and Bloedel, Gutmann and Schiffnie, and Margarete Steiff energetically continued their peaceful conquest. In Sonneberg, the great doll-producing center, many firms dealt specially with export to France. Protected by the imperial government and Chamber of Commerce, they received important bonuses. Nüremberg, Eisfeld, Georgenthal, Ilmenau, Naustadt and Walterhausen sent dolls by the thousands to France. German cheapness was often the consequence of the resaler's demands. The factories on that side of the Rhine were highly efficient in producing articles. Thanks to their improved materials and their steadiness of production, they couldn't be opposed. By the beginning of the war, the situation was critical.

---

[3] Saxony delivered heads to Paris at 0 francs 10 each, all costs included. The same head, produced in France, cost 0 francs 40. One of the main reasons for this difference was that the Saxon kilns were built to simultaneously bake doll heads (inexpensive articles) and porcelain (luxury articles).

A worker attaching and styling a doll's wig at the rue Montempoivre factory.

Les habilleuses

De l'atelier des perruques elle passe à l'habillement, où on s'occupe d'abord de ses dessous et ensuite de ses robes.

Dressmakers creating outfits for the dolls.

A worker putting shoes and stockings on a doll.

Le magasin des poupées.

Après ces diverses opérations, les poupées sont entassées par catégories dans le magasin d'où elles partiront pour être livrées à la vente.

After being assembled and dressed, the dolls were piled in categories for the stores where they would be distributed for sale.

The proposal Fleischmann made to his associates, as to their merging into a trust, allowed them to eliminate numerous expenses such as rent and travel which burdened them individually. Cleverly directed, the *Société Française des Bébés et Jouets* doubled its turnover in 15 years; this was about five million in 1914, employing 2,000 workers. Shareholders' dividends were between eight and nine percent.

One fifth of its turnover represented the volume of primary materials bought in Germany in 1915. This was enormous, but no one could oppose Salomon Fleischmann's policy. His "associates" were ruined, and the appraiser's report remarked that "costs absorbed about everyone's profits, except for one."

At the beginning of the century, around 1905, Fleischmann imported from Germany a big stamping machine of Bavarian origin. This made 400 doll bodies per hour instead of 25 done by hand. Wooden limbs for the middle category dolls (those completely articulated with nine pieces: two arms, two forearms, two hands, two thighs, two legs and one torso) came from the Ain and Nièvre factories. In 1913, the Montempoivre factory (the old Fleischmann and Bloedel Company factory) still made about five

Photographs from the rue Montempoivre doll factory which Fleischmann contributed to the S.F.B.J.
CLOCKWISE:
Dolls before entering the wig workshop.
Worker attaching legs to bodies.
Arm and leg workshop with doll hands drying in the foreground.
Legs workshop

and a half million clay dolls. This factory was featured in an article written by Leo Clarétie, which appeared in the 1902 paper *Femina*.

The initial factory, that of the *Bébé Jumeau*, where the S.F.B.J. was originally installed, was greatly transformed from 1899 to 1913. For example, the two meter kiln was replaced by two kilns, each of six meters, which allowed the S.F.B.J. to produce 30,000 heads at once. When reading these figures, it is easy to understand why so many S.F.B.J. dolls exist today. However, discards sometimes represented 30 percent of gross production, at various levels.

Speaking of kilns and baking, Germany had an advantage over France; German porcelain clay baked at 200 degrees less than the French clay which resulted in great savings. Firing expenses had to be doubled to prolong the baking time. In temperatures over 1000 degrees, the consumption of coal was out of proportion with the heat obtained. The S.F.B.J. clay composition baked at 1,200 degrees, that of Germany, around 1,000 degrees.

This and other reasons such as a fast and efficient assembly line system, made Germany an important exporter of doll heads. The clear difference in price was a determining factor in Salomon Fleischmann's choice to order German doll heads. Up to World War I, S.F.B.J. dolls were produced in large numbers outside of France.

Introduction to Part II
by Ann Marie Porot

The S.F.B.J.'s production, like its history, was the meeting of two important toy greats, two nationalities until then competitors, and two very different conceptions of production and commerce. When we say "toy," it is to respect the company's title, but *the S.F.B.J. was essentially a doll making consortium.* Fleischmann kept his toy business separate from the S.F.B.J. and the co-founders were practically all doll merchants. It was a successful combination from which a new production was achieved, but with the persistent stamp of each member.

To attain optimum production, several targets had to be aimed for. First, to select from each manufacturer the object which sold the best or was the cheapest to make. These became *the surviving brands and products within the S.F.B.J.* But the unprofitable had to be rejected, and *their production ceased in 1899.*

Upon attaining a certain growth, the industrial trust presented new creations (essentially character dolls). So the *S.F.B.J. talent itself* was most important. The S.F.B.J.'s talent, as that of other producers, naturally expressed itself largely by *patent petitions and trademark registration.* This aspect is so important, that we will dedicate a special chapter to it.

II

La Fabrication S.F.B.J.
The S.F.B.J. Production

by Ann Marie Porot

Anatomie des Poupées et Bébés de la S.F.B.J.

The Anatomy of the S.F.B.J. Dolls

The S.F.B.J. manufactured dolls for nearly 60 years. During this period, its manufacturing developed and diversified or simplified according to changing styles. It also adapted to material and technical changes, yet at the same time followed market fluctuations. This aspect of diversity is quite useful since each new and different characteristic allows us to date the S.F.B.J. dolls.

It is therefore necessary to define the anatomical types that correspond to different eras and price categories and to be able to label these anatomical types in clear terms. This is difficult, however, because of the confusing labels and changing terms used by the manufacturers and old and recent catalogs.

We must accept the fact that we do not all speak the same language. Each profession has its own jargon, consequently, we sometimes use familiar terms improperly. This is especially noticeable when talking about the words *poupée* and *bébé*. In principle, the term *poupée* refers to a rigid or semi-articulated figure that represents older girls or women, and the term *bébé* refers to very young infants. However, though the difference lies in the age limit, the distinction is not precisely defined. From 1855-1900, the distinction prevailed that *bébé* referred to a young infant and *poupée* to a little girl or lady. The term *bébé* is of the masculine gender, and therefore refers to a being whose gender is not yet defined, because in the French language, the masculine gender is dominant. In the 19th century, as well as in the beginning of the 20th, boys also wore skirts and dresses during their early infancy.

Even today, we are still debating about which term to use. At the end of the 19th century, the term *bébé* was of considerable importance. It was, without a doubt, significant of the fact that the term *bébé* was an expression of tenderness, which clearly revealed the maternal relationship established between the little girl and her doll. In 1899, when the S.F.B.J. first began manufacturing, all the products were called *bébés* including the *incassables* (unbreakable dolls) and the *marcheurs* (walking dolls); the term *poupée* was not used in commercial language. Even the name of the company prefers to use *bébé* instead of simply *poupée*.

The *bébé* with a character head was introduced about 1910, thereby creating a new category: character *bébés* which were distinguished from the ordinary *bébés*.

Felt dolls first appeared on the market around 1922, and were called *poupées*. Confusion in the catalog reached its peak towards 1935. The terms used in the catalogs are sometimes inaccurate. However, the term *bébé* is used in connection with the celluloid doll.

We are grouping together all of what French manufacturers call *incassable* (or unbreakable dolls) and character *bébés*, under the title chapter *bébés*. All the other subjects will be grouped under the title *poupées*. The confusion of terms is further aggravated by the use of the term *incassable*. In advertisements and in the French manufacturers' old catalogs this term serves as a kind of classification and needs clarified because it did not represent the same thing during different periods. First of all, the term *incassable* (unbreakable) indicates that the *bébé* itself was manufactured in non-fragile material; this is easy enough to understand. However, around 1880, the term *incassable* signified that the whole body of the *bébé* was assembled in a way that made it more durable. Therefore, it could subsequently be easily repaired because it was assembled from multiple articulated components. From that time on, the term *incassable* was also associated with the term, *bébé*. The use of the two-word term *incassable bébé* (unbreakable baby doll) to designate a new creation had consequently become largely widespread among manufacturers; so much so, that the business directory (in France called *le Bottin*) created a special classification

for it next to the one for *poupées*. This designation was used until 1953 or 1954. And vice-versa, the term *poupée* was used again with the remarketing of stuffed dolls (felt or fabric), even though they were not assembled from articulated components, and so were not able to be dismantled. The term *incassable bébé* is practically synonymous with that of articulated *bébé*. We will see later on that the articulation methods used for these components result in various anatomical structures.

When talking about the anatomy of *poupées* and *bébés*, we must never separate the *corps* (body) from the *tête* (head), and we must give equal attention to both. Admittedly, they are manufactured separately, often from different materials. Few collectors really know how to appreciate the beauty of a body. Harmony and logic must merge together to form a necessary relationship between the head and the body. This marriage can result in a perfect union, a legitimate hybridization, or an outrageous and grotesque assemblage.

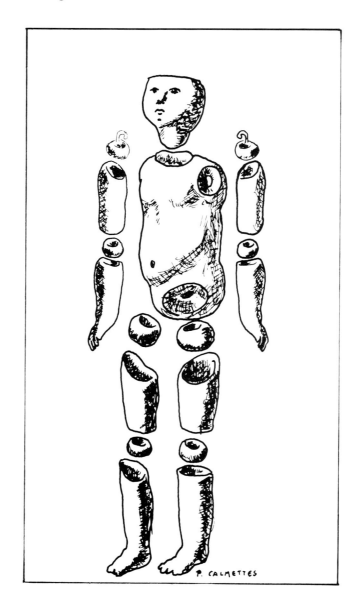

P. CALMETTES

Les Corps
The Bodies

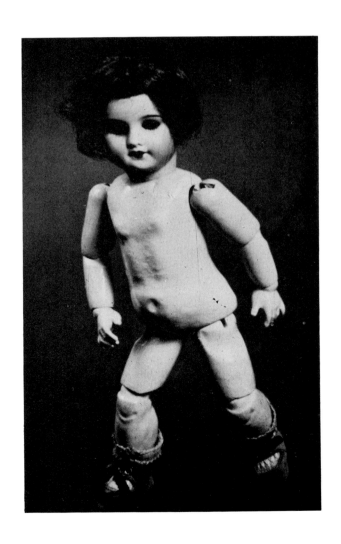

Le Corps du Bébé Articulé Incassable Ordinaire
The Articulated Body of the Ordinary Doll

The doll body's essential characteristic, its articulation, is what precisely defines it and consequently determines who produced it and when. Therefore this particular aspect must be examined closely. Manufacturers in the past took note of this, and called their dolls *bébés articulés incassables* (unbreakable articulated baby dolls).

When talking about the S.F.B.J., the body type determined the *bébés* quality and selling price. The ordinary *bébé articulé incassable* body was derived from a Jumeau body. It had been produced before the S.F.B.J. *bébés* and was manufactured for a long time.

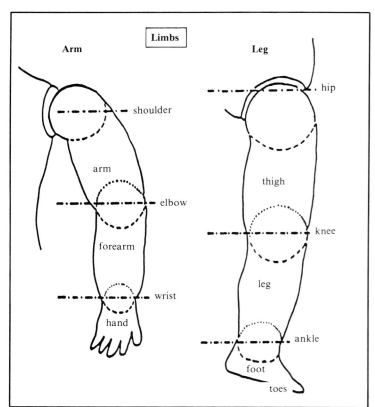

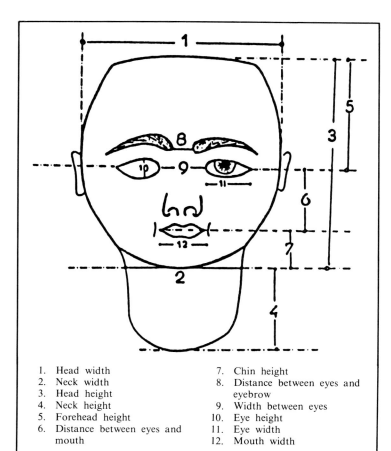

1. Head width	7. Chin height
2. Neck width	8. Distance between eyes and
3. Head height	eyebrow
4. Neck height	9. Width between eyes
5. Forehead height	10. Eye height
6. Distance between eyes and	11. Eye width
mouth	12. Mouth width

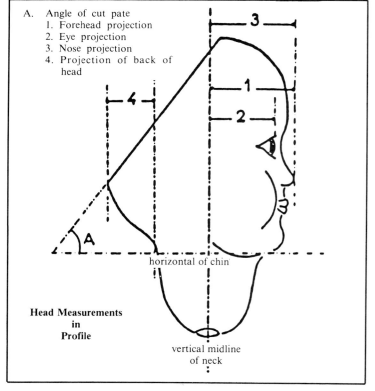

A. Angle of cut pate
  1. Forehead projection
  2. Eye projection
  3. Nose projection
  4. Projection of back of head

Head Measurements in Profile

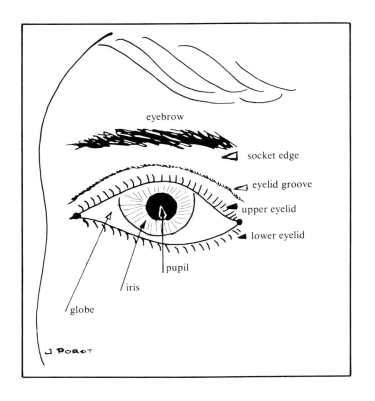

eyebrow

◁ socket edge

◁ eyelid groove

◀ upper eyelid

◀ lower eyelid

pupil

iris

globe

J POROT

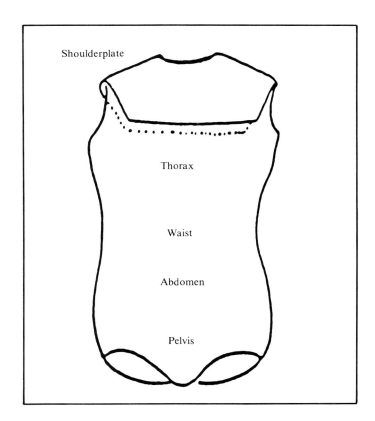

Shoulderplate

Thorax

Waist

Abdomen

Pelvis

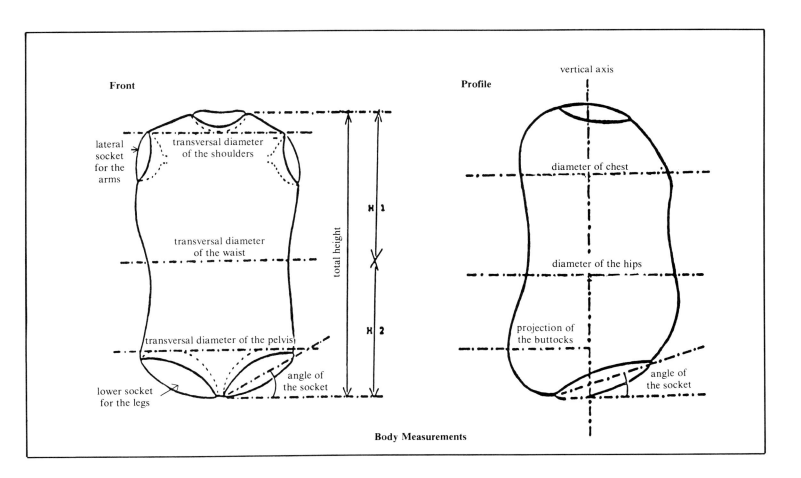

Front

lateral socket for the arms

transversal diameter of the shoulders

transversal diameter of the waist

transversal diameter of the pelvis

lower socket for the legs

angle of the socket

total height

H 1

H 2

Profile

vertical axis

diameter of chest

diameter of the hips

projection of the buttocks

angle of the socket

Body Measurements

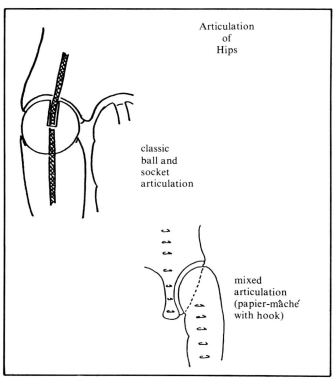

Articulation
of
Hips

classic
ball and
socket
articulation

mixed
articulation
(papier-mâché
with hook)

Diagram showing hip articulation.

Angles of Articulation

slight
angle

steep
angle

with
button

Diagram illustrating three angles of leg joints.

Baby doll body can be identified through anatomical details, such as measurements of different structures. The police, doctors and artists are familiar with the type of anthropometry. The following tables of reference points are useful for this type of exercise. Several kinds of character *bébé* bodies subsequently followed.

Five Kinds of S.F.B.J. Body Articulation

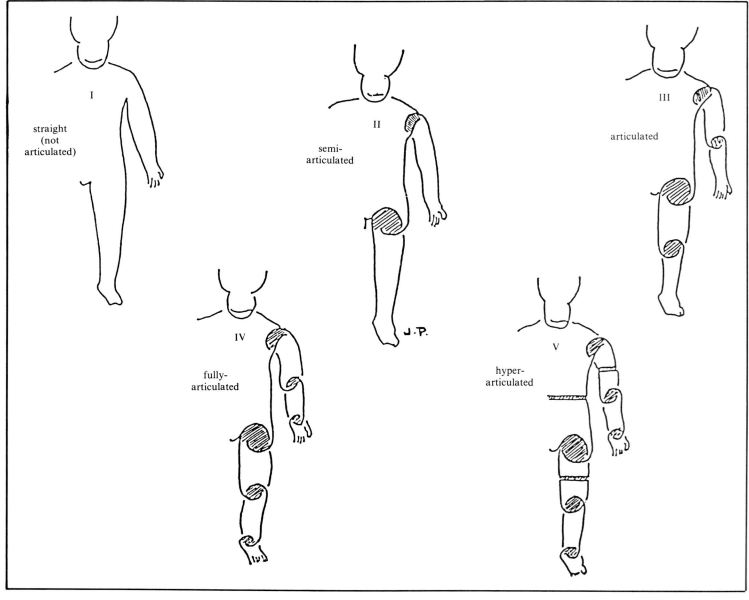

I
straight
(not
articulated)

II
semi-
articulated

III
articulated

IV
fully-
articulated

V
hyper-
articulated

J.P.

Le Bébé Incassable tout Articulé
The Fully-Articulated Incassable Body

The bodies of this category evolved according to manufacturing requirements rather than style changes. The fully-articulated *bébé*, which in fact was Jumeau's, was quite suitable for child's play. It could sit, and if we believe the advertisements, it could also kneel. However, its cost of production was high because it required specially selected materials and more labor, the main difference between Jumeau's and Fleischmann's manufacturing process. The S.F.B.J. oscillated between these two trends but never completely discarded this type of body. In the beginning, both Jumeau's and Bru's molds were used. However, Bru's molds were quickly replaced by Jumeau's.

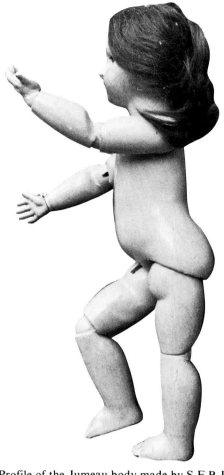

Profile of the Jumeau body made by S.F.B.J.

Doll with a head marked "D.E.P." and a Jumeau body made by S.F.B.J. Stamped "Tête Jumeau," it is size 10, 55cm (22in) high.

The Jumeau Body Type

Jumeau's body type was used regularly until 1910, sometimes bearing the blue stamp. Most often, however, it bore the pink oval label, placed on the small of the back and marked, "*Bébé Jumeau Diplôme d'Honneur.*"

Consequently, the outward appearance of the body leads us to believe that there was confusion between Jumeau's later *bébés* and the ones first produced by the S.F.B.J. This was especially evident in that the S.F.B.J. heads bore the stamp, *Tête Jumeau* (Jumeau head). However, the outward appearance was of no importance, as the assembly was not the same. It is therefore necessary to either open or x-ray the subject to identify the maker.

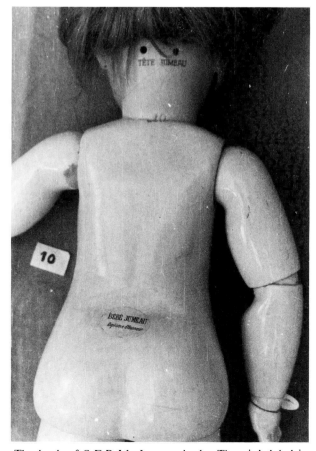

The back of S.F.B.J.'s Jumeau body. The pink label is printed "*Bébé Jumeau, Diplome d'Honneur.*"

1899-1914

In the S.F.B.J. body derived from the Jumeau type, the limbs were still thick and heavy, the calves were large, but the forearms thinned down into articulated wrists. The feet were well formed with the toes visibly defined; hands were detailed and the fingers were clearly separated. Finally, the upper extremities of the thighs were still visible and were lightly marked by a fissure which, with time, became more apparent; the contours were toned down and softened; the inner side of the thighs were emphasized by two grooves representing rolls of skin.

Little by little, a different body took shape. As before, it was made of molded carton or pasteboard. However, the lower abdomen was less indented by the hips, and its form was less trapezoidal. The trunk was still detailed, carefully pumiced and painted, and quite smooth to the touch.

Towards 1910, the thighs were a little longer than the lower legs. (This particular aspect was less noticeable in German dolls.) This was a device due to the fashion of the period when skirts were knee length. As the waist of the dress was still low, esthetically speaking, this fashion style did not suit the dolls very well. Therefore, the thighs were lengthened in order to regain a balance between the skirt and the bodice. Evidently, the quality of the anatomy reflected this effect, and in France this device was discarded as soon as the waist regained its importance.

From 1899 to 1914, the *tout articulé bébé* (fully-articulated doll) had its trunk in molded carton, its limbs in turned and hollowed wood; legs in wood or in molded carton, and its hands in composition. These bodies were assembled with French or German (Simon and Halbig) bisque heads, or with heads manufactured from unbreakable material — a type of composition.

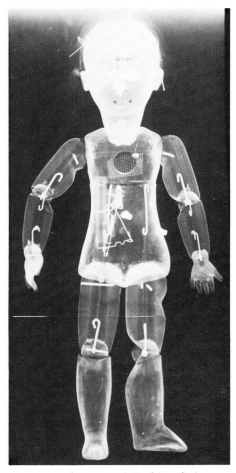

X-ray showing how a doll with an independent head connection is assembled. The papier-mâché trunk has a wooden bar to which the long leg hooks are connected. The S.H. head has eyes patented by S.F.B.J. in 1904.

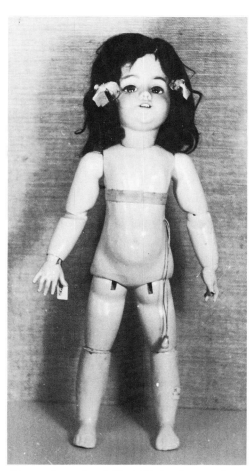

Front view of a S.H. 1039 head on a first model S.F.B.J. body.

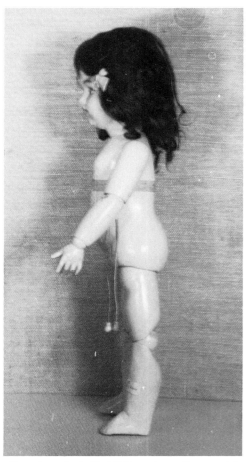

Side view of a S.H. 1039 head on a first model S.F.B.J. body.

1914-1925

After World War I, high-waisted, short dresses were in style for little girls. The knee was therefore exposed, and so *bébés* also showed their knees. The molding, being more realistic, revealed the projection of the kneecap.

The torso was still fabricated in molded carton. However, bodies in composition were beginning to be manufactured: they were heavier, less realistic and more rectilinear: the hips were almost perpendicular to the shoulders. The body also consisted of a small chest, a large stomach, and a hollow navel. The back was straight, hardly arched. The limbs were less well proportioned. The arms were short and straight with no roundness to the shoulders. The forearms were rectilinear and tubular. The hands were small, and no longer showed apparent wrists. The upper limbs attained only hip articulation.

The lower limbs were also rectilinear. The plane and the groove which completed the rounded upper extremity (condyle or ball joint) were quite marked on this model. Over the years, this became more accentuated, marking a straightforward cut, *en coup de hache*, or hatchet cut. This plane was a release area which allowed for the flexing of the limb.

The assembly was connected with elastic. In the *bébé* body of molded carton with a wooden crosspiece, the legs hung onto the crosspiece through long hooks and rubber cords. The same system was applied to the Jumeau *bébé*. The head was held by another rubber cord connecting the two arms. The S.F.B.J. discarded the big Jumeau spring used for the head, as well as the springs used for the forearms. There was also a head-to-legs connection, thus leaving the arms independent. In the very first few years, there was an independent fastening device for the head.

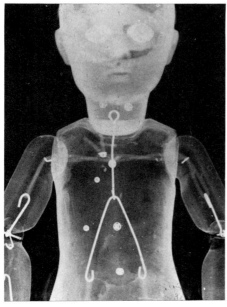

Assembly of an S.F.B.J. doll with the head marked "1907."

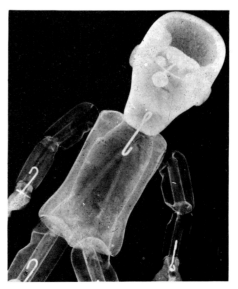

Assembly of an S.F.B.J. doll with the head marked "UNIS."

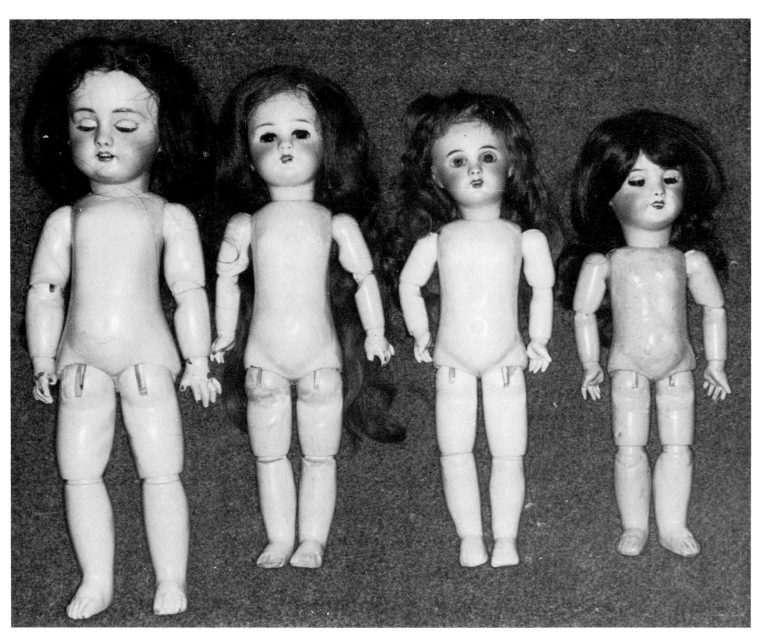

Front view of S.F.B.J. bodies showing the evolution of the Jumeau type. The doll on the left has the first model body and the doll on the right has a body made after World War I.

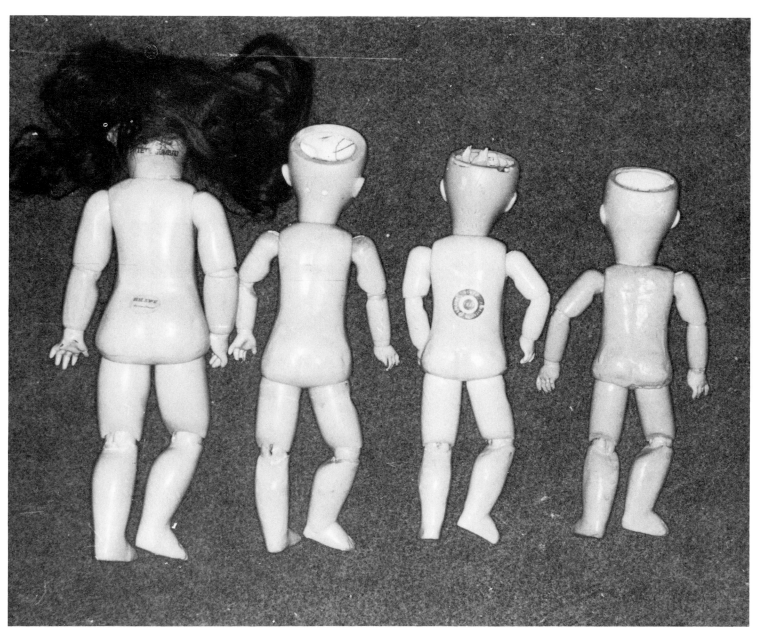

Back view of S.F.B.J. bodies showing the evolution of the Jumeau type. The doll on the left has the first model body and the one on the right has a body made after World War I.

1925-1930

Another fully-articulated *bébé* appeared towards the year 1925. The trunk was manufactured in molded carton and divided into two parts which were then joined together by staples in the middle of the front and of the back. This trunk was straight and round, with hardly any contours, and ended in a point, or rather in a V. The upper limbs were manufactured in wood, and were spindly.

The lower limbs were manufactured in molded carton and were fastened in the front and in the back. The thighs appear to be long because their articular side faces inside and not up; the hip articulation is vertical and no longer horizontal. This enabled the assemblage elastic to pass directly from one hip to another.

This type of articulation was already known at the end of the 19th century. Denamur used it to assemble his *Le Bambin*. It offered the double advantage of avoiding the inelegant opening at the top of the thighs and, especially, of maintaining the legs in a sitting position. The legs, manufactured in wood, had a glued wooden condyle. The contours of the kneecap were apparent; the insteps revealed the folds of flection. The feet had little detail.

Occasionally a number was engraved on the soles of these *bébés* feet. This same number appeared on the side of the bust: it corresponded to the size of the *bébé*.

The assembly of this model was very simple: a long linkage system, made of rubber, joined one wrist to the other by crossing the arms and the bust. The same system was used for the lower limbs in which the elastic tie joined one knee to the other through the lower abdomen. This procedure caused the *bébé* to be rather fragile and difficult to repair.

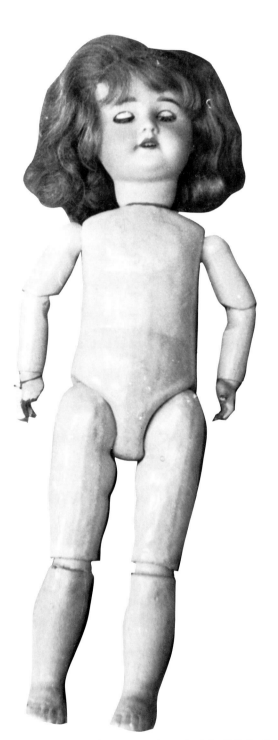

48cm (19in) doll with the head marked "S.F.B.J. 60 Paris 2." The papier-mâché body with hooks dates between 1925 and 1930.

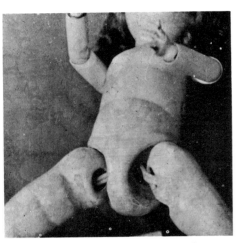

Detail of how the legs and trunk were assembled circa 1925.

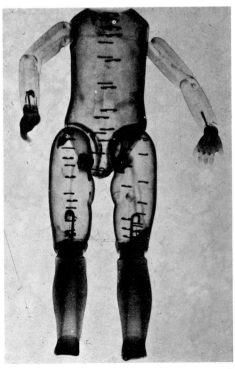

X-ray showing how the 1925 papier-mâché body was assembled.

le Bébé Incassable semi-Articulé
The semi-articulated incassable bébé

The preceding body was also produced in the semi-articulated form. In this case, the semi-articulated *incassable bébé*, the limbs were in composition. The lower limbs were rectilinear and coarse, the upper limbs were slightly curved and the hands were non-articulated. The finish was coarse. These *bébés* were inexpensive and were not meant to be undressed. They were sold outfitted in ethnic costumes and uniforms typical of occupations such as soldiers and nurses.

The semi-articulated *bébé* body was the same one used by Fleischmann at the end of the 19th century. The trunk and the limbs were manufactured in molded composition. This *bébé* was called *en pâte* or *bébé pâte* (pâte meaning "paste"). The upper limbs were slightly bent, the hands were fixed, and the lower limbs were rectilinear and revealed no contours. The trunk was long, tubular and ended in a point, since the hip articulation was at a wide angle. The assembly did not utilize much elastic cord, and did not require much labor. Several patents were taken out in order to economize rubber and labor.

Though these *bébés* were sold by the millions, relatively few are found among collectors and in auction rooms. Though these dolls managed to survive in the hands of children, they were prey to the predilection of parasites, worms, and other insects, and did not survive.

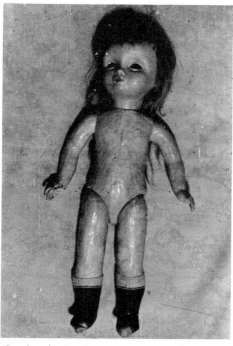

Semi-articulated composition body of the Fleischmann and Bloedel type.

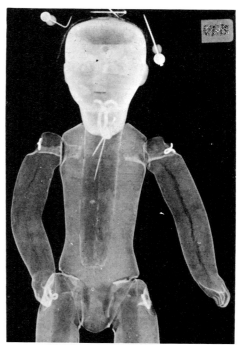

X-ray showing how a semi-articulated composition body with a head hook patented by S.F.B.J. is assembled. The head is marked "UNIS FRANCE."

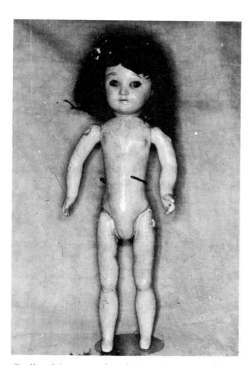

Doll with a semi-articulated composition body and an unbreakable head marked "S.F.B.J." It dates between 1930 and 1940.

Front and side views of a doll with a semi-articulated composition body. The head is of hard plastic and is marked "Jumeau" in relief which dates it to around 1950.

le Corps des Poupées Marcheuses
The walking bébé body (Bébé Marchant)

The S.F.B.J. first tried to use the fully-articulated body for walking dolls, but realized later that by allowing the knee to bend, the walk would be defective. Therefore, in 1905, the S.F.B.J. took out a patent, number 351,452 (see patents chapter), *"dans le but d'éviter que la jambe n'oscille librement, on produit un frottement elastique entre ce levier et les parois de la fente."* (In order to prevent the legs from swinging freely, we produce an elastic friction between the lever and the wall of the opening.) Thus, the leg was rigid for walking and bent for the sitting position. This is a detail which is very important for dating and identification, and can only be seen through an x-ray. However, this system did not show itself to be very resistant to heavy usage, and was not marketed for very long. The S.F.B.J. followed Girard and Fleischmann in returning to rigid legs.

The legs of these walking dolls were manufactured in molded carton, but in order to obtain a better cohesion in the hip, the upper part was manufactured in wood. The trunk of these *bébés* differs slightly from others since they were a little larger and of a trapazoidal form. The abdomen lowered into the sides in order to give support to the metallic axial bar by which the thighs oscillated.

Poupées a Corps de Femme
Dolls with a woman's body

One body model had limbs typical of turn-of-the-century production, but with a rather particular torso. The waist was very small and the shoulders were almost as wide as the hips, which gave an unusual hour-glass look. In addition, the torso was long: the wrists were well above the level of the hips. This was much more a woman's body than that of a little girl. It has a *Bébé Jumeau* label on its back, but it does not seem to be mentioned in Emile Jumeau's inventory. This body is rare and has a Simon and Halbig or S.F.B.J. head with a Jumeau face. We have also found it with character head number 306.

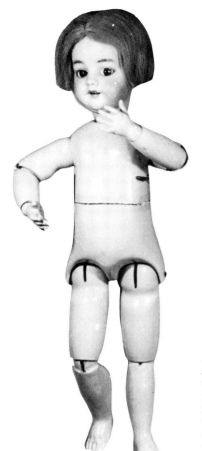

Bébé marcheur is an articulated walking doll with a system patented by S.F.B.J. in 1905. The head, marked "S.H.," turns and both hands throw kisses. It has a voice box and flirty eyes.

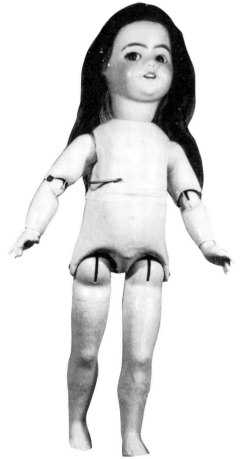

The bébé marcheur walking doll with straight legs and an S.F.B.J. head, size 8, which turns. It throws kisses and has a voice box and flirty eyes.

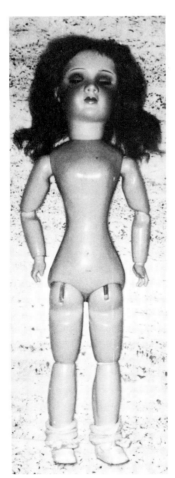

FAR LEFT: Front view of a doll with a woman's body. The head is marked "306."

LEFT: Back view of a doll with a woman's body.

Le Corps du Bébé Caractère
The Body of the Character Doll

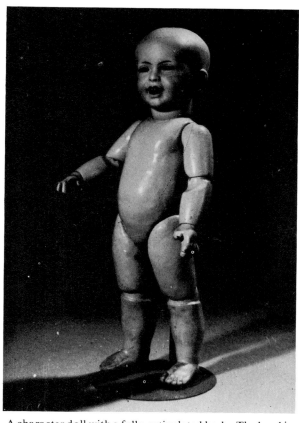

A character doll with a fully-articulated body. The head is marked "235." *Sambat Collection, photo by Doumic.*

When the manufacturing of character *bébés* first began, the heads were fit onto *entiérement articulés*, fully-articulated bodies. In 1911, *la marque deposée* (the registered trademark) was a dirigible showing a baby with bent limbs. This particular model was to be introduced in the 1912 catalog of the big department stores. That year Galeries Lafayette introduced its newest item, a character doll with sleeping eyes, bent limbs, and a chemise identical to one printed on S.F.B.J. boxes. We believe that it must have been head model number 236.

The character bébé body with straight limbs, either fully or semi-articulated

The anatomy of this body resembled the body of a toddler: a thick and straight torso with a large stomach, protruding or flat; short limbs, thick-set with skin folds, plump calves and feet; the big toe turned up. The knee was accentuated by lateral dimples.

The body was heavy, but was neat, pumiced and painted. A touch of rose color was frequently applied to the knees, the elbows, the topside of the feet and the back of the hands.

There were two variations within the semi-articulated category: stiff legs with arms fully-articulated, or stiff legs with arms articulated only at the shoulders, rarely at the wrists.

The hip articulations were of the articulation plane type.

The manufacturing materials used for this category varied according to the era. Composition was first used for fully-articulated bodies. Next, semi-articulated *bébé* bodies were made in composition. Their upper limbs were fabricated either in wood or in composition. Finally, the body was fabricated in molded cardboard and stapled. The stiff lower limbs were fabricated in composition, and the upper limbs in wood (fully- or semi-articulated). This particular *bébé* body was very realistic, and had been manufactured for a long time. In the Bazar de l'Hôtel de Ville gift catalog of 1931, it was referred to as *bébé articulé, gros corps, tête caractérisée* (articulated baby-doll, large body, character head). It was produced in all sizes, from 28cm (11⅛in) to 67cm (26⅜in).

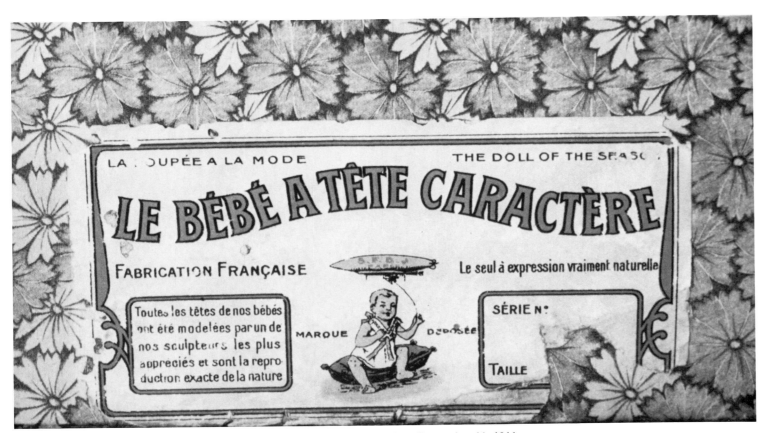

Paper label from an S.F.B.J. character doll's box. It has the mark patented on September 11, 1911.

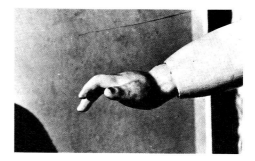

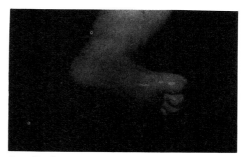

Details of a character doll's hand.

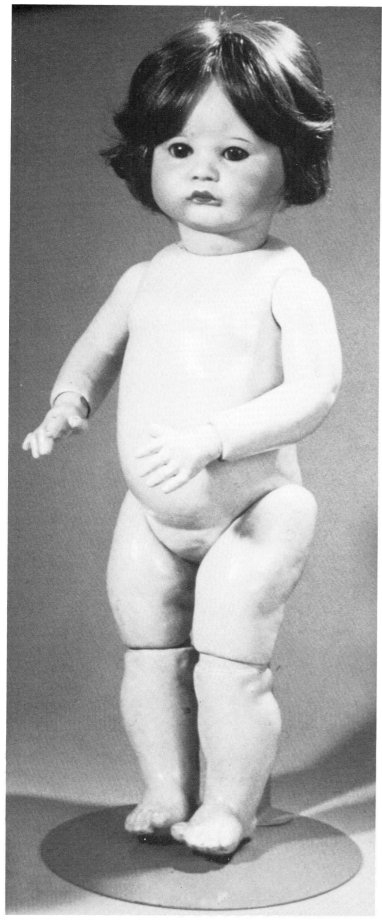

Fully-articulated body of a character doll. This model has bent arms without elbow joints. The bisque head is marked "252." *Sambat Collection, photo by Doumic*.

Detail of a character doll's foot.

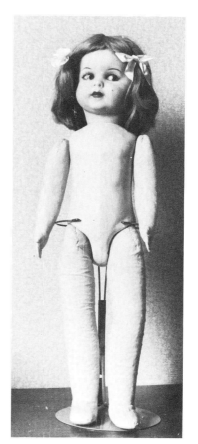

Doll with a papier-mache body and arms and legs of stuffed fabric. The felt head is marked "247."

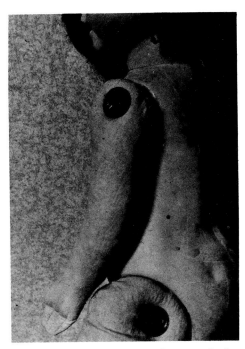

A detail of the buttons used to attach the arms and legs to the body of the doll shown below.

18 — JS — 37245. BEBÉ articulé, gros corps, tête incassable, chemise barboteuse. 0ᵐ28. **17.25**		19 — JS — 37246. BÉBÉ complètement articulé, gros corps, tête caractérisée incassable, yeux dormeurs à cils, perruque fine, chemise soie, ruban assorti dans les cheveux. 0ᵐ30 0ᵐ33	
0ᵐ32	0ᵐ36	0ᵐ40	
21.75 0ᵐ45	**26.»** 0ᵐ50	**31.50**	**29.50** .0ᵐ37 **36. »** 0ᵐ43 0ᵐ49
37.50 0ᵐ55	**44.50** 0ᵐ62		**44. »** 0ᵐ51 **55. »** 0ᵐ58 **65. »** 0ᵐ67
55. »	**70. »**		**70.»** **93.»** **120.»**

Christmas catalog from the Bazar de l'Hotel de Ville, Paris, 1931.

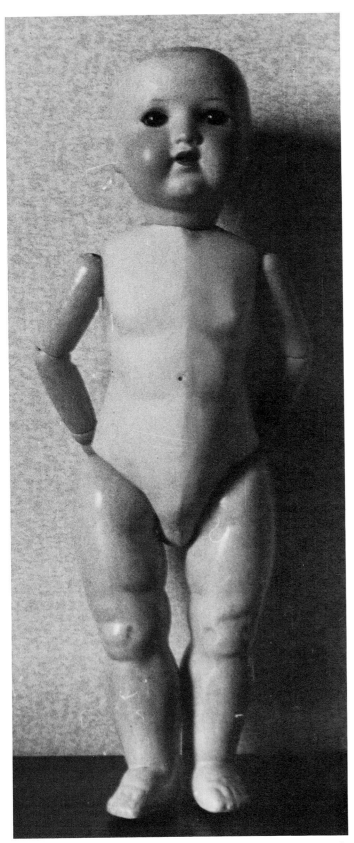

A character doll with a papier-mâché body, straight legs of composition, fully-articulated wooden arms and an unbreakable head marked "287."

The semi-articulated character bébé body with bent limbs

This *bébé* body was manufactured by the S.F.B.J. in 1912. It corresponded to the body of a new-born baby. This was the specific body of *bébé* number 236. The chest was straight ending in a V, the stomach was round and the back was flat. The upper limbs were bent while the hands were fixed, and the lower limbs were *torses*, or bent; the inside of the thighs were marked by rolls of fat typical of a healthy baby; the knees and the elbows were marked by small dimples on the sides; and finally, the feet were curved, like the feet of a baby. The fingers were separated (with the exception of the smaller models, whose fingers were molded together); the index finger was always turned up, as was the big toe.

This body was fabricated in composition, and was finely finished. It was assembled with a connection which crossed through at shoulder level. The head was linked to the legs by one elastic cord. The articulation of the thighs was *a bouton*, with a button.

This bent-limb body was manufactured in all sizes (0-12), from 18cm (7⅛in) to 62cm (24⅜in).

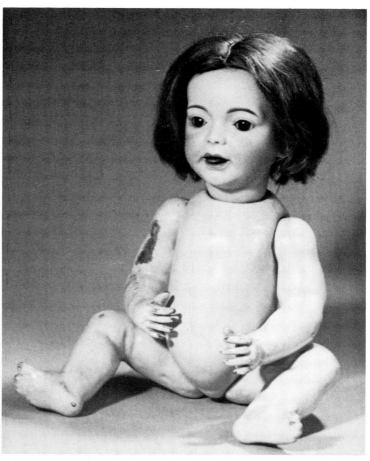

Character doll with the head marked "234" and a bent-limb composition body. *Sambat Collection, photo by Doumic.*

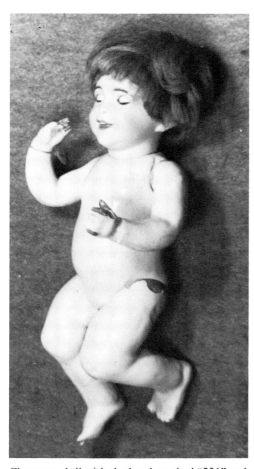

Character doll with the head marked "236" and a semi-articulated composition body.

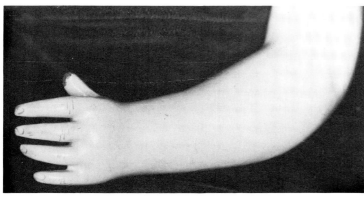

Arm and hand detail of a bent-limb body.

Character doll with a bisque head marked "252" and a semi-articulated bent-limb composition body. *Sambat Collection, photo by Doumic.*

An S.F.B.J. *incassable* (unbreakable) doll with a head marked "235" and a fully-articulated body, dating circa 1925. *Sambat Collection.*

The ordinary and unbreakable bébé body (fully- or semi-articulated)

This body has been previously described. It was not usually combined with character heads. However, certain model number heads were used with semi-articulated bodies of composition origin, for example, model number 239, called *le Poulbot*. This *bébé*, which was sold with a very unique outfit, was not meant to be undressed. The body, therefore, was not of great importance, and the accent was placed on the facial expression and costume.

We find three previously described models in the category of fully-articulated character *bébé* bodies: two S.F.B.J. types derived from Jumeau, and the 1925/1930 type.

An unbreakable S.F.B.J. doll with the head marked "245" and a fully-articulated body. This second model has a composition trunk with arms and legs of wood and composition. *Sambat Collection.*

Black version of an S.F.B.J. incassable doll. The head is marked "227" and the body is fully-articulated and an example of the first model. *Sambat Collection, photo by Doumic.*

Les Têtes
The Heads

The 247 character head of pressed felt.

BÉBÉ maillot

7.90   11.50   14.75

BÉBÉ marcheur

23.50

Le même   15.90

BÉBÉ marcheur

10.75

BÉBÉ marcheur

10.75

BÉBÉ

5.90 6.00 8.90 10.50 13.50

BÉBÉ promenette

4.90   6.90

BÉBÉ articulé

1.75 2.25 2.95 3.90 5.75

NOS BÉBÉS MODERNES

BÉBÉ   POUPÉE   "LA MODE DE BÉBÉ" BÉBÉ

18.50   18.50   16.50 19.75   13.75 15.50

BÉBÉ réclame

9.90

BÉBÉ-PRINTEMPS

4.90 5.90 7.50 8.75 9.75 11.50

13.75 16.75 19.75 25. 34. 43.

BÉBÉ 3 têtes

15.75   19.75

BÉBÉ-PRINTEMPS

17.50 19.90 25.

Printemps department store catalog from 1912. More than half of the dolls on this page are character dolls. The three-face doll is advertised as "new."

Têtes des Bébés Caractère
Character Doll Heads

The character *bébé* was the principal item manufactured by the S.F.B.J. It was the company's most original product, and in general, was of a good quality. The character *bébé* was responsible for the fame enjoyed by the S.F.B.J. and today, is still responsible for its prestige among contemporary collectors.

The term *caractère*, refers to the head, and more precisely, the face. During a period of 30 years, from 1910 (the date of their first appearance) until World War II, the S.F.B.J. did not stop creating these varied head models. What appears to be most important, innovative and original was that the character *bébé* borrowed very little from its predecessors: the Jumeau or the German product. It was a creative phenomenon that an anonymous company, whose partners had been previously known, could succeed in creating a new personality. This phenomenon was a product of collective thought and ingenuity. Possibly, Jumeau continued to impose his ideas on the partnership...or it could have been Fleischmann. Or possibly after having observed each other as rivals before becoming partners, both of them succeeded in bringing about a miracle that produced one common way of thinking.

All of these *bébés* represent the expressions of the young child. It is this quality that moves us, for these are the very expressions we see reflected in our own children. These expressions may sometimes be dreamy or naive; they are most often gay, alert and clever. Nevertheless, one fact is certain: the S.F.B.J. character *bébés* are so realistic, that we seem to recognize them in our own children, and we are often tempted to say about Sophie, Mathieu or Jean-Luc, "he's a real 236!"

This constitutes great art, and we can appreciate the everlasting passion that collectors feel for the S.F.B.J. character *bébés*, which touch reality so closely.

Many artists have shown their interest in this doll, from Carrier Belleuse to A. Marque. The S.F.B.J., as one of its former directors concurred, always insisted that its models be drawn or sculptured by artists, known or unknown. The two most reknowned artists were Poulbot and Lejeune. As far as art and expression are concerned, there was a noticeable difference between Jumeau's models and those of the S.F.B.J. The first ones were not really babies, but were little girls. Quite often, they were caricatures, sometimes grinning rather unpleasantly.

The nursing baby of the 19th century held little importance in the family and social life of the bourgeoisie. The middle class was virtually the only class concerned by the doll business. The nursing baby, relegated to the cares of the nurse because of its daily constraints and demands, was only capable of sounds and a gestural language that the family could not yet understand, and therefore, interested no one. After 1900 however, the role of mothering was returned to the mother, and consequently, rediscovering the mother-baby relationship revealed the beauty of the infant face.

At the risk of clouding even further an already confusing terminology, perhaps the Jumeau doll such as number 217 which represented the toddler with its cheerfulness and its tantrums, was the real character *bébé*; whereas the S.F.B.J. *bébé* was rather a portrait. In order to avoid confusion, the Jumeau doll could be labeled *bébé mimique*, and the S.F.B.J. baby doll *bébé beauté*.

The changing mother-infant relationship, was first brought to attention by Hippolyte Rigault in 1855 in one of his *Literary and Moral Conversations*, in which he concluded that the doll was the child's child. In that era, such a statement was a revelation.

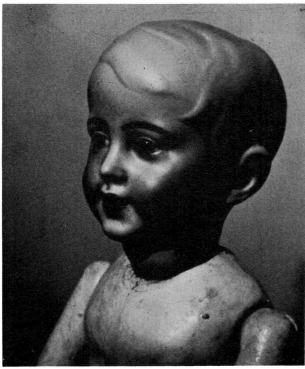

Doll with a bisque head marked "*S.F.B.J. 237.*" *R.B. Collection.*

N° 48001. *Nouveauté.* BÉBÉ caractère. yeux dormeurs, perruque fine.

Hauteurs	0"20	0"25	0"31	0"37	0"42	0"48	0"65
Prix	2.90	4.25	5.75	8.50	10.50	14.50	18.75

N° 48002. BÉBÉ caractère, yeux dormeurs, perruque fine, habillage tricot soie, se déshabillant.

			0"31	0"37	0"42	0"48	0"65
Prix			10.75	15.75	19.75	26.50	35. »

Galeries Lafayette department store catalog from 1913 showing the novel semi-articulated body.

There were also important material differences between Jumeau's heads and those of the S.F.B.J. Jumeau for all practical purposes produced only decorated bisque heads. They were manufactured in beautiful bisque, and were quite lovely. The S.F.B.J. heads differed in that their fabrication utilized materials other than bisque. There are three kinds of S.F.B.J. bisque heads.

The first type, the most beautiful ones, were manufactured at what once had been the Jumeau factory, at Arago Street in Montreuil. The second type, heads that were of inferior quality, were manufactured during several periods. The inferior quality depended upon the number of successive copies extracted from the same mold. And the third kind were the heads which were being imported from Germany. Contrary to the writings of Clarétie, du Maroussem or Calmette, this was a common business practice that was largely widespread. According to these authors, Fleischmann, prior to 1899, had undertaken a large scale operation in which bisque heads were copied from French models, fabricated in Hamburg or in Fürth, and finally resold in France. Consequently a shadow of doubt was cast on Fleischmann's name, although it was never proved that fraudulent plagiarism was an issue.

These character heads, imported from Germany, were in bisque. They were unsigned, and only bore the mold number incised in italics. It was also believed that heads bearing two holes on the top part of the nape, were manufactured in Germany. This was by no means unique. The purpose of these holes was to secure the eyes for long distance shipping, with the help of a string. We find this same system in French heads as well, especially in those from Limoges. The use of these imported heads probably extended over a rather short period of time, from 1910, the beginning of S.F.B.J. character bébés, to 1916.

As it was necessary to meet growing demands, the S.F.B.J. first built a 9 m 3 oven in 1909, in Montreuil. A third oven was built in 1915. Thus, demands were satisfied, and texts published at that period all agreed that after World War I, France was no longer dependent on Germany for its doll heads.

The S.F.B.J. did not limit its manufacturing to bisque-head bébés and character bébés. It also produced unbreakable and washable heads, manufactured from a patented composition, such as carton (see patents chapter). These heads were of a remarkable soft and smooth texture, and lent themselves quite well to careful painting.

The S.F.B.J. also began to produce felt-pressed heads in 1923, and plastic heads in 1950.

It is quite difficult to date the character bébés. In principle, numerical order should have followed chronological order. However, that was not always the case. At times, one model required more finishing time than another, and was therefore marketed at a date well beyond its chronological order.

There are only two model numbers of whose dates we may be certain: the 239, called the Poulbot, beause of the publicity and other published texts that date from 1913; and the 242, bébé têteur, the nursing baby, whose patent was filed in October 1910. The manufacturing had to be undertaken within the following two years in order to maintain the patent's validity.

Nevertheless, we can notice that the coloring of the bisque heads was modified over the years.

Around 1910, some heads were completely rosy and even mauvish. Others, especially the baby-dolls marked Unis France, were coral colored only on the cheeks. These probably date from the 1930s.

Nouveauté.
ÉCOLIER ou ÉCOLIÈRE, tête expressive d'enfant, perruque fine, tout articulé, habillage soigné, se déshabillant. Hauteur 0m34 . . . . **6.75**

La Samaritaine department store catalog for 1912. It advertised a schoolboy and schoolgirl with fully-articulated bodies. They are 34cm (14in).

3022. **NOUVEAUTÉ**. - Petit bébé articulé, tête caractérisée, culotte avec bretelles promenettes.
Hauteur 0m21 . . . . **1.45**

3023. **Le même, robe tissu fantaisie et tablier blanc.**
Haut. 0m21.
1.45

A la Ville St-Denis department store catalog for 1911.

BÉBÉ tête
expressive, absolument incassable
et lavable, avec costume
et tablier *"Se déshabillant"*.

Hauteurs . .	0ᵐ35	0ᵐ44
	3.90	**5.90**

BÉBÉ tête
expressive
d'un jeune enfant, perruque
fine, *entièrement articulé.*
chemise avec broderie.

Hauteurs :

0ᵐ36	0ᵐ43	0ᵐ51
3.90	**4.90**	**5.90**

La Samaritaine department store catalog for 1913.

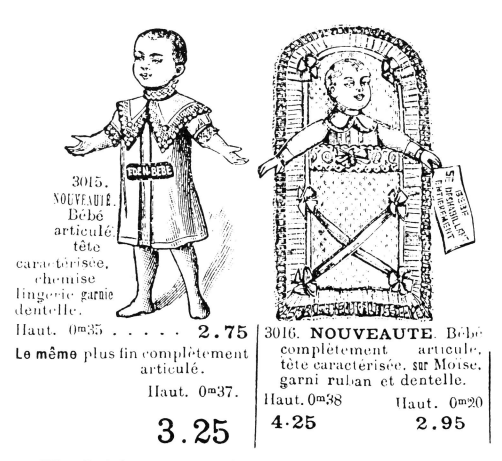

3015.
NOUVEAUTÉ.
Bébé
articulé
tête
caractérisée.
chemise
lingerie garnie
dentelle.

Haut. 0ᵐ35 . . . . . **2.75**

Le même plus fin complètement
articulé.

Haut. 0ᵐ37.

3.25

3016. **NOUVEAUTE**. Bébé
complètement articulé.
tête caractérisée. sur Moïse.
garni ruban et dentelle.

Haut. 0ᵐ38	Haut. 0ᵐ20
4·25	**2.95**

A la Ville St-Denis department store catalog shows a character head doll and one marked
"Eden Bebe."

In numerical order, number 226 is the S.F.B.J.'s first character *bébé*. It's a doll with a boy's head, said to be inspired by the German character doll, the *Kaiser Baby* by Kämmer and Reinhardt which bears the number 100. The 226 has a solid head, set glass eyes, an open/closed mouth with a molded tongue. It has a pointed chin, and very pronounced facial sculpturing.

It can have painted hair, either with regular brush strokes forming strands around the forehead, or uniform color with a slight point on the forehead, or finally, flocked hair.

The eyebrows are painted in one stroke that rises slightly towards the temples. The eyelashes are painted downwards with dark little strokes. The upper lid is slightly lowered, showing a clear palpebral furrow.

This *bébé* can be found with different bodies: that of the unbreakable *bébé* completely or semi-articulated, or the baby body with bent arms and legs. It exists in all sizes, but the most common are sizes 4 through 8, that range between 35cm (12¾in) and 52cm (20½in) tall.

There is also a mulatto or black one.

Some of these *bébés* with an S.F.B.J. body are not marked on the nape, but bear only a mold number. They are smiliar, at least for the eyelashes, eyes and mouth, except that the eyes are a little more closed on the unmarked version than on the marked S.F.B.J. model. We have noticed that in the unmarked models, the hair is painted in small regular lines, and the top and back of the skull has furrows in the bisque. These unmarked models would be the imported ones made for the S.F.B.J.[4]

---

[4]David and Jo Barrington, "Doll in Profile," *International Toy and Doll Collector*, No. 10, April/May 1981, p.34

46cm (19in) bisque head marked "S.F.B.J. 226, Paris 8." *Galerie de Chartres* 1978.

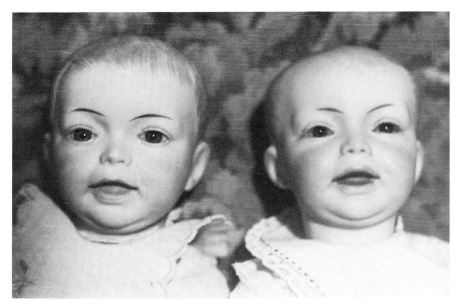

Two 226 heads. The one on the right is marked S.F.B.J., the one on the left is not signed. *Sambat Collection, photo by Doumic.*

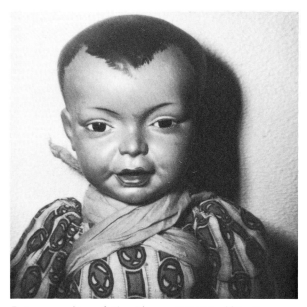

Brown version of the bisque S.F.B.J. 226. *Sprenger Collection.*

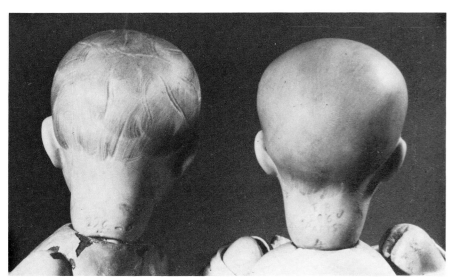

Back view of the two 226 heads. The one on the right is marked S.F.B.J. Notice that the hair parts are different. *Sambat Collection, photo by Doumic.*

227

Number 227 is a happy boy *bébé* with a solid bisque head, and paperweight eyes. The mouth, with a plump upper lip, opens with a frank smile, revealing six upper teeth. The nose is a bit flat, and the eye slit more closed than the 226. The eyebrows are painted with one stroke slightly arched, and the lashes are painted in little oblique strokes.

On the outside of the head there are rather pronounced round bumps. The hair is painted with little strokes toward the front either of a faded tint, or flocked with a point in front.

It can be found with different bodies: bent arms and legs, completely or semi-articulated, which make the different sizes approximate measurements. It exists in sizes from 18cm (7⅛in) to 52cm (20½in). The *bébés* of small size (18cm [7⅛in]) have painted eyes, and the S.F.B.J. called these *bébés mignonnettes pâte*, the body being composition.

The 227 is a rather common *bébé*; there is also a black version. Some of these *bébés* are not marked S.F.B.J., but bear on the nape, in italics, only the mold nmbers and size. These are heads made in Germany for the S.F.B.J.

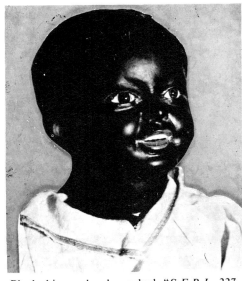

Black bisque head marked "*S.F.B.J. 227, Paris, 8.*" The doll is 50cm (20in) tall. *Sambat Collection.*

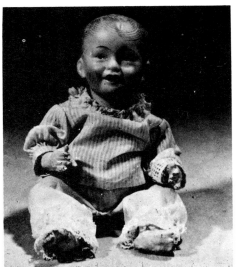

Small, seven inch high doll has a bisque head with painted eyes. It is marked "*227*" but has no S.F.B.J. signature. *Sambat Collection, photo by Doumic.*

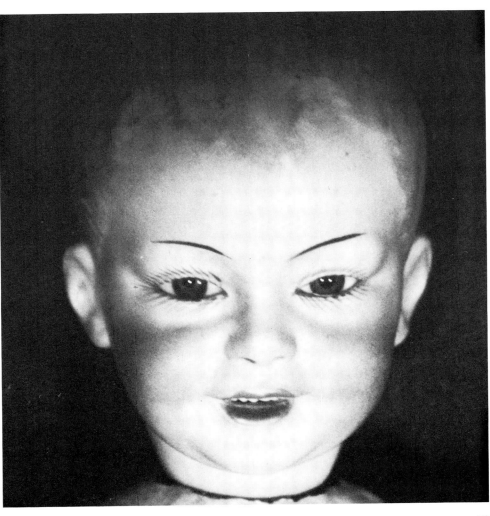

S.F.B.J. 227 showing details of the head molding.

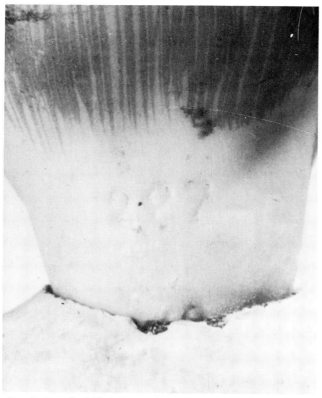

Small size of a 227 doll showing the mark. It is not marked S.F.B.J. *Sambat Collection, photo by Doumic.*

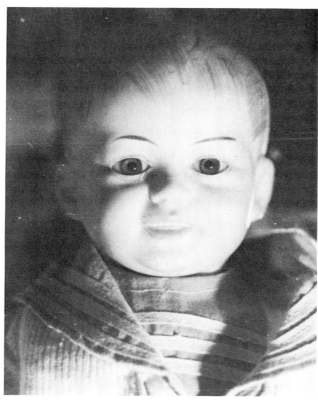

227 head not marked S.F.B.J. *Galerie de Chartres* 1980.

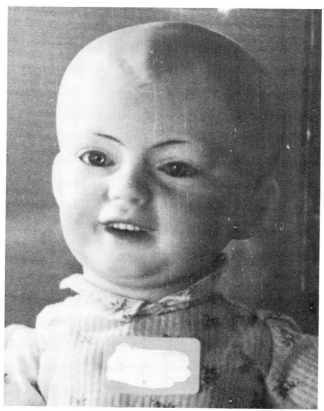

227 head marked S.F.B.J. *Galerie de Chartres* 1978.

227 head not marked S.F.B.J. Notice the different hair treatment. *Galerie de Chartres* 1979.

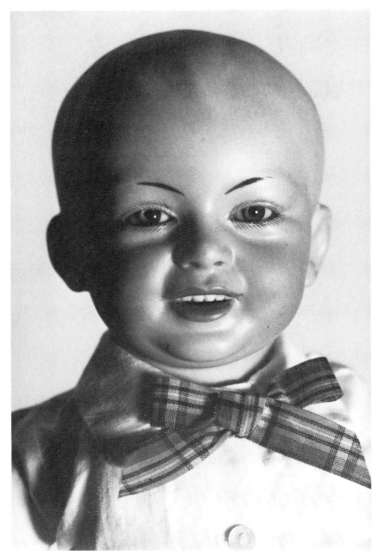 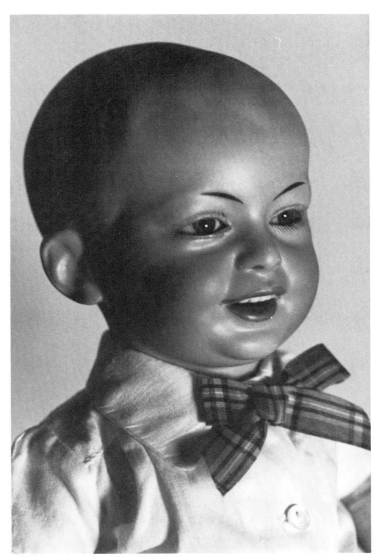

Head marked S.F.B.J. 227 PARIS 6. *Photo by Cook*. S.F.B.J. marked 227. *Photo by Cook*.

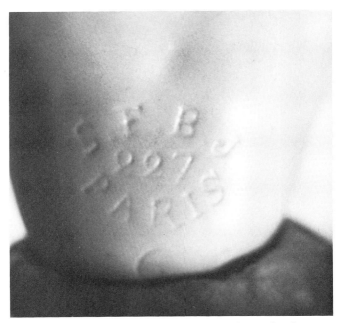

Incised mark on the S.F.B.J. 227 doll shown in the two photographs above. *Photo by Cook*.

228

The 228 *bébé* has a face with very prominent features, more so than the 226. It has a double chin, small eyes with lashes painted in oblique lines, and brows rising towards the temples.

The mouth is slightly open with a round hole in the middle; the swollen cheeks make one think more of a whistling child.

It is unknown to this day in France. It is mentioned in the publication by Marlowe Cooper, *Doll Home Library Series*, Volume I.

229

The 229 can be a girl or boy *bébé* with a wider smile than the 227. The bisque head is cut for a wig. The mouth is open with upper teeth. It has a rather marked double chin and small, half-closed paperweight eyes. The eyebrows are short, the lashes painted with small, oblique lines.

The body is completely articulated. It can be a walker, in which case the legs are straight. It is very rare, and generally of a small size: 4, or 32cm (12⅝in).

S.F.B.J. 229 doll. *Galerie de Chartres* 1980.

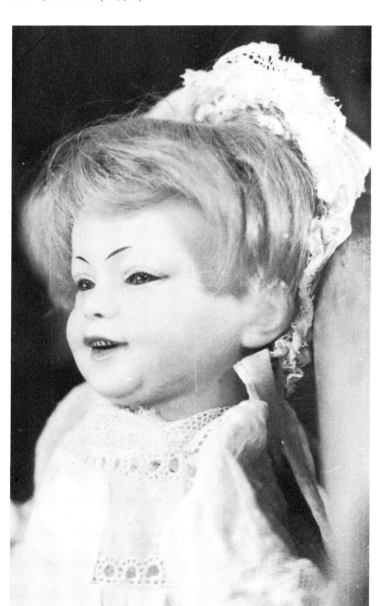

S.F.B.J. 229 doll. *Galerie de Chartres* 1980.

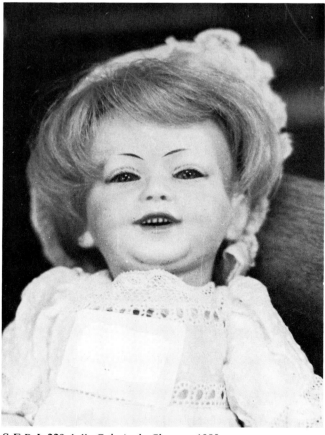

S.F.B.J. 229 doll. *Galerie de Chartres* 1980.

230

The 230 is not exactly a character *bébé* after the S.F.B.J. fashion. It is rather the portrait of an attentive young girl similar to those made by Emile Jumeau.

The bisque head is cut high for a wig. The eyes can be paperweight or movable glass. The mouth is open with six upper teeth; the lips are well drawn and a beautiful coral color. The forehead is high and clear. The ears are applied and pierced in the lobe.

The eyebrows are molded and painted with several strokes of bright brown. The lashes are painted with straight lines for set eyes; for movable eyes only the lower lashes are painted, and natural lashes are placed on the upper edge of the lids.

The body is articulated, or with straight legs if it is a walking baby. This is a relatively common *bébé*. It can be found in all sizes from 4 to 15, that is, between 30cm (11¾in) and 85cm (33½in). The most common size is 10, or 60cm (23⅝in) high.

These *bébés* appeared early; some are marked with an inscribed concave circle; others are more classically marked: "JUMEAU 230 PARIS," the letters in an oval. This is one of the rare *bébés* marked JUMEAU which was made by the S.F.B.J.; the other rarity is the 306.

Bébés with set eyes are not walkers, those with flirty eyes are usually walking babies and they bear a round label on the nape with the abbreviations *Bté SGDG* (*patented sans gurantie du gouvernement*, without guarantee of the government): this patent is for the flirty eyes.

The *bébés* of the 230 model were made for a long time with variations and with different quality bisque and decoration.

Face detail of head mold 230. *Sambat Collection.*

Detail of the mark on a Jumeau 230 head. *Sambat Collection.*

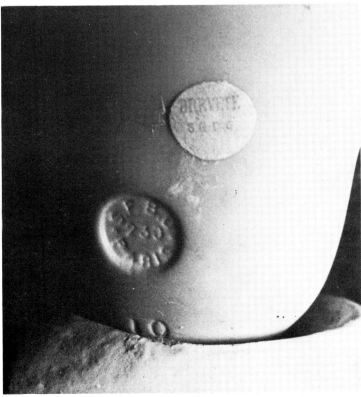

Detail of the mark on an S.F.B.J. 230 doll. It has a paper label marked "Brevete S.G.D.G." for the 1904 eyes system.

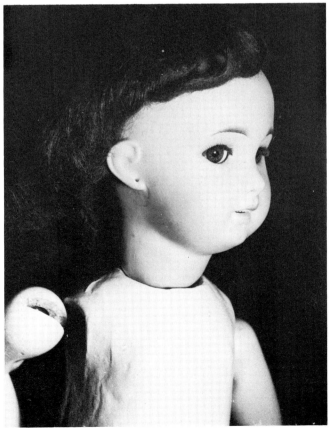

S.F.B.J. 230 face with flirty eyes.

233

The physiognomy of the 233 corresponds to a crying or singing *bébé*. It is a boy, with a solid head in bisque with molded hair which is sometimes flocked, and with the beginning of a part on the right side and a lock across the forehead towards the left temple.

The mouth is wide open, and deep, with a molded tongue and a row of upper teeth and four lower teeth. The eyelids are slightly closed; the set eyes are paperweight. The brows are painted with a single stroke and are not symmetrical. In some models the eyelid is more closed than others. The ears are well turned in, the chin well formed.

The body is completely articulated. This expressive *bébé* is found in sizes 4 through 8, which correspond to 35cm (13¾in) to 50cm (19⅝in).

It is one of the three interchangeable doll heads, and it is also found on automatons. This model is found about as often as the 226.

Detail of the face on an S.F.B.J. 233. *Sambat Collection, photo by J. Porot.*

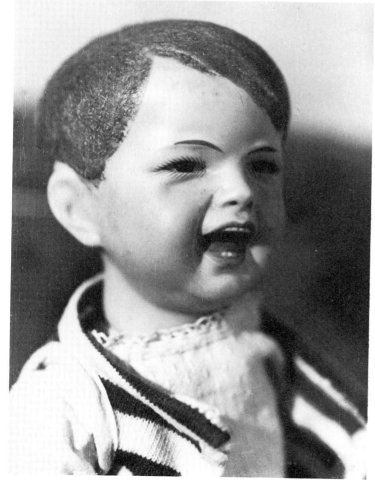

Detail of the face of an S.F.B.J. 233 doll. *Sambat Collection, photo by J. Porot.*

234

The 234 *bébé* has a curious expression due to its wide open eyes and open mouth with a movable tongue. There is a certain resemblance to the 251, but the 234 has no teeth, and its face has more relief and rounder eyes. It has chubby cheeks with dimples. The lower lip is rolled towards the bottom: one has the impression it is sticking out its tongue.

The bisque head is cut horizontally, quite high, and bears a wig. The glass eyes sleep.

The brows are painted with several long, brown, horizontal strokes. The lashes are painted in oblique little strokes. The eyelid is largely open, but the hollow remains perceivable.

It can be found with bent arms and legs in small sizes. It is very rare.

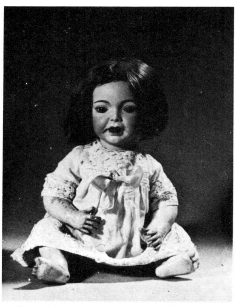

A 234 with a bent limb baby body. *Sambat Collection, photo by Doumic.*

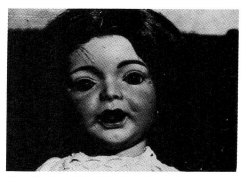

Detail of the 234 doll. *Sambat Collection.*

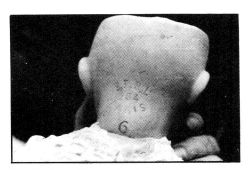

Detail of the 234 mark. *Sambat Collection.*

A 234 doll with a bent limb body. *Photo by Jackson.*

Close-up of the 234 doll
with a bent limb body.
Photo by Jackson.

The 235 boy *bébé* is smiling like the 236. He shows two upper teeth; but, different from the 236, his fixed eyes are "jewel" paperweight and he has a solid bisque head.

His hair is molded with a lock falling towards the left, it can be flocked. One also finds him with painted hair, small strokes falling to the left. These are *bébés* which are not marked S.F.B.J., but with heads made in Germany for the S.F.B.J.

The ears are well formed. The fixed paperweight eyes are partly open and show a characteristic slight upper eyelid; the lashes are painted oblique lines. The eyebrows are short, painted with a single brown line, and are sometimes slightly asymmetric. They look a bit like a circonflex accent (⌃). The 235 is also found with classical brows painted with several strokes following the eye-socket shape.

This *bébé* has a body with bent arms and legs or a straight semi-articulated or fully-articulated body.

It exists mostly in small sizes. At 17cm (6⅜in), it has painted eyes and hair. The S.F.B.J. called these tiny dolls *mignonnette pâte*, even though the head was of bisque. Some of these *bébés* are marked with an incised 235, and without the S.F.B.J. mark. These are heads made in Germany for the S.F.B.J.

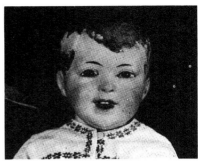

Detail of a doll from the 235 mold, not marked S.F.B.J. It has paperweight eyes. *Galerie de Chartres* 1980.

Face of a small 235 which is not marked S.F.B.J. It has painted eyes. *Sambat Collection.*

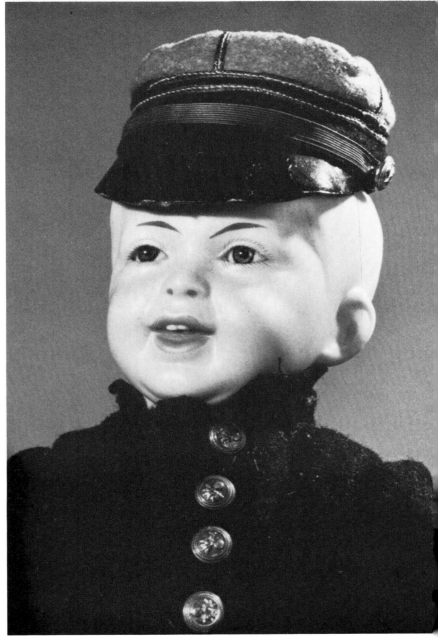

Detail of the face of a 235 in military costume. The 48cm (19in) doll probably dates from the first World War and is all original. See color plate 6. *Sambat Collection, photo by Doumic.*

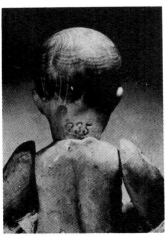

Back view of the small 235 not marked S.F.B.J. *Sambat Collection, photo by Doumic.*

Doll marked "*S.F.B.J. 235.*" *Galerie de Chartres* 1978.

The 236 is the most classic and most popular of the S.F.B.J. character *bébés*. It seems almost superfluous to describe it. It is a joyful child, with an open pate and short wig. Its mouth is partly closed with two upper teeth and rising corners of the mouth.

Its eyes are always glass and can sleep. The look is slightly fixed and convergent. The tongue, slightly out, is molded with the lower lip, which gives the characteristic thick-lipped look. It has a double chin.

It habitually has a baby's body with bent arms and legs, even in large sizes, but one also finds it with a character *bébé's* completely articulated body. It exists in all sizes from 0 to 12, or 19cm (7½in) to 62cm (24⅜in) high for *bébé* bodies. It also exists as a 17cm (6¾in) *mignonnette pâte*.

During the 30 years the doll was made, the color of the bisque varied from pale to a purplish-red.

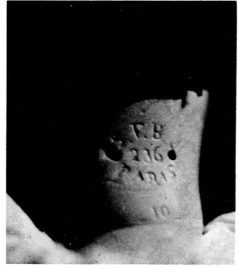

Detail of the 236 mark.

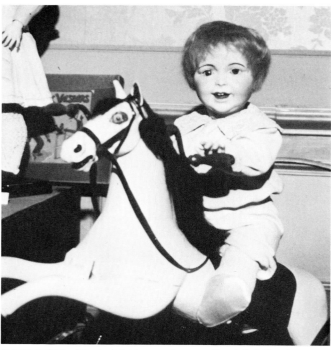

S.F.B.J. 236 with straight legs and arms. *Pesché Collection.*

236 head.

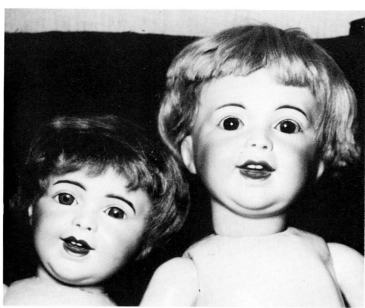

Two different size heads from mold 236. *R.B. Collection.*

S.F.B.J. marked 236 PARIS. *Photo by Cook.*

The 237 is a boy with a solid bisque head — a child who looks quiet and reflective, well combed and good-mannered. The hair is molded with a right part, waving to the left, and sometimes flocked on the heads not bearing the S.F.B.J. mark, both painted and flocked hair can be found.

His jewel eyes have the upper lids raised to show a pronounced furrow. The brows, continued to the outside are barely arched, and are painted with several fairly thick lines on the heads not bearing the S.F.B.J mark. They are placed low on the socket edge. The upper lid has an undulating outline on a central hollow, wide and deep. The mouth is partly open, hardly showing four teeth.

The *bébé* body is classic, semi or fully-articulated. This *bébé* is found in small sizes: 4 to 6. It is rather rare and sought after.

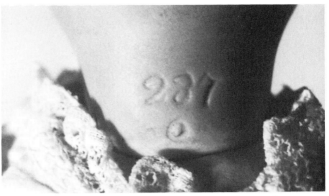

Close-up of a 237 not marked S.F.B.J. *Photo by Cook.*

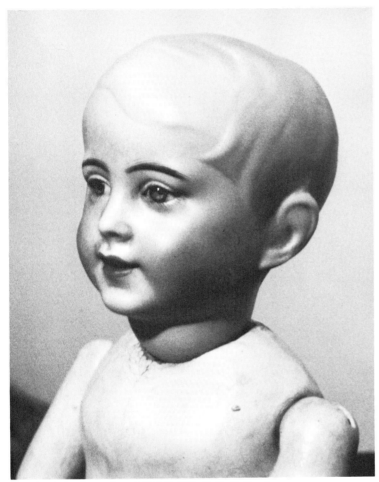

Detail of the face of an S.F.B.J. 237. *R.B. Collection.*

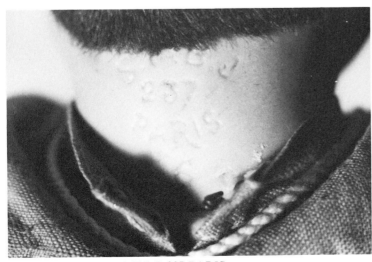

Close-up of a marked S.F.B.J. 237 PARIS.

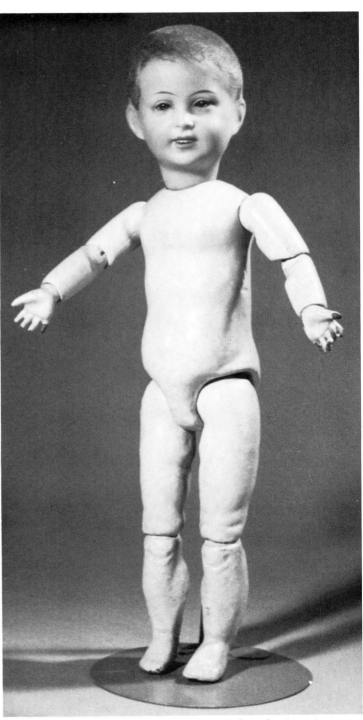

Unmarked S.F.B.J. 237. *Sambat Collection, photo by Doumic.*

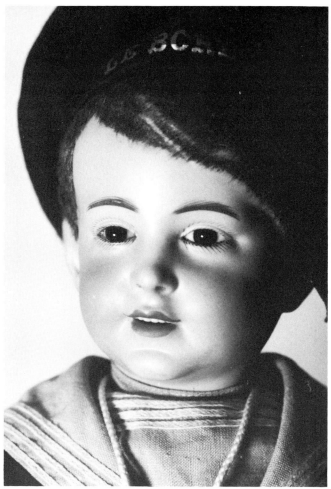

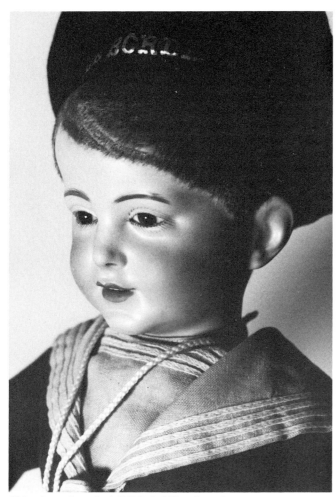

Marked S.F.B.J. 237. *Photo by Cook.*

Side view of marked S.F.B.J. 237. *Photo by Cook.*

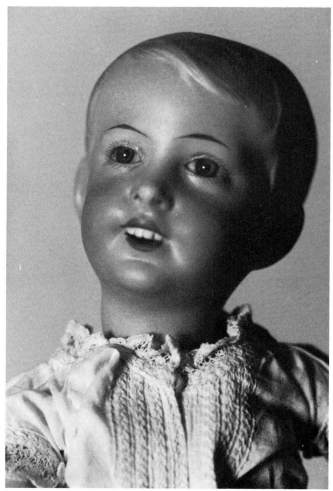

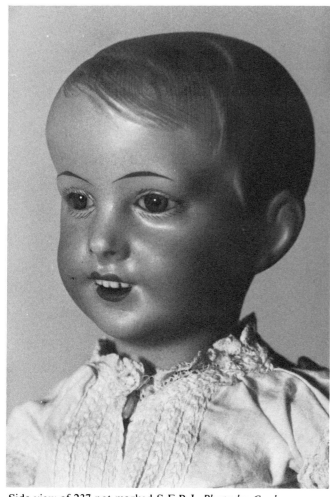

237 not marked S.F.B.J. *Photo by Cook.*

Side view of 237 not marked S.F.B.J. *Photo by Cook.*

The 238 *bébé* has a very special expression, a distant and dreamy look: widely separated, clear eyes and a nose which is thick at the base. The face could be that of a girl as well as that of a boy.

The bisque head is cut high on the pate. The open mouth is small, thin and narrow, the upper teeth crowded and leaning backwards. There is no tongue. The chin is rather pointed, without a dimple.

The jewel eyes are small. The lashes are painted in oblique lines, the brows of bright brown, are painted with several strokes along the socket edge. The eyelid is quite marked. The ears are well contoured and defined.

The body is fully articulated of ordinary stapled cardboard. This 238 is not rare, but its unusual appearance makes it a *bébé* sought by collectors. It exists from size 4 to size 10.

Face detail of a doll from mold 238. *Galerie de Chartres.*

47cm (19in) size 6 S.F.B.J. 238 doll. *Sambat Collection.*

S.F.B.J. 238. *Brisou Collection.*

The 239 depicts the Poulbot boy and girl named *Nénette* and *Rintintin*. It is, in fact, Poulbot who, in 1913, created the model made by the S.F.B.J. Francisque Poulbot is mostly known for his drawings of children in Montmartre, whose misery and vagrancy inspired a tender pity.

The names Nénette and Rintintin were also known in popular songs and within the intimacy of the Poulbot couple, *he* was called Nenette and *she*, Rintintin. Mrs. Poulbot, "Rintintin," designed the first clothing for the dolls during a holiday on the seashore. The dolls were much talked about before their production and they were probably the stake in one of the goodwill campaigns Poulbot initiated in favor of the Montmartre child.

These dolls are curious and surprising, as much for their sickly, roguish little children's faces, as by their hair, of an unexpected "carrot" red, which evokes the famous character *Poil de Carotte* by Jules Renard, but which the store catalogs called "ardent blonde."

The head is clearly triangular with a large skull, the forehead high on a face a bit flattened, eyes widely separated, a pressed-in nose: all stigmas of a deprived childhood. Besides a sickly coloring, it has no lashes or brows. In contrast, the slender mouth, closed in a thin smile, is of infinite grace. The eye itself, with a barely opened lid, has the sparkle of attentive intelligence: the best portrait of the *Titi Parisien* or cheeky Parisian youth. A characteristic detail, very apparent on a photo of the plaster mold which the Poulbot family furnished us: the mouth is asymmetric, pulled towards the right.

Its body may have been created articulated, but it is always found now with a semi-articulated composition body.

The Poulbot signature, is found in the hollow on the nape, below the number 239. Poulbot had registered a trademark August 1913. This *bébé* exists, as far as we know, only in two sizes: 36cm (14⅛in) and 40cm (15¾in).

It is very rare and very appreciated by collectors.

The dress, originally conceived by Mrs. Poulbot, contains a "magnificent blue girl's apron, and a boy's superb sailor outfit, which Poulbot decorated with beautiful white anchors."[5] But, when commercialized, the boy's outfit was slightly modified: striped shirt, tie, and double, large button suspenders, a silhouette not without comparison to "the Kid," but minus the hat.

[5] *Art and the Child*, Vol. IX, No. 51, Nov/Dec 1913.

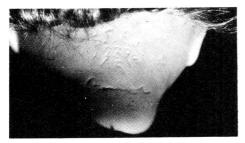

Nénette and *Rintintin* dressed by Madame Poulbot in 1913. The fully-articulated body and the clothing are different from the dolls sold in the department stores. *L'Art et l'Enfant*, November/December 1913.

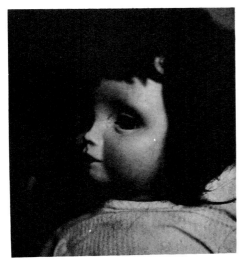

Poulbot signature on a 239 head.

S.F.B.J. 239 doll. *Sambat Collection.*

Au Bon Marche department store catalog, Paris 1914.

La Samaritaine department store catalog, Paris 1914.

Original plaster model of the S.F.B.J. 239 from sculptor Poulbot. *Document and photo J. Cheval.*

Poulbot and *Poulbote.* Note the difference in body size. *Sambat Collection, photo by Doumic.*

The Poulbot, S.F.B.J. 239. Photo by Griffith.

242

The 242 doll is *bébé têteur*, the nursing *bébé*, whose patent number 432,650 was petitioned October 8, 1910. Up until 1910 the S.F.B.J. produced the nursing *bébé* patented by Bru, but with a completely articulated cardboard and wood body. This is not a simple renewal of Bru's device which has a sucking tube in the head, controlled by a metallic stem. The originality of this one lies in having the sucking tube in the trunk instead of the head, which leaves space free for the eye mechanism. (See the patents chapter for information on the exceptional preoccupation of eye assembly by the S.F.B.J.)

The physionomy of this *bébé* is classic: a round head, a small and flat closed mouth which is pierced with a single hole for the nipple or cigarette stem in the "smoking" version. The stomach bulges because it is the location of the sucking mechanism. The bottom of the torso in back has the shape of a skirt with a particular horizontal edge of German inspiration, instead of buttocks. The upper torso has wide falling shoulders, in the Bru manner.

This *bébé* comes in three sizes: 30cm (11¾in) with bent limbs, and 38cm (15in) and 44cm (17¼in) completely articulated. It is quite rare.

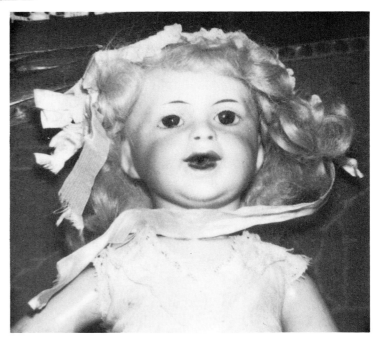

S.F.B.J. 242 doll.

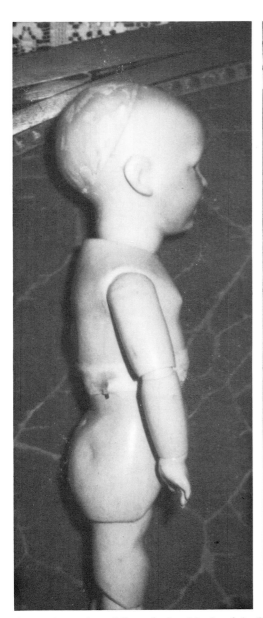
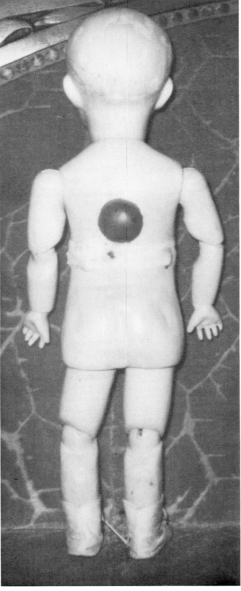
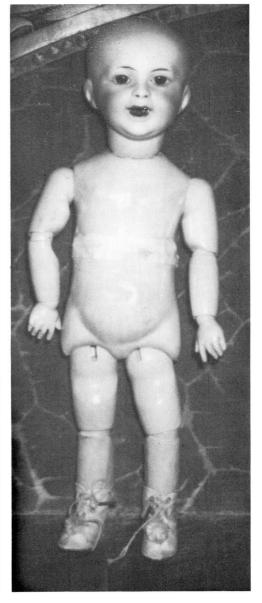

Three views of the fully-articulated body of the S.F.B.J. 242. *Theimer Documents.*

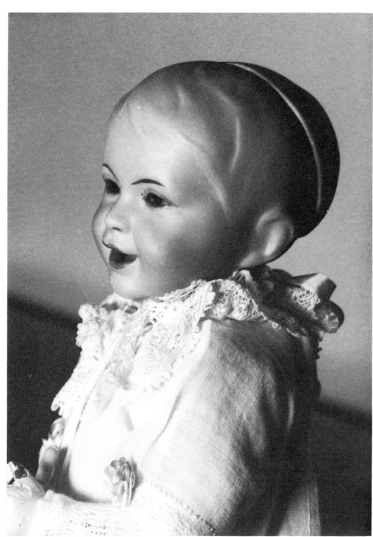

S.F.B.J. 242 nursing doll. *Photo by Cook.*

242 Nursing doll showing how back of head was sliced to install mechanism. *Photo by Cook.*

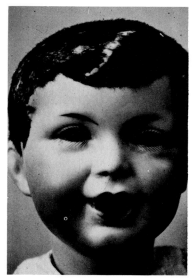

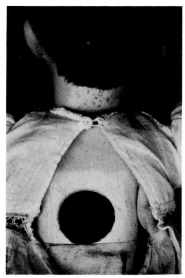

S.F.B.J. bisque head 242. *Photo by Bazin.*

The S.F.B.J. 242 showing the hole in the back of the torso which when pressed activates the mechanism. *Photo by Bazin.*

245

The 245 is known in Anglo-Saxon countries as a "Googly-eyed" *bébé*. This type of doll was very much in style in the 1920s in Germany and America. All doll producers made a doll of this type (Armand Marseille, Stobel and Wilken, Heubach and so on).

The S.F.B.J. owed it to itself to follow the movement with originality. This *bébé* has a round head with the crown cut high. The eyes, like loto balls that roll and take up a large part of the face, have enormous pupils and a perfectly circular eye opening. It is an amusing caricature. The upper lashes are painted directly on the socket in little vertical lines arranged in a circle. There is no eyelid. The eyebrows are short and tend towards the vertical, barely painted with a few brown lines.

The nose is flat, the cheeks well rounded. The mouth, laughing with a large upper lip, is hardly open but shows four upper teeth. The lips are painted in rosy red and outlined in a darker red. The body is an ordinary completely articulated *bébé* body. It is found only in size 4, or 32cm (12⅝in). It is quite rare.

Detail of the face of an S.F.B.J. 245. *Sambat Collection.*

246

The 246 is a joyous tiny tot. It has a high forehead, sleep eyes with natural lashes, though the lower lashes are painted vertical lines. The brows are short, painted with several horizontal lines drifting towards the temples. The mouth is open/closed with a drooping lower lip. The very conspicuous tongue gives the impression that this *bébé* is sucking on its tongue. The upper lip is well defined and shows two teeth. This *bébé* is quite rare.

The 247 exists in three versions: a porcelain head, a composition head and a pressed felt head.

The porcelain head version is a charming *bébé* that is similar to the 235 and 236 but with a more turned-up nose and round, deep eyes. Its little face is definitely that of a relaxed, serene, pensive *bébé* with an attentive look. It is probably the liveliest of all S.F.B.J. character *bébés* due to the absolutely realistic proportions of the mold.

The opening in its head is cut high with the forehead quite convex. The coral mouth is open/closed with two upper teeth. It has sleep eyes. The brows are short, and painted towards the side; the lower lashes are painted vertically. The neck is short.

It was made with both a bent limb body and with a fully-articulated character baby body. It exists in sizes from 4/0 (15cm or 5⅞in) to 11 (65cm or 25⅝in). The sizes below 20cm (7⅞in) are *mignonnettes pâte* with painted eyes. The most common size is 8 or approximately 44cm (17¼in).

Some of these *bébés* bear the Unis France brand, indicating they were made after 1925; others bear the numbers of the years 1921 and 1922. The 247 is a common mold number.

The second version has a head of composition or *carton-pâte*, a compound that is clay dried and baked and which looks similar to pressed cardboard. These heads were called *incassables et lavables* or "unbreakable and washable." Sometimes the eyes were painted looking to the left; sometimes they were in moveable glass like the porcelain heads.

One can also find charming heads in pressed felt in this model. The body is stuffed cloth, semi-articulated or made of a stapled cardboard torso and articulated composition wood limbs. These *bébés* measure generally 50cm (19⅝in) to 60cm (23⅝in).

An S.F.B.J. 247 with painted eyes.

Face detail of mold 247; bisque head. *Sambat Collection.*

S.F.B.J. mold 247 with a semi-articulated body. *Sambat Collection, photo by Doumic.*

An S.F.B.J. 247. *Photo by Cook.*

Close-up of the 247. *Photo by Cook.*

Mold 247 with a felt head and stuffed fabric body.

Details of the felt head of an S.F.B.J. 247.

Another view of the facial details of the felt version of mold 247.

248

The 248 is a *bébé* with a very unusual expression: it looks angry. Its lowered eyebrows and tight lips with dropping corners give it an almost aggressive air. It has a bisque head with the opening cut high. The face is basically round with a short chin. It is quite rare.

S.F.B.J. 248. *Ralph Griffith Collection.*

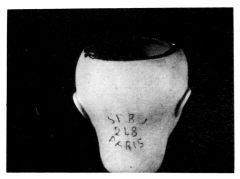

Detail of the mark on an S.F.B.J. 248. *Azou Collection.*

The 250 character *bébé* is also quite rare. It's a young girl with smiling face, rather heavy classical features which are relatively unexpressive.

The opening in the bisque head is cut high. The eyes are glass and sleep. The lashes and eyebrows are painted. The mouth is open with four teeth. The ears are pierced.

This *bébé's* body is fully-articulated.

Detail of the face of an S.F.B.J. 250. *Photo by Simon.*

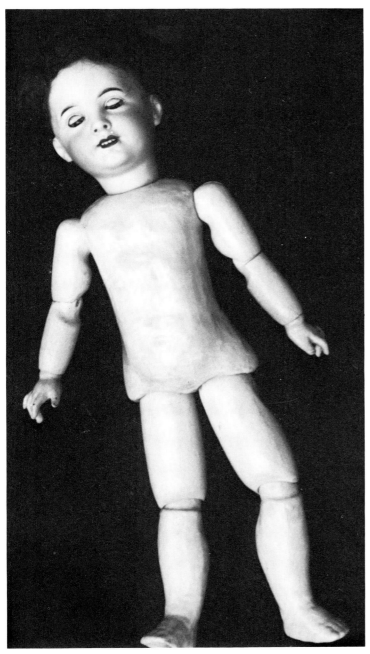

A view of the body of the S.F.B.J. 250. *Photo by Simon.*

S.F.B.J. 250. *Ralph Griffith Collection.*

251

The 251 *bébé*, which is sometimes referred to as a *demi-boudeur* or "half-pouty," has a frozen, rather dreamy expression. It is quite common.

It has a cut pâte, weighted sleeping eyes with real upper lashes and vertically painted lower ones. The eyebrows are short and painted with several horizontal strokes. The nose is flat. The open mouth is coral-colored with two upper teeth and movable tongue.

This *bébé* has beautiful, fat, vermillion cheeks with dimples. The bottom of its face is as wide as the temples.

The body is either that of a *bébé* with bent limbs, or that of a fully-articulated *bébé* with a fat stomach.

It was made in the 1920s. Some bear the numbers of their production year, 1921, 1922, 1923, or 1924, while others made after 1925 carry the mark Unis France. The 251 is rather common and found in all sizes between 30cm (11¾in) and 70cm (27½in).

It is found in two versions: the porcelain head and the *incassable* (unbreakable) composition head.

S.F.B.J. mold 251. *Galerie de Chartres.*

An S.F.B.J. 251 showing the "wobble" tongue. *Photo by Cook.*

252

The 252 *bébé* is named *le boudeur* or "the pouty" due to its pursed lips. This is a name that suits it: its expression is quite realistic and appealing.

The pate of the head is cut out, and the glass eyes sleep. It has no eyelid, and the upper and lower lashes are painted in little oblique strokes. The brows are short, painted with several strokes right above the eye.

The forehead has two curious bumps, rather unexpected and uncommon, above the flat nose. The closed mouth with falling corners makes it appear sad. It has a small chin. The beauty of this *bébé* is in its look.

Its body has bent limbs. It can also be on a semi- or fully-articulated character *bébé* body and is found in all sizes, from 0 to 10 or 21cm (8¼in) to 50cm (19⅝in). It is rather rare and from the same period as the 250 and 251.

S.F.B.J. mold 252. *Sambat Collection, photo by Doumic.*

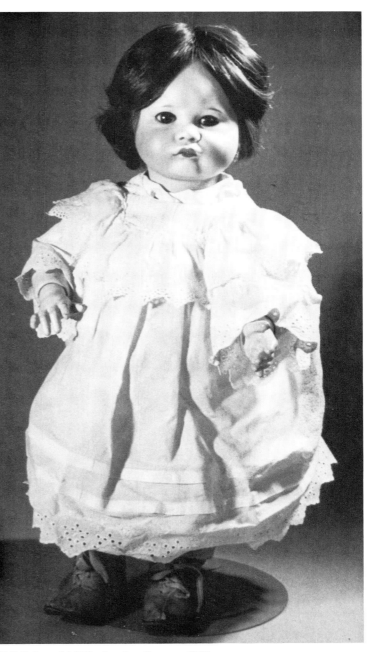

S.F.B.J. mold 252. *Auction Bourges* 1979.

253

The 253 is a full, very elongated clown's head, made in composition. The eyes are painted and enlarged by a very accentuated make-up. The brows are important and traced in a half-circle above the eyes. The nose is long and the mouth closed and well-drawn. This *bébé* has the complete face of a Pierrot.

It is mentioned in Marlowe Cooper's publication, *Doll Home Library Series*, Vol. I.

Two 252 character dolls. *Sambat Collection, photo by Doumic.*

255

The 255 is not exactly a character *bébé* since this number corresponds to a clown head. It is found either on automatons, or on toy clowns who have cymbals controlled by pressure on the body.

Its face is white, decorated with red designs on the cheeks, chin, the outer edge of the eyes and on the ears, with points at the base of the nose, between the eyes and on the forehead. The brows are thick and slightly wavy. The lashes are painted with oblique lines and the eye contours are outlined. The mouth is closed in a slight smile and painted coral red.

This is neither a *bébé* or an adult, but more like an adolescent. The size is small: marked 10/0.

S.F.B.J. mold 255. The clown has hair of two colors. *Bailly Collection.*

257

The 257 has the head of a clown, with an open/closed mouth.

259

The 259 number has a very lively child's face with an open mouth connecting with the inside of the head, two teeth and well-drawn lips. Unknown in France, it is mentioned by Marlowe Cooper.

262

The 262 is again a child's face. The mouth is open with four upper teeth. The face has full cheeks and thick eyebrows. It is at this time unknown in France.

S.F.B.J. mold 255. *Bailly Collection.*

The 263 is a fat *bébé* with a full *composition-carton* head and molded hair. The mouth is open and shows two upper teeth and a movable tongue. The glass eyes sleep and have silk lashes. The lower lashes are painted vertically and quite short.

The neck is short and wide at the base for attachment to the body by sewing. The mark, "S.F.B.J. 263 Paris," is impressed on the nape of the neck.

The body is of stuffed cloth and is jointed at the hips and shoulders. The hands are composition.

It is found in size 11, or 62cm (24⅜in).

11
S.F.B.J.
263
PARIS

Detail of the mark for mold 263.

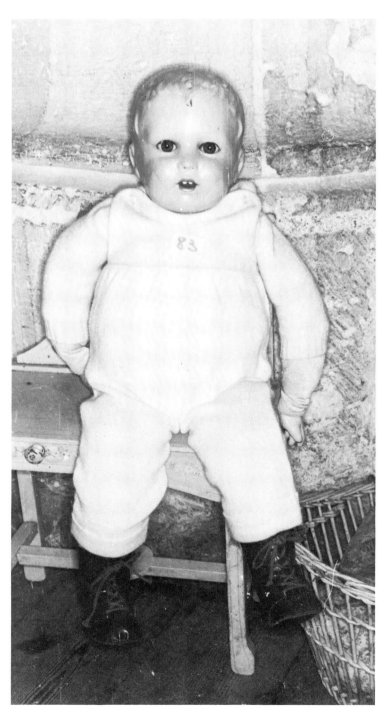

S.F.B.J. mold 263. *Galerie de Chartres.*

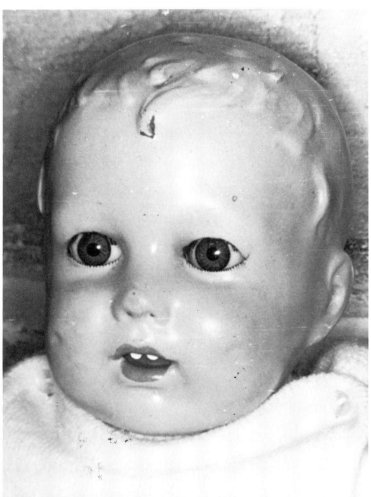

Detail of the head of mold 263. *Galerie de Chartres.*

271

The 271 character *bébé* with a solid bisque head has a newborn look similar to Armand Marseille's 351. The skull does not have hair, but is tinted an ochre yellow. It has an open mouth, without teeth and with semi-mobile tongue.

It is small in size: 20cm (7⅞in) to 30cm (11¾in). The 21cm (8¼in) *bébés* have painted eyes, the others have sleeping glass eyes. The outer edge of the eye socket is prominent.

Its body is a composition *poupon* body. This *bébé* is rare. It was made in the 1930s to 1940s, and marked in the nape hollow: "UNIS FRANCE, Paris 271."

 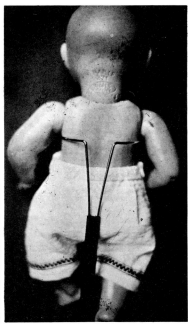

RIGHT: 27cm (11in) mold 271 with a closed dome bisque head marked "UNIS FRANCE 271." It has an open mouth, sleep eyes and a bent limb baby body. *Godard Collection.*

FAR RIGHT: A back view of the 271 baby. *Godard Collection.*

272

The 272 is a *bébé* in swaddling clothes. The body is very simple: it is simply a sewn bag. Only the head is in bisque, the hands are composition. The head is round, full, and bald. The eyes are small and sleep. The mouth is open with a movable tongue and without teeth.

It is marked on the nape: "UNIS FRANCE 272." It exists in size 2, or 21cm (8¼in). It is rare.

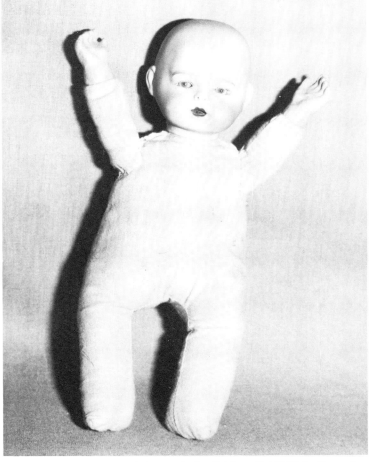

Swaddling baby, mold 272, marked "*UNIS FRANCE.*" *Photo by Chauveau.*

Swaddling baby, mold 272. Marked "*UNIS FRANCE.*" *Photo by Chauveau.*

Back of the head of S.F.B.J. 272. *Photo by Chauveau.*

164144

UNIS FRANCE

278

The 278 is a character *bébé* with a solid head in an unbreakable material, identical to the *Bambino* of the 1940s. It has the face of a newborn, with sleeping eyes and an open mouth without teeth. It is rather highly colored. At the end of the neck, a half-ring is molded with the head, for attaching it to the body.

Its body is composition, semi-articulated with bent limbs. It is signed in the hollow of the neck: "JUMEAU 278." In size 3 (26cm) or 10¼in), it was the model for the last *Bambino* made by the S.F.B.J. for *la Semaine de Suzette* (Suzette's Week). In fact, in 1955, *la Semaine de Suzette* presented the great novelty of *Bambino* with an unbreakable head.

It is rare.

284

The 284 has a sad, but nonetheless attractive face of a little girl. The head is of a composition which resembles cardboard called *incassable,* or unbreakable.

The eyes are very large, open, with noticeable eyelids, and traces of make-up on the upper lid. They sleep and bear lashes.

The head is round. The mouth is small, closed and pinched, painted in two tones of red, the lower lip paler. The brows are thin, horizontal, and rather high.

The head is stamped near the upper opening: "UNIS FRANCE 284." This kind of marking is often masked by paint and glue. It is seen better on the inside, but it appears backwards.

The body is quite ordinary, composition or stuffed cloth like the later dolls made before the last war.

Its size is quite large: about 60cm (23⅝in), and it is a rare model.

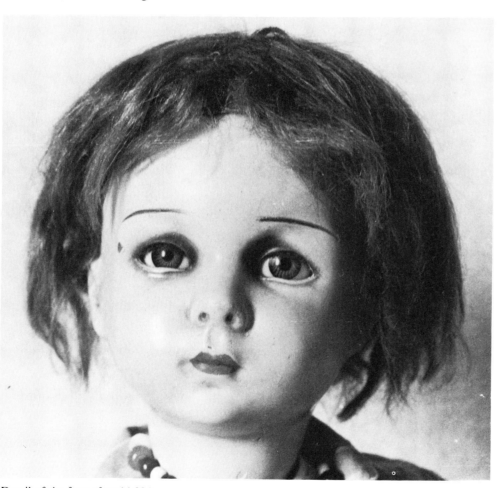

Detail of the face of mold 284.

Detail of the mark inside the head of a 284 doll.

287

The 287 has a rather special face: a large round head with a small mouth very much withdrawn as if buried between two fat cheeks and an ample chin. The head, made of cardboard-composition and said to be *incassable et lavable* (unbreakable and washable) has a high cut opening.

The mouth is open with two upper teeth and a movable tongue. The nose is flat. The sleeping eyes are slightly outlined with make-up on the outer part, like the models of the 1940s. They are fixed according to the patented bridge-lid system. They bear natural lashes. The lower lashes and painted brows are indicated in a rudimentary manner.

The body is a character *bébé* body from the last period: the upper limbs completely articulated, the lower ones straight, and the torso is stapled cardboard.

This *bébé* exists in size 10, or 62cm (24⅜in). It is relatively rare and little known.

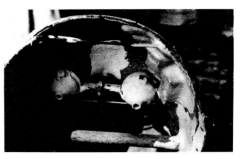

Detail of the sleeping eyes of S.F.B.J. mold 287.

The 287 doll.

Mark inside the head on a 287 doll.

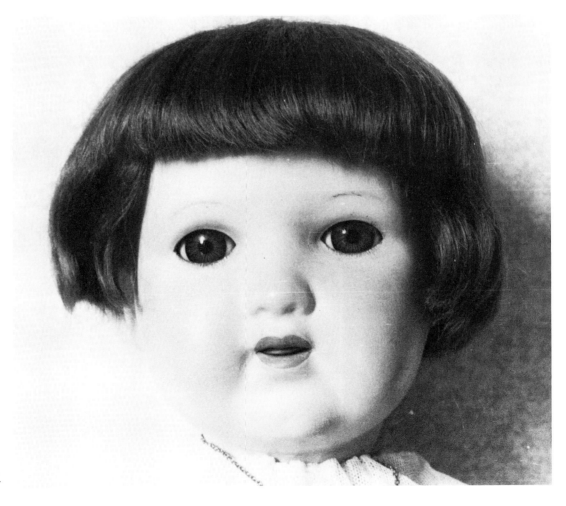

Face detail of mold 287.

288

The 288 is a character baby with the face and body of a *poupon*, a very young baby with bent arms and legs. It has a solid dome head of composition. The hair is molded in relief and painted and styled with a lock on the left side. The doll has sleeping glass eyes, thin eyebrows, an open mouth with a tongue, and applied ears.

The composition body is jointed at the shoulders and ankles. The mark on the nape of the neck is:

288   8
71   (UNIS FRANCE)   149

The 8 is the size number which corresponds to 40cm (15¾in).

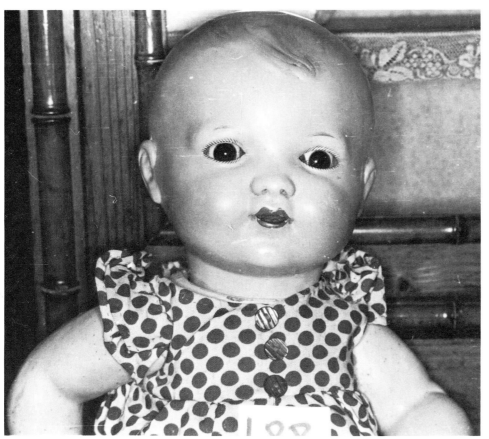

The 288 character baby.

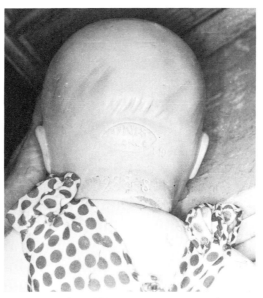

Back view of the 288 character baby showing the head markings.

290

The 290 has a bisque head with the face of a young girl. It has sleeping glass eyes and well-drawn, rather thick eyebrows. The mouth is open with a semi-mobile tongue and two upper teeth. The ears are not pierced. It has an open pate and is marked UNIS.

The composition body is fully jointed with a flat stomach and sharp lower end.

298

The 298 has a cardboard-composition solid dome head. The hair is molded in relief and painted in a style with a lock falling over the forehead. It has sleeping glass eyes.

The semi-jointed body is made of stuffed fabric with pasteboard limbs. Number 298 is marked in the hollow at the nape of the neck.

301

The 301 is not a character *bébé*, but the face of a young girl doll, quite common, like the number 60, which one finds in the chapter on heads of ordinary dolls.

The head has an open pate. The brows, rather short, are molded and painted with several strokes. The eyes can be either set or sleeping. The lashes are painted with oblique lines. The nose is short and turned up. The mouth is small and open with four upper teeth. The cheeks are full.

The body is a *bébé* type, unbreakable and fully-articulated. This baby can be a walker which throws kisses and has flirting eyes.

Certain models bear a production year (1922-1926), others the brand Unis. Often, as well as the brand, three letters are incised: ERT. This may indicate the year of fabrication, or may indicate the foreign origin of these heads. They were made in all sizes from 4/0 (14cm [5½in]) to 16 (90cm [35⅜in]).

The 301 heads are found in bisque or in unbreakable cardboard composition, called *carton-pâte*. They were also made tinted black or mulatto with matching bodies.

One can find these 301 heads with bodies marked *Bébé Vrai Modèle, fabrication Jumeau*. The brand, Jumeau, had been registered several times by the S.F.B.J.; Jumeau is thus a simple commercial name, and not related to the quality or production of Emile Jumeau. 301 heads often bear a superimposed stamp *TÊTE JUMEAU*.

Face of S.F.B.J. mold 301. It dates from the beginning of the 20th century.

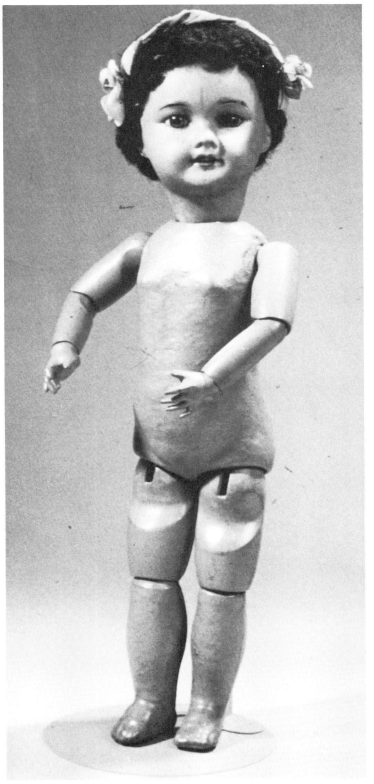

Brown version of S.F.B.J. mold 301. It dates before 1910.

Detail of the mark on an S.F.B.J. 301 head.

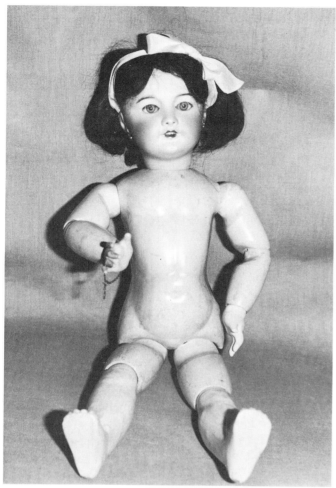

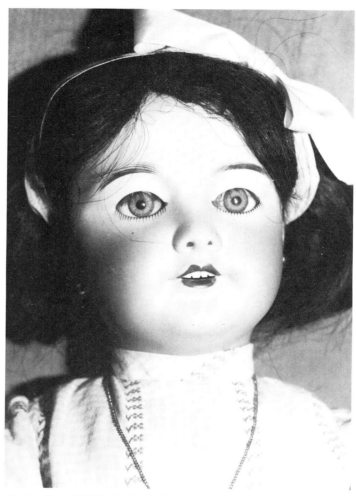

60cm (24in) doll dated 1948 and marked "*UNIS FRANCE 301.*" It has an unusual body. *Photo by Chauveau.*

Detail of the 1948 Unis France 301 doll. *Photo by Chauveau.*

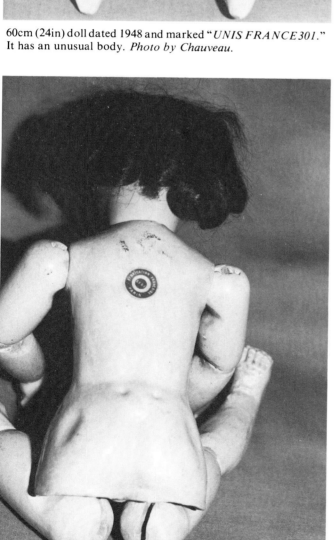

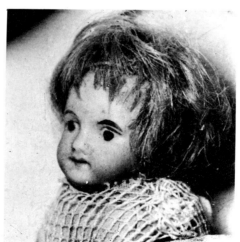

Small composition doll from mold 301 with painted eyes.

16cm (6½in) composition doll marked "*UNIS FRANCE 301.*"

Back of the Unis France 301 doll. It has the tri-color cockade sticker denoting French production. *Photo by Chauveau.*

306

The 306 model was manufactured after the visit of the English sovereigns to France in 1938. It reproduces, in a smaller size, the two large dolls, *France* and *Marianne*, offered by French school children to the young princesses Elizabeth and Margaret, during the visit of King George VI and Queen Elizabeth.

The head has an open pate and is made in colored bisque. It has the beautiful face of a young girl about ten years old, the age of the princesses. The face is well proportioned and the careful make-up reflects the look of movie stars of the period.

The mouth is closed and painted in two tones, the lower lip paler. The glass, flirting eyes are wide open with natural lashes on top and painted vertically on the bottom. There is a touch of make-up on the upper part of the socket.

The heads are marked in the hollow of the nape UNIS FRANCE and JUMEAU 1938 PARIS. These dolls had blonde or brown hair, styled according to the period: a part on the right side with short curls around the face.

The body is completely articulated in wood and composition; the upper limbs are slender. They are made in two sizes of 45cm (17¾in) and 90 cm (35½in). The dresses were long and of rose or pale blue organdy. These dolls had a great deal of success, and it is not uncommon to find them.

The 306 doll pictured in *Le Jouet Francais* (Toymaker Magazine) May 1949.

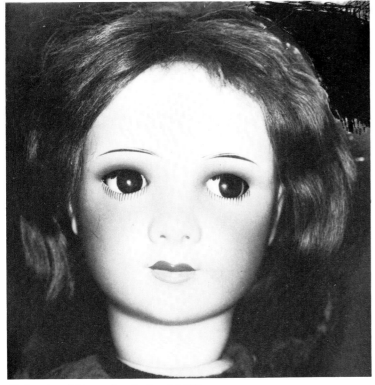

Pink colored bisque head of mold 306.

Front and back view of the 306 head. *Fichter Collection.*

316

The 316 is one of the S.F.B.J.'s last doll models. These dolls are in small sizes like many of the dolls of the period, 1950 through 1958.

The round face, without dimples or furrows, is smooth and has a high, convex forehead. The face is not long, the neck is slender.

The sleep eyes have a simple bridge lid and long lashes. The brows are barely indicated with a red line. The mouth in the shape of a closed heart, is colored with a single tone of bright red. The molded ears are not clearly defined.

The head is made of the unbreakable composition papier-mâché *carton-pâte incassable*, in two stapled parts. It is stamped in back, near the pate opening: S.F.B.J. 316 with a size number.

The body is a composition character baby body, articulated at the shoulders and hips. The limbs are partially bent. The hands made with thick, short fingers and painted nails.

30cm (12in) 1952 creation, *Christine*, with an unbreakable head and composition body. Head marked "*316.*" *Photo by Chauveau.*

S.F.B.J. mold 316. *R.B. Collection.*

S.F.B.J. mold 316. *R.B. Collection.*

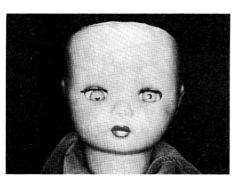

Detail of the head of a 316 doll.

The 318 is also one of the S.F.B.J.'s last models. It represents a young girl of the 1950s. The head and body are made of a plastic which imitates celluloid. This model is identical to 316, but in a different material.

The body is articulated at the shoulders and hips and has partially bent limbs with dimples at the knees and elbows.

This model is signed in relief on the neck: JUMEAU 318/4. This last figure indicates the size which corresponds to 30cm (11¾in), a common size of that period.

Side view of mold 318, *Babybotte.* The shoes are marked "*Jumeau.*"

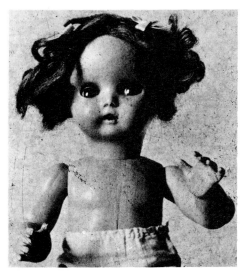

An example of the 318 with a plastic head.

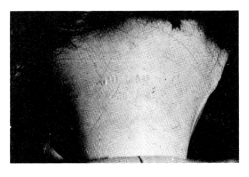

Detail of the Jumeau mark on the S.F.B.J. 318.

Tête marquée de deux chiffres
Heads marked with two numbers

These heads are generally made of *carton-pâte* with glass eyes. They are marked S.F.B.J. Paris and stamped with the size number. Another number shows the year of production, in this case, 1948.

These heads were placed on ordinary jointed composition bodies.

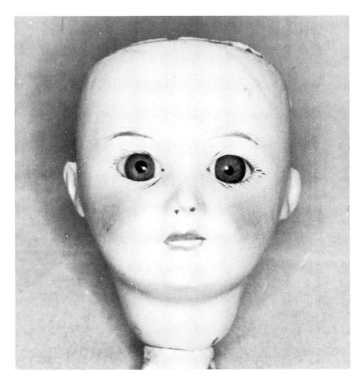

Doll with a head of *carton pâte* (cardboard), glass eyes and a closed mouth.

Bébés Caractère à Têtes Interchangeables
Character *Bébés*
with Interchangeable Heads

These *bébés* are quite curious and rare. They were only advertised for one year, 1912/1913, in the department stores' New Year's catalogs the same as the Poulbot. This model must not have had the expected success.

Its price was nonetheless quite reasonable for such a curiosity: hardly ten percent more than a character *bébé* of the same size dressed in the latest style, and the same price as a 62cm (24⅜in) Jumeau product in a chemise.

Changing the heads was probably not easy for young children, and the risk of breakage quite important. The linking system is an application of the Bouchet 1894 patent explained by J. Porot in *Poupées articulées*.

The three interchangeable bisque heads are three different character *bébé* models: a smiling model, a pensive model and a shouting model, or numbers 227, 233, 235 and/or 237.

The body either has bent limbs, or is fully-articulated. These baby dolls were made in 34cm (13⅜in) and 37cm (14½in).

C. C. 44101. Nouveauté. Jolie BOITE contenant un trousseau et un bébé entièrement articulé, avec trois têtes caractères de physionomies différentes interchangeables.

Hauteur du bébé :
0 34   0 36
15.75   **19.75**

Advertisement from Grands Magazins for the interchangeable doll.

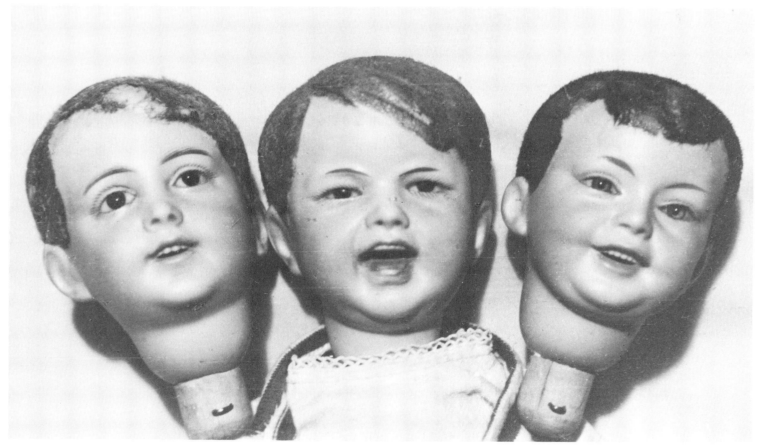

Three "interchangeable" heads, numbers 237, 233 and 227. *Sambat Collection, photo by Doumic.*

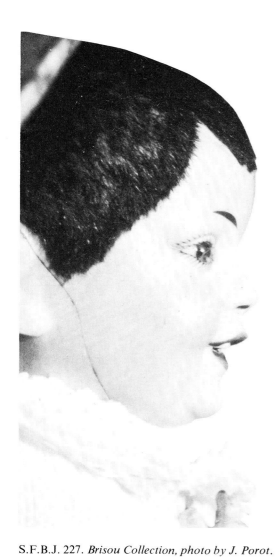

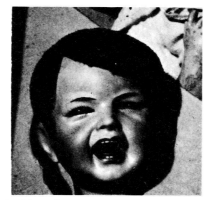

Doll head from S.F.B.J. mold 233. *Brisou Collection.*

S.F.B.J. 227. *Brisou Collection, photo by J. Porot.*

S.F.B.J. 235. *Brisou Collection, photo by J. Porot.*

Original box with heads 233, 227 and 235. *Brisou Collection, photo by J. Porot.*

Têtes des Bébés Ordinaires
Ordinary Baby Doll Heads

Têtes allemandes
German Heads

In the course of the S.F.B.J.'s history there was a great demand for their products, but they were not well enough equipped to manufacture all the heads for their *bébés*.

The only kiln available to them at the beginning was 7m3 in size, built by Emile Jumeau in the factory in the Rue François Arago, and therefore their first problem was to replace this one with another of 9m3. This was done in 1909, and they had plans for yet another to be built in 1915. Thus while waiting for the time when they would be equipped to turn out four million heads per year (a figure which would be reached after World War I), the S.F.B.J. was forced to look further afield for someone to meet their demand, and at a realistic price. This could only be achieved through a liaison with Germany, where Fleischmann, who had kept his establishment at Fürth, was in a good position to strike a bargain with them.

So German dolls' heads began to be imported in large quantities. The main suppliers were Simon and Halbig who had an extremely good reputation among doll manufacturers. Their bisque was very fine, and it was this which brought them closest to the French manufacturers in terms of quality. Many German doll manufacturers, such as Kämmer & Reinhardt, Bergmann, and Handwerck, ordered their dolls' heads from them.

So the S.F.B.J. began to use Simon and Halbig's heads. These heads usually bear the word DEP and a mold number: 1039, 1078 or 1079 as well as the letters S & H or the whole name. However, this mold was not reserved exclusively for the S.F.B.J. because many other French and German manufacturers also used these heads: for example, the firm of Decamps used S & H's numbers 1039 and 1079.

Another head model which was manufactured in Germany is that which is stamped DEP, and may also carry a red stamp bearing the words TÊTE JUMEAU. There are, incidentally, two kinds of red stamp marks: the coral-red *baveux* or "blurred" mark which may sometimes be completely ineffectual; and the garnet-red stamp, which is very clear and is in bold characters. It is still not known who was manufacturing these heads, but it seems very likely that it was also Simon and Halbig. Nor was this mold exclusive to the S.F.B.J. for one may find DEP heads mounted on German bodies, and other manufacturers could easily have purchased these heads.

It is, therefore, the body which allows us to recognize an S.F.B.J. *bébé* carrying a German head, because the S.F.B.J. bodies are different from those made in Germany. These DEP dolls are highly sought after because of the quality of the bisque and the coloring of the face.

1905 doll with a Simon and Halbig 1039 head and an S.F.B.J. body.

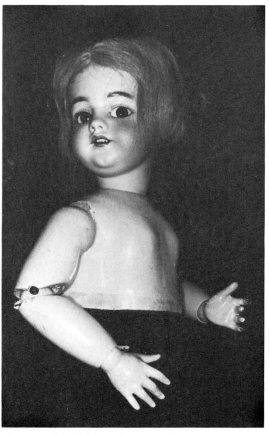

Simon and Halbig head, size 10½.

Simon and Halbig mold 1039 in original dress. It dates from 1905.

D.E.P. "*Tête Jumeau*."

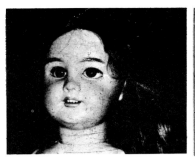

D.E.P. doll marked with a red stamp "*Tete Jumeau*."

Back view of the D.E.P. doll on the left showing the stamp and mark.

Detail of the Simon and Halbig 1039 head showing the paper "*Breveté*" label and the sleeping eyes system which the S.F.B.J. used in 1904.

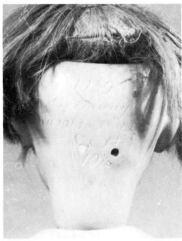

Detail of the Simon and Halbig mark.

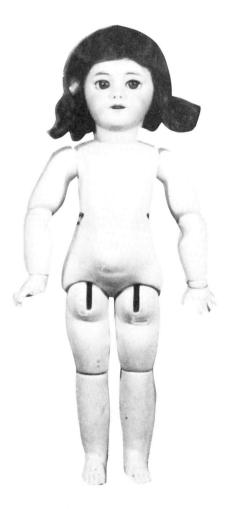

D.E.P. doll marked "*Tête Jumeau*."

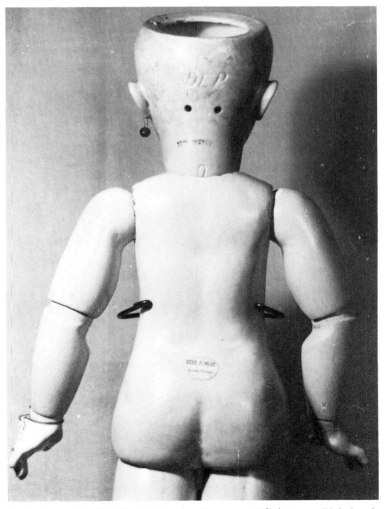

Back view of the D.E.P. doll showing the paper "*Bébé Jumeau*" label and the red "*Tête Jumeau*" stamp.

Têtes françaises
French Heads

The *bébé* heads S.F.B.J. 60 or UNIS 60 are of two kinds: made of either bisque or of *composition-carton* and were inspired by the German heads produced during the first years of the 20th Century. The heads have the pate cut high. The mouths are open showing four upper teeth. They may have sleeping eyes. The quality of the bisque is not always very high. This model also exists in the form of black or half-caste *bébés*.

The size numbers of these *bébés* do not correspond to the usual ones. For example, the 13/0 is 24cm (9½in) high, the 10/0 is 30cm (11⅞in) and the 2/0 is 37cm (14½in). Size 2 measures 48cm (18⅞in) and size 13 measures 75cm (29½in).

The earliest models must have been made at the end of World War I, and together with model 301, were the most numerous of the S.F.B.J. *bébés*, and probably continued to be made right up until the end of the firm's career. Model number 60 was usually kept for the cheaper dolls, and model 301 was used for the more expensive of the *bébés*.

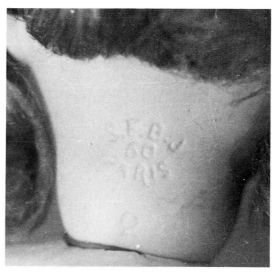

Mark on an S.F.B.J. 60 doll, size 2.

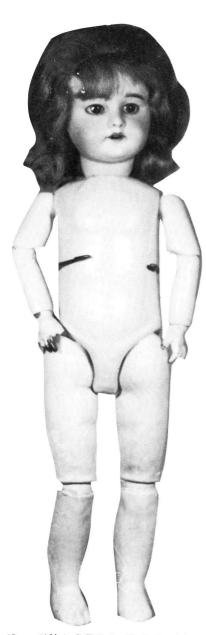

48cm (19in) S.F.B.J. 60 doll with a bisque head and cardboard body, size 2.

Brown version of mold 60 wearing the original dress. It is 21cm (8in), size 12/0.

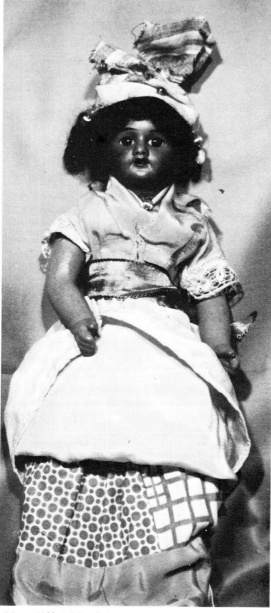

30cm (12in) Martinique doll with a brown bisque head marked *"UNIS-FRANCE,"* in the original dress, 1935.

Composants de la S.F.B.J.
Members of the S.F.B.J.

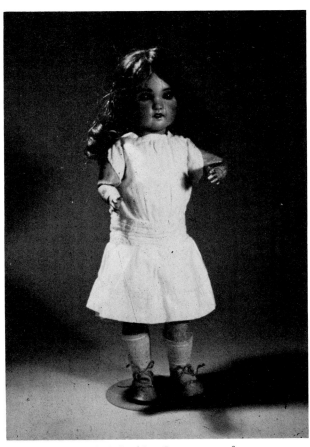

A marked S.F.B.J. doll with a Jumeau type face.

Les Bébés Jumeau dans la S.F.B.J.
Jumeau *bébés* in S.F.B.J.

Emile Jumeau played an important part in the history of the S.F.B.J. since he supplied the company with the bulk of his models, trademarks and materials. He was perhaps the only one to have turned over almost all of his stock to the S.F.B.J. His name already carried a great deal of prestige when he entered into the commercial side of the business, and he had a large stock of finished products. For this reason, it is hardly surprising that his name was long used in the manufacturing, and one could almost say that these were Jumeau's own products which were being marketed by the S.F.B.J. during their formative years. It is extremely difficult for an amateur of today to distinguish between the *bebes* which were made by Jumeau himself, and those manufactured by the S.F.B.J. at this early period.

The other founding members of the S.F.B.J. were much less significant than Jumeau in regard to their contribution to the Société's production.

Fleischmann and Bloedel's factory was equipped for the manufacture of semi-articulated composition *bébés*. The manufacture of fully-articulated *bébés* was very rare, and not profitable. Furthermore, very few finished products are listed in their inventory.

The Maison Bru, which had been bought by Girard in 1890, was steadily declining, although their advertisements still boasted of their *Bébé Bru* on which their reputation had been founded. Monsieur Girard and his son had completely modernized their methods through the manufacture of a fully-articulated unbreakable *bébé*, based on Jumeau's model, and they later produced and patented a walking *bébé* which functioned without the use of a key. But their output was very small compared with Jumeau's and their inventory made no mention of either body molds or head models.

The contribution of the Société's other partners to the manufacture of fully-articulated *bébés* was relatively insignificant. Wertheimer was responsible only for the boxes and labels. Gobert, Remignard and Bouchet contributed some of the molds for ordinary *bébés*. Genty's factory at Limeil, which rivalled Jumeau's in 1890, was only producing equipment for the manufacture of dolls made of kid, and the materials for the pouring of porcelain heads. Pintel and Godchaux provided only the *bébé* molding machines.

Thus, in practice, it was Jumeau's own factory which kept the S.F.B.J. going. An inventory of some hundred pages describes in minute detail the raw materials, loose parts, finished products and the working stock itself. At least in terms of high quality products, it was this acquisition which would set the S.F.B.J. in motion.

At the lower end of the market, Fleischmann's Picpus factory would continue to produce the composition *bébé* bodies which were then completed by Pintel, Bouchet and Gobert.

And it was the well-known *Bébé Jumeau*, first registered as a trademark by Jumeau in 1886, which would later be exploited. This name was to be stamped on the body either by means of a blue stamp or, more often, by means of a pink label stuck on the back. By the last years, Jumeau had already stopped stamping the heads with the mark: "DEPOSE, BREVETE S.G.D.G." It is also known that some of these heads, those which were of second- or third-class quality, were not marked at all. Although the advertisements of this period state that these heads were of the same standard as the others, they were not impeccably finished and their decoration left much to be desired. This is not to denigrate the overall strength of their appearance, but since Jumeau's reputation was based on the high quality of his goods, he preferred not to put his name on anything which was not up to standard; and it was financial pressures which forced him to put these second-class goods on the market.

It is still not known what exchange of ideas took place during the drawing up of the Société's constitution, nor how this dictated the choice of models which were to be manufactured. For the sake of the company's profitability, it must doubtless have been their policy to simplify things as far as possible. An examination of the *bébés* made between 1900 and 1910 shows that the S.F.B.J. was using the same mold for heads that Jumeau had used in 1895, a fact which can be taken as certain, whether or not the heads are stamped. Nevertheless, some of these unstamped heads are marked 1907 on the nape of the neck. However, there are also heads obviously made in Germany which bear the red *TÊTE JUMEAU* stamp. All of these heads have open mouths with teeth, which were known as *bouche à dents* at the time.

The bodies may or may not bear the pink label or stamp which was mentioned earlier. It is here that the problem of identification arises. It is not impossible that some *bébés* heads made before 1900 may have been broken and replaced by others, and so it is important to pay special attention to the bodies, because the body types fall into distinctly defined chronological categories. How can a Jumeau *bébé* dating from the end of the 19th century be distinguished from an S.F.B.J. *bébé*, marked Jumeau, but dating from the early years of the 20th century?

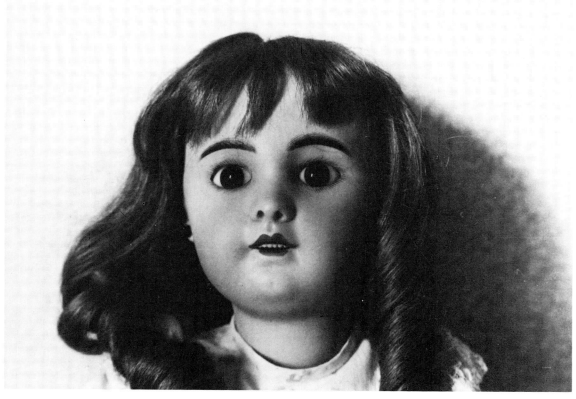

S.F.B.J. 1907 bisque head with pierced ears and paperweight eyes.

Le Corps
The Bodies

The body of the S.F.B.J.'s model was the same as Jumeau's, and bears the pink label, but there is an important difference in the method of mounting. The S.F.B.J. no longer used the spring method of mounting the hands, a system which had been patented by Cordier and was used by Danel in 1889 and by Jumeau after 1892. The hands are joined directly to the forearms by the same piece of rubber that links the arms to the trunk of the body. The head was no longer attached to the crosswise rod in the thorax by a large spring which was characteristic of Jumeau's style, but was mounted either by a short link or else was connected directly to the limbs.

Les Têtes
The Heads
Decorated *bébés* and Jumeau models (with or without his stamp)

If the *bébé* has the type of mounting described above: with the style of head which Jumeau was manufacturing in the last years of the 19th century, including the high cut-out in the pate which is almost horizontal, and with a large internal border, then one can rest assured that this is a *bébé* manufactured by the S.F.B.J. On the other hand, if the cut-out in the head has only a shallow slope, then this would not be the case. Only the thickness of the border could sway the argument in favor of this being an S.F.B.J. *bébé*.

But in absolutely no case should any pressure whatsoever be applied to the stamp on the body or to the head in an attempt to ascertain whether or not the *bébé* is a genuine Jumeau. Before coming to any conclusion, the mounting of the body must be examined as closely as the shape and decoration of the head.

Decorated *bébés* and Jumeau models stamped "1907"

There has been a great deal of discussion of these 1907 *bébés*, and the question has arisen: were they made by Jumeau himself or by the S.F.B.J.? For two reasons, one can be sure that these *bébés* were manufactured by the S.F.B.J. First, no mention of these 1907 heads is made in Emile Jumeau's finely detailed inventory which was used in the constitution of the Société. Secondly, we have had confirmation of our belief from the daughter of a former worker in the S.F.B.J. that 1907 was indeed the year in which this mold was made.

On the other hand, there are 1907 heads which were made in Germany and do not correspond to Jumeau's style. Their origin is unknown. The cut-outs in these heads are high, but the heads are of lower quality. Their bisque is of a pinkish color, dyed in bulk, and even the inside is pink, something which is very unusual in old bisque. These 1907 *bébés* should not be confused with those of the same year which are stamp-marked "R/A DEP" and were manufactured by Recknagel.

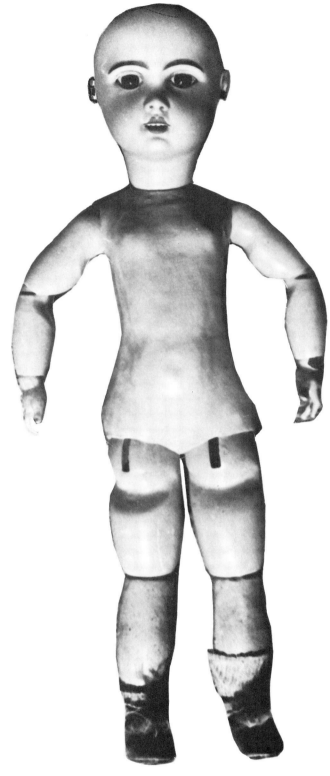

S.F.B.J. 1907 with the first model S.F.B.J. body.

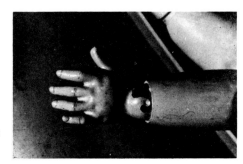

Detail of the hand on an S.F.B.J. 1907.

Different *bébés*, made in the Jumeau mold and stamp-marked "TÊTE Jumeau"

In this case too, the stamp-mark has caused some confusion, although there is no doubt that these *bébés* are the work of the S.F.B.J. The heads can be easily recognized: the coloring of the head is occasionally high, taking on the shade of carmine pink; the mouth is open showing four upper teeth, and the eyebrows are molded in relief and painted. They often bear the stamp "DEP."

The cut-out is high in the head, and there are two small holes in the nape of the neck. No really satisfactory explanation has been found yet for this latter feature, but it was frequently used by German manufacturers and was later adopted by the French. Some experts have theorized that a thread through these holes served to secure the sleeping eyes when the doll was transported. Others think that they would have been used to hold the head during its manufacture, either for the drying or the decorating. We tend to lean towards the former explanation, because these heads seem to have nearly always been fitted with movable eyes (though it is true that in some cases the French manufacturers used the technique of attaching a thread to the eyes through the mouth). The presence of one or more of these characteristics must serve as a strict warning to the amateur that this is a head made not by Jumeau but by the S.F.B.J.

A distinction must be made here between the terms stamp-mark (or trademark) and manufacture. Jumeau's fame often caused confusion and was exploited to such a great extent that little girls no longer said, "my doll" or "my *bébé*," but "my Jumeau"; much as the French are now in the habit of referring to all refrigerators by the tradename of "Frigidaire."

Bébés whose heads are stamped "Jumeau 230" on the nape of the neck.

This number indicates that this is a character *bébé*, in fact an S.F.B.J. character *bébé*, though the truth is that the face is not really a character at all; it is the face of a good little girl, the classic face of the *incassable bébé* of this period.

Although some of these heads are stamped with Jumeau's name, they were nevertheless manufactured by the S.F.B.J. Those made by Jumeau himself all bear the red stamp-mark, "Depose Brevete S.G.D.G.," and Jumeau's molds made before 1900 are numbered from 200 to 225.

Moreover the heads numbered 230 are different from Jumeau's and have all the characteristics of the S.F.B.J.'s manufacturing process: the eyebrows are molded in relief and painted, and the cut-out in the head is high and almost horizontal.

Bébé heads stamp-marked JUMEAU 306 in the hollow of the neck.

This model is a late S.F.B.J. model, dating from 1938. The details of its history will be found in the chapter on character *bébés*, but at this point it should just be added that the date of manufacture is also stamped on the head, and the presence of the letters UNIS-FRANCE confirms that this is indeed an S.F.B.J. head.

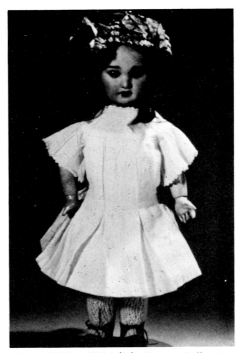

31cm (12¼in) 230 *bébé*. *Chovet Collection, photo by Doumic.*

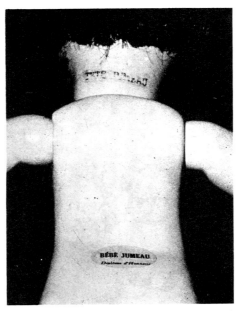

Back view of the 1934 S.F.B.J. doll marked "*Jumeau*" on both the head and the body.

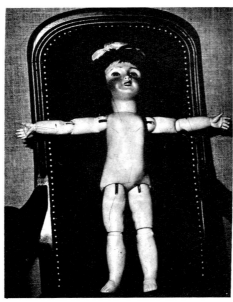

A 1934 S.F.B.J. doll marked "*Jumeau*."

How to recognize Jumeau *bébé* heads manufactured by the S.F.B.J. whether or not they bear a stampmark

When there is no stamp, look for another indication, either on the head or on the body:
- a red stamp, either *sans netteté* (blurred) or sharp and of a dark red color, or applied by means of a transfer.
- the presence of two holes in the nape of the neck.
- the cut-out high on the head, either almost horizontal or at a steep slant; and always with a large, overhanging ledge on the inside of the cut-out.
- eyebrows molded in relief.
- a small mouth, always open, coral in color, showing four upper teeth.
- paperweight eyes, or glass eyes of an irregular design.
- brighter coloring of the bisque.

If one or more of these specifications is met, then the *bébé* was definitely manufactured by the S.F.B.J.

Doll with the Jumeau mark from L' Illustration, December 15, 1934. *Maciet Collection, Musée des Arts Décoratifs*, Paris.

Other types of *bébés*, or dolls stamp-marked JUMEAU during the S.F.B.J.'s period of production.

The numbers 278 and 318 can be seen in the chapter on the heads of character *bébés*.

The last of these dolls were normally of a composition material or later of plastic. The plastic dolls made by the S.F.B.J. were always of a very small *mignonnette* type, with jointed shoulders and hips. At the top of the back between the shoulder-blades, the words JUMEAU MADE IN FRANCE are molded in relief. These, too, must be called S.F.B.J. dolls and not Jumeau dolls.

Other articles manufactured by the S.F.B.J marked with the names Jumeau or *Bébé Jumeau*.

For example, the flowered chemise, which was first worn by Jumeau's own *Bébé Jumeau*, was adopted by the S.F.B.J. without any alteration whatsoever, and is to be found in all the *Grands Magasins* New Year's gift catalogs from 1899 to 1930. The typical chemise (but not the dress) usually had a label on the belt bearing the words "*Bébé Jumeau*" in gold lettering on a black background, and was worn by all of the most luxurious models of fully-articulated *bébés*. For commercial reasons these were listed in the catalogs as "made by Jumeau," but it can be stated with complete certainty that these dolls were made by the S.F.B.J.

On the other hand, the use of the tradename *Bébé Jumeau* is perfectly lawful because the S.F.B.J. registered it four times after 1911. This mark is found on all the doll bodies and heads made by the S.F.B.J. in their first ten years and on all their chemises made in the following thirty years. The name is to be found, even after this date, on not only the items themselves, but also on the accompanying labels. Thus it is not infrequent for S.F.B.J. dolls made after 1930 to have a circular, oval or square label attached to one of the hands. These may be marked "*BÉBÉ JUMEAU*" "*Poupée Jumeau*," "*Fabrication Jumeau*" or "*Jumeau Paris*," and the lettering is either red, gold or black on a white, red or gold background. During the S.F.B.J.'s last years a label was often attached to the doll's dress. Once again, these specifications do not mean that the doll was made by Jumeau himself, but that it was made by the S.F.B.J. under his trademark which they re-registered in 1956, 40 years after Jumeau's death.

The S.F.B.J. also molded Jumeau on the white plastic shoes which were issued with the plastic dolls (especially model number 318) and were made for the S.F.B.J. by Maison Babybotte.

The dressed "Jumeau" doll shown at the bottom of page 118.

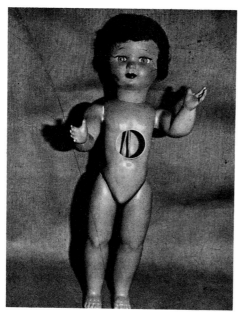

Front view of *Sylvie. Photo by Chauveau.*

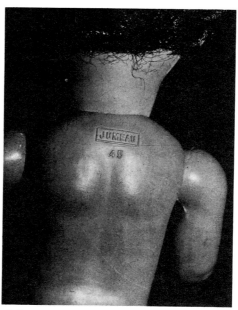

Sylvie doll of painted plastic from 1957 showing its Jumeau mark. It was pictured in the Galeries Lafayette department store catalog in 1958. *Photo by Chauveau.*

Two mignonnettes, small plastic dolls marked *"Jumeau." R.B. Collection.*

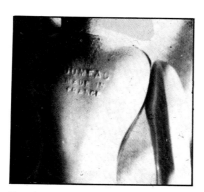

Detail of the mark on the samll dolls above: *"Jumeau. Made in France." R.B. Collection.*

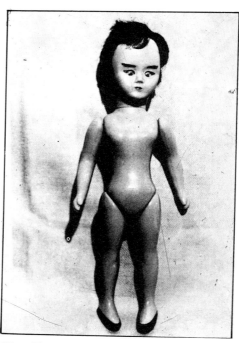

17cm (7in) small plastic doll marked *"Jumeau." R.B. Collection.*

40cm (16in) "*D.E.P. Tête Jumeau*" with original dress and box cover. The doll is size 5.

Nº 48588.

BEBE jum.eau entièrement articulé, cheveux naturels.						
0ᵐ37	0ᵐ41	0ᵐ45	0ᵐ49	0ᵐ53	0ᵐ58	0ᵐ63
7·90	8·90	11. »	13. »	16.25	19.50	23.»
Parlant, yeux dormeurs.						
Prix	14·50	17·50	21. »	24. »	28.»	

Typical Jumeau dress used by the S.F.B.J. from 1899 to 1930.

MAISON JUMEAU
Première Manufacture du Monde pour la Fabrication des Beaux Bébés

National
JUMEAU
yeux naturels

Le **Bébé Jumeau** est le JOUET NATIONAL par excellence; il est partout, il a figuré à toutes les grandes Expositions françaises et étrangères, et a toujours obtenu un éclatant succès. Ses victoires ne se comptent plus, et dans ces luttes commerciales il a largement contribué à propager en pays lointains la renommée de la fabrication française.

D'une fabrication **extra supérieure**, il est unique en son genre, et absolument parfait; et si nos charmantes fillettes l'ont adopté avec joie et bonheur, c'est qu'il réunit toutes les qualités indispensables à cette perfection : **Beauté, Solidité, Légèreté**.

Le **Bébé Jumeau est beau**. — Il doit cette qualité à son heureux modèle exécuté par le gracieux maître statuaire *Carrier-Belleux*, et sa tête, en fine porcelaine, possède un décor idéal qui la distingue de toutes les autres.

Le **Bébé Jumeau est solide**. — Il doit cette solidité à son genre de construction. Tous ses membres sont faits en bois de deux essences différentes, mortaisés et collés ensemble, ce qui les rend insensibles aux variations atmosphériques et aux ...

Le **Bébé Jumeau est léger**. — Quoique nécessitant un travail difficile, cette légèreté est obtenue en enlevant aux membres ... partie de leur poids par un creusement, fait avec précision, avant la réunion des deux bois nécessaires à leur construction.

Avec toutes ces qualités le **Bébé Jumeau** se place de lui-même au premier rang de la fabrication française et ... largement revendiquer le nom de **Jouet National**. *Dans leur carton, les Bébés sont toujours placés les pieds du côté de l'étiquette extérieure.*

GARANTIE	La tête du Bébé Jumeau a été réclamée propriété exclusive de la Maison par jugement confirmé par arrêt de la Cour d'Appel de Paris.	DÉPOT	La forme de son nouveau corps a été l'objet d'un dépôt au Conseil des Prud'hommes.	**BÉBÉ JUMEAU**

LE BÉBÉ JUMEAU EST VENDU PAR LES MAISONS DE PREMIER ORDRE

Paper label from the inside of the box cover used by the S.F.B.J.

Plastic doll made between 1952 and 1958 which has a paper Jumeau label. The label is red and gold and states: "*Incassable- lavable- in- inflammable-Jumeau- Paris.*" Photo by Chauveau.

Babybotte mark on the shoes of a plastic Jumeau doll.

De Danel a Jumeau et a la S.F.B.J.: Paris Bébé

From Danel to Jumeau and the S.F.B.J.: the *Paris Bébé*

The name *Paris Bébé* has given rise to a lot of confusion because it was registered by two manufacturers: first by Danel & Cie in 1899 and then by the S.F.B.J. in 1900. It is therefore necessary to give a brief resume of the history of Danel's company.

In 1888 Anatole Ludovic Danel was commercial director of Jumeau's company. For reasons which are still unknown, he left Jumeau the following year to set up his own rival company, forming a partnership with Jean-Marie Guépratte who was Jumeau's principal supplier of eyes and shoes. Danel lured a group of workers away from his former employer, and by means of the molds which they bought with them from Jumeau's factory, was able to turn out exactly the same products as Jumeau. A walk-out on this scale was bound to have serious reasons.

This was followed in 1891 by a memorable court-case between the two companies, a case in which Jumeau alluded to one of his advertisements. Jumeau won the trial, although Danel was only punished by an order to break the molds. Even though their firm was a commercial success, the light sentence led Danel and Guépratte's company into difficulties. In 1892 the company was liquidated and then dissolved. We have not yet been able to find official documentation proving that Jumeau's company bought back the raw materials, finished products, stamps and patents after the demise of Danel and Guépratte, but we do know that Jumeau's *bébés* manufactured after 1892 bear in the arm the spring which was used by Danel. Jumeau's inventory dating before 1899 (the year of the S.F.B.J. foundation) mentions the *Paris Bébé* dolls, the trademark which had been patented by Danel's company in 1899.

Emile Jumeau had not seen fit to re-patent the *Paris Bébé* trademark, but the S.F.B.J. re-registered it three times: in 1911, 1926 and 1941. On the other hand, Jumeau had registered the trademark of *Bébé Français* in 1896 for his packaging. This mark had most certainly been registered by Danel's company in 1891, it was only used for seven months at the most. All this evidence gives good reason to suppose that Jumeau absorbed Danel and Cie.

How can the *Paris Bébé* dolls marketed by Danel be distinguished from those of Jumeau and the S.F.B.J.?

Danel's *Paris Bébé* dolls are easily identified by an examination of the head, body and shoes, and also by the box, if there is one.

La Tête
The Head

As was established during the trial, if the head is indeed a copy of the Jumeau, the decoration of the head will be different: the eyebrows are not so well-defined, the eyes are of the set paperweight type, the iris is usually radiated, and the mouth is closed. The red stamp on the nape of the neck is always *PARIS BEBE tête deposée*.

Le Corps
The Body

There are some details of the trunk and limbs which are characteristic of Danel's method of manufacturing, although they would not be easily spotted by an amateur. There is not room here for a detailed analysis, but one thing to bear in mind is that Danel's *bébés* have movable hands which are mounted by means of metal springs rather than rubber cords.

The trunk bears a blue or violet stamp of the Eiffel Tower on the back, and the words "*PARIS BÉBÉ Breveté*." This stamp-mark is not always immediately visible, but exists on *all* Danel's *bébés* and will never be found on any other make of doll.

Les chaussures
The Shoes

Danel's company was the first to sell what were known as *bébés dits nus*, bare *bébés*, wearing only a chemise and shoes. To mark this innovation, a special stamp-mark on the sole of the shoe was added to the marks already printed on the body and head. This mark is in the form of a five-pointed star of which each point bears the initial of Danel and his partners. Thus the inscription reads: C. (for company) D, L, G, R. Therefore these stamped shoes form an intrinsic part of the whole *bébé* (if they have not been lost in the course of the years) and the current price of the doll should be guaged according to whether or not it has shoes.

Les emballages
The Wrapping

Danel's company was well-protected because they had registered as a trademark the inscription on their boxes. Apart from the words *PARIS BÉBÉ*, this inscription consists of a drawing of the Eiffel Tower, both of which date from 1889, and a detailed description of the extra-special, patented mounting of this model of *bébé*. These days this box is difficult, even impossible to find.

Les Paris Bébé de Jumeau et de la S.F.B.J.
The Paris Bébé of Jumeau and the S.F.B.J.
La Tête
The Head

The date of this head mold can definitely be fixed at between the time of the trial and the founding of the S.F.B.J., or at the latest, during the first years of the S.F.B.J.'s existence. However, because the trademark was renewed three times, it is clear that the *bébés* made in 1926 will have different faces from those made in 1941. The S.F.B.J. even used heads with the DEP stamp for this model of doll.

The *Paris Bébé* heads manufactured by Jumeau and by the S.F.B.J. always have the mouth open and the teeth showing; the eyes may be sleeping or fixed, but they are never of the radiated style. These heads usually bear the stamp *PARIS BÉBÉ* incised on the nape of the neck.

Le Corps
The Body

These *bébés* always have either the Jumeau or the S.F.B.J. body, and sometimes even have a pink label marked *BÉBÉ JUMEAU*. The hands are always movable, and the mounting is usually effected by means of rubber cords.

Les Chaussures
The Shoes

The original shoes should be engraved with the bee-stamp which was first registered by Emile Jumeau as a trademark in 1891 and later by the S.F.B.J. in 1906 and 1921.

Les emballages
The Wrapping

At first glance this could well appear to be Danel's, but a closer examination of the wrapping will reveal a drawing of a "phoenix rising from the ashes" on the small side of the box. The graphics of this design are identical to those on Jumeau's boxes, which are also stamped "Jumeau" on the inside.

With the knowledge that Danel's emblem was the Eiffel Tower, it is particularly significant that Jumeau chose the phoenix. It was never registered as a trademark, and no one has been able to offer a satisfactory explanation for it, but it could well be that it is a reference to the revival of the *Paris Bébé* after Danel's downfall. Whatever the meaning of this emblem, the *bébés* stamped *PARIS BÉBÉ* must be subjected to close scrutiny before being attributed to Danel's short period of manufacture (1889-1892), since they were also made by Jumeau and then by the S.F.B.J.

Given all these indications, no amateur of today should ever make a mistake in identifying these *bébés*. It is not uncommon to come across dolls stamped *PARIS BÉBÉ* on the head and even on the clothing, and in their original box, which were actually made by the S.F.B.J.

Eden Bébé (Fleischmann) dans la S.F.B.J.
Eden Bébé (Fleischmann) in the S.F.B.J.

In 1890, Fleischmann had registered the trademark *Eden Bébé*, and the S.F.B.J. acquired it and re-registered it three times: in 1905, 1938, and 1953. Thus it can be seen that the S.F.B.J. was using this mark right up until the firm closed. One may still find these *Eden Bébé* dolls, and they can only be correctly identified if they are still wearing the original shirts with which they were issued.

It is difficult to distinguish between Fleischmann's *Eden Bébé* and the S.F.B.J.'s, and there are few clues to facilitate this process. Before 1899, Fleischmann bought heads from the Gaultier brothers and eyes from Guépratte for use on his most superior model of *bébé*. *Eden Bébé* heads can be recognized by their decoration: the eyebrows are usually heavy and arched and follow the line of the eye socket; the lips are very strongly defined (like those of the last F.G. *bébés*), and the mouth may be closed, but is usually open.

Fleischmann was making cheap goods above all, and in the doll line he was producing a semi-articulate pasteboard *bébé*. The body of this *bébé* is fairly crude and the bisque head is not of very high quality. The hands were made and decorated in Germany where Fleischmann had also registered his *Eden Bébé* trademark.

With the help of Pintel and his associates Fleischmann's factory continued to make inexpensive, fully-articulated *bébés*. These dolls are to be found in the catalog of larger shops, especially in that of A La Ville St. Denis, and may be recognized by the linen of their chemises.

Paris Bébé in original box with the Jumeau mark, but made by the S.F.B.J. The bisque head is marked "*D.E.P.*" and has sleeping eyes. Size 2. *Galerie de Chartres.*

Paper label on a *Paris Bébé* doll box with the S.F.B.J. Phoenix design. *Galerie de Chartres* 1983.

Jumeau shoes marked with the bee. The bee was a mark registered by Jumeau and used by the S.F.B.J.

Doll head with the *Eden Bébé* mark. *Pesche Collection*.

Eden Bébé dress shown in the La Ville St-Denis department store catalog, 1913-1914.

Étrennes 1913

16013-P. BÉBÉ articulé, demi-*fin*, bouche à *dents*, chevelure flottante, chemise garnie, et *chaussé*.

Hauteurs. 0^m51 0^m4

Prix. . . 3.90 1.95

ABOVE and BELOW: Aux Classes Laboroeuses department store catalog advertisements.

Z — 157. BÉBÉ articulé, tête fine, chemise lingerie et dentelle.

0^m51	0^m45
3.25	1.60

Les mêmes, fermant les yeux.

0^m48	0^m41
3.25	1.60

Bru (Girard) dans la S.F.B.J.
Bru (Girard) in the S.F.B.J.

The Maison Bru, which was then directed by Paul Girard, the successor, made a relatively insignificant contribution to the S.F.B.J.'s constitution: they owned only 110 shares in the company, as opposed to 1320 owned by Jumeau, so it is hardly surprising that its manufacture formed only a small part of the S.F.B.J.'s total production.

However, the Girard family were always faithful to the S.F.B.J. (as was Fleischmann): Paul Girard's grandson, André, was one of the last directors of the S.F.B.J. resigning as late as 1958.

The S.F.B.J. only used the Maison Girard's walking and nursing *bébés*.

Le bébé marcheur Bru
Bru's walking *bébé*

The Maison Bru were the only ones to ever have the idea of a walking *bébé*. Apparently Fleischmann had bought the patent from Simonot in 1892, and he himself took out two patents in 1894 and 1897, of which the main one was based on Simonot's model. Perhaps the mechanics of this system were too complicated, for it was not used by the S.F.B.J.

Emile Jumeau tried rather belatedly to manufacture a walking *bébé*: its automatic system was probably derived from that patented by Roullet and Decamps, and we think that they must also have supplied the mechanism itself. This system was not adopted by the S.F.B.J.

Thanks to x-ray photography, it has been possible to examine the internal mechanism of the model which was patented by Eugène Frédéric Girard (Paul Girard's son) on March 13, 1897. It is this model of *bébé*, a predecessor of the S.F.B.J.'s which is to be found in the 1902 Bon Marche New Year's catalog.

The heads of these dolls may be stamped *Bru Jne* or *S.F.B.J.*

56cm (22in) Girard walking doll in the original dress. It is size 9 and was made between 1902 and 1905.

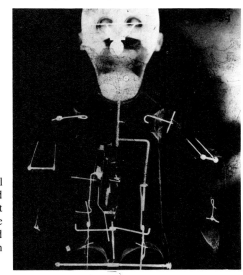

X-ray of the walking doll patented by Girard and made by the S.F.B.J. It has flirty eyes, a voice box, turns its head and throws kisses with both hands.

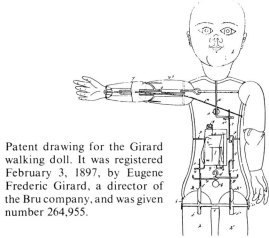

Patent drawing for the Girard walking doll. It was registered February 3, 1897, by Eugene Frederic Girard, a director of the Bru company, and was given number 264,955.

Nᵒ 1906. BÉBÉ MARCHEUR yeux mobiles, bouche à dents perruque flottante, chemise satin. *Haut.* 0ᵐ57. **8.75** BÉBÉ articulé chemise soie et dentelle. *II.* 0ᵐ57. **5.90**	Nᵒ 1907. BÉBÉ articulé yeux mobiles à cils, bouche à dents, costume soie. 0ᵐ28 6.50 0ᵐ40 10.75 0ᵐ31 8.50 0ᵐ43 12.50 0ᵐ35 9.75 0ᵐ47 14.50	Nᵒ 1908. BÉBÉ JUMEAU avec cheveux naturels. chaussés

The doll advertised on the left is a walking doll with a Bru label on the belt. On the right is a *Bébé Jumeau* made by S.F.B.J.

Front view of the nursing Bru. *Bourges Auction.*

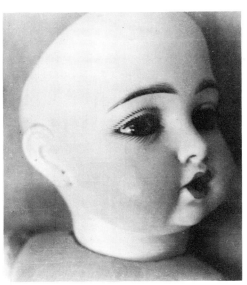

Three-quarter view of the nursing Bru.

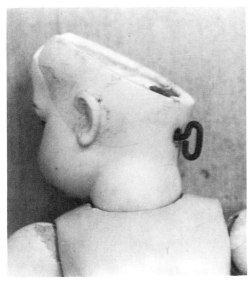

Back view of the nursing Bru showing the key.

Le bébé têteur Bru
The Bru Nursing *Bébé*

The nursing *bébé* patented by Bru on October 3, 1879, had a visible pear-shaped piece of rubber inside its head. This system was modified by a patent of 1882 so that the rubber was no longer visible, but became a metallic rod which applied pressure as it protruded behind the head.

The bodies of the first Bru nursing *bébés* were made of kid, but were later of a type known as *bébés incassables* or unbreakable baby dolls. These dolls are rare today, although according to the advertisements they were on sale right up until the last years before the formation of the S.F.B.J.'s constitution. The inventory for this period lists several molds for bisque heads and pasteboard bodies, of which one series was nursing *bébés*.

The S.F.B.J. used this Bru model for several years, and it is to be found in the Grands Magasins' catalog. These *bébés* were usually mounted on a Jumeau style body. This model would cease to be produced when the S.F.B.J. began manufacturing its own special model, which is number 242 in the character *bébé* series. (See the chapters on character *bébés* and on patents for additional information.)

An advertisement from the Grands Magasins de la Place Clichy department store catalog, Christmas, 1903.

BÉBÉ têteur avec biberon pneumatique et récipient contenant le lait.

0ᵐ34	0ᵐ38	0ᵐ42	0ᵐ47
4.90	5.90	6.90	8.75

BELOW: Patent addition number 132,998 registered by Casimir Bru on February 21, 1882.

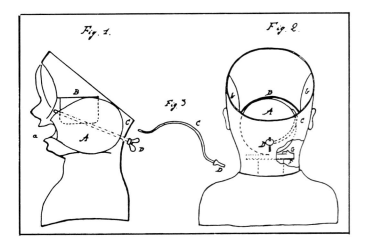

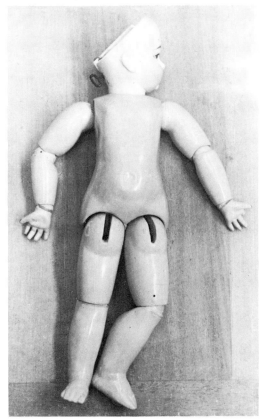

Nursing doll with a bisque head marked "*Bru Jne,*" and a Jumeau body which is assembled in the S.F.B.J. manner. *Bourges Auction.*

Lang dans la S.F.B.J.
Lang in S.F.B.J.

Lang's contribution to S.F.B.J. (1923) overlaps with his later production of stuffed dolls. His short time with S.F.B.J., 1923-1928, overlaps with his creation of the Société des Bébés Jumeaux, which produced stuffed dolls and other stuffed toys. The patents taken out by S.F.B.J. at this time (see Part IV) are the result of Lang's hot embossing of fabric.

Autres Fabrications
Other Manufactured Products

Felt doll from mold 247. It has a fabric body.

Poupées Marcheuses ou Bébé Marchant
Walking Dolls

The S.F.B.J. made quite a large number of mechanical dolls and walking *bébés*, but there was not much difference between the model designs. The S.F.B.J. owned very few of the patents of invention for this kind of doll: nearly all those manufactured by them had already been designed before the amalgamation of the company.

Fleischmann

The only model of Fleischmann's retained by the S.F.B.J. was that which had a clockwork motor. The body and legs were made of a single piece of molded pasteboard; the articulated arms were made of wood. The bisque head was of the S.F.B.J. type, with sleeping eyes and an open mouth. It was stamped "Deposé S.F.B.J. 9" in a hollow on the nape of the neck. This baby doll was 59cm (23¼in) high.

The arms were jointed at the shoulders and elbows, activated by the motor, and were attached to the body by the same metal frame that fixed the head to the body. The mechanism was a spring-motor, set in motion by a large key on the left flank and controlled by an off-switch on the right hip. The drive spring consisted of two long vaucanson chains which led down into the feet to operate two cogged wheels which set the doll walking (see photo of detail). The walk, actually more of a glide, was aided by the presence of a roller at each end of the sole of the foot. By means of adapted crank-arms, the mechanism also controlled the movement of the arms, the turning of the head and a classic talking bellows; in fact, the doll was almost an automaton. This model was only produced for a short period and is not often found in collections.

The Fleischmann and Bloedel walking mechanism. The head on this doll is marked "*Depose/S.F.B.J./9.*"

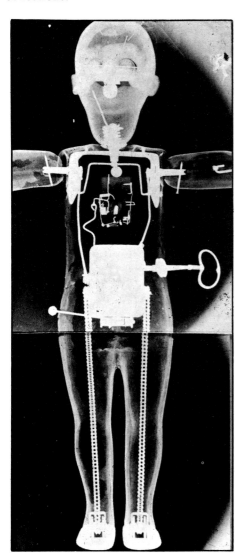

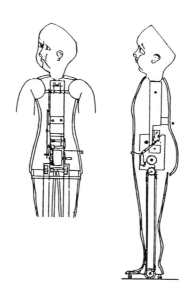

X-ray of the walking doll made by the S.F.B.J. using the 1894 Fleischmann and Bloedel system.

Drawing for patent number 243,005, registered by Fleischmann and Bloedel on November 20, 1894.

Detail of the feet of a walking doll made by the S.F.B.J. using the Fleischmann and Bloedel system.

Le Système Girard
The Girard system

In the walking doll from Girard, the arms were mounted by means of a rubber cord, with a special device at the elbows to allow for a kiss-throwing gesture. The mechanism consisted of a simple metal rod which crossed the top of the thighs and which was linked to the lower part of the body (see x-ray). Two small crank-arms were fastened to the metal rod and embedded in the top of the thighs. The crank on the right side activated the talking mechanism, that on the left controlled the kiss-throwing movement. This model was produced until 1905 when the S.F.B.J. took out a patent for a simplified design of the model.

Et les Systèmes S.F.B.J.
The S.F.B.J. system

The essential difference between the S.F.B.J.'s model and Girard's lay in the part which formed the crank-arm and how it was embedded in the top of the thighs by means of a tight fit (see x-ray). This part was described in patent number 351,452 of February 4, 1905. This particular walking *bébé* had stiff legs. Another similar model, but with flexible legs, was also produced.

The S.F.B.J. took out a patent which would have allowed the knee-joints to be governed by the same part of the mechanism as the hip, but in practice the knees were nearly always jointed by the classic method of a rubber cord attached to a hook. In addition to this, there was also a fixed metal bolt which was inserted into a slot in the knee to prevent complete rotation (see x-ray).

Another model unique to S.F.B.J. did not have movable arms or head. A much simplified mechanism produced an alternating movement in the legs, giving an approximate imitation of walking. This system also operated the talking mechanism.

The x-ray shows that the peculiarity of this model, as with Girard's, is that the mounting of the main crank-arm was effected by means of a long metal spindle which crossed the thighs and then, instead of being fixed directly to the sides, was taken up by two rods which were mounted inside the trunk. Since the crank-arms were sealed into the top of the thigh in this model, the *bébé* had no means of sitting down.

There was one other very simple model which was produced during a long period. It was able to sit down, but did not always have a talking mechanism. The crank-arms were embedded in the thighs, and also controlled the turning of the head. The left crank-arm, which was held at the end by a ring, controlled the movement of the right arm for throwing a kiss by the relay of an interior thread. This system was also found in models stamped "UNIS FRANCE," where the trunk and arms were made of two housings joined by hooks.

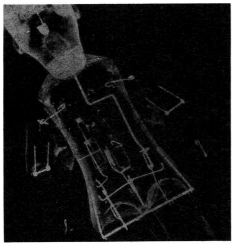

Girard walking doll on an unmarked S.F.B.J. body. *Galerie de Chartres,* September 1979.

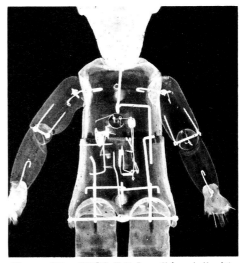

X-ray of the 1905 S.F.B.J. walking doll with straight legs. The head is marked "*Déposé S.F.B.J. 8.*"

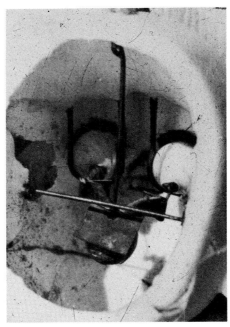

Head interior showing the sleeping eyes patented in 1904, number 3601, the second addition to the patent number 341,108.

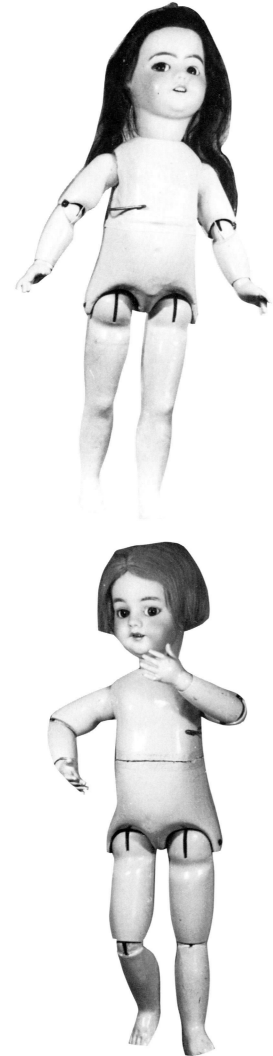

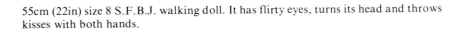

55cm (22in) size 8 S.F.B.J. walking doll. It has flirty eyes, turns its head and throws kisses with both hands.

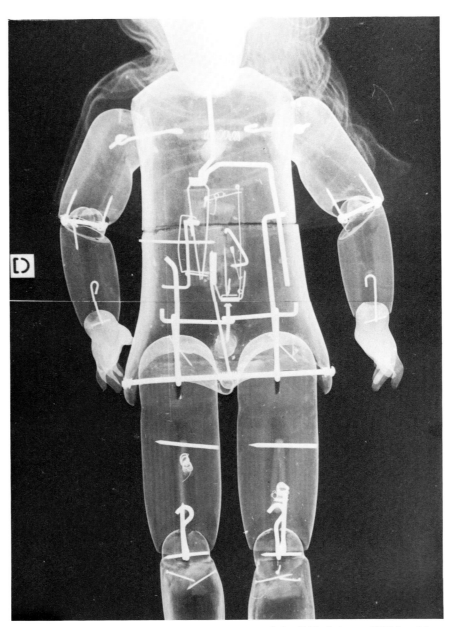

X-ray of the walking doll patented by the S.F.B.J. in 1905. It has a 1039 head by Simon and Halbig and jointed legs. The head, arms and voice box are activated by the walk. Notice the nail in the thigh to hinder the leg rotation.

Walking doll patented by the S.F.B.J. with jointed legs, flirty eyes, and the ability to throw kisses with both hands. The bisque head is mold 1039 by Simon and Halbig.

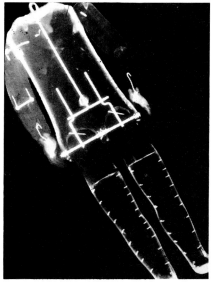

X-ray of the simple walking system in a doll marked "*UNIS FRANCE.*"

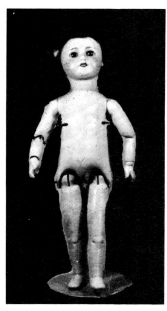

Walking doll of the simple system patented by the S.F.B.J. It has a cardboard body and legs connected with hooks. The head is a mold 60 Unis France.

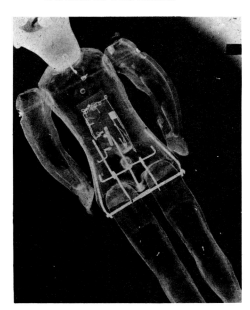

An x-ray picture of the S.F.B.J. walking doll with a simple system derived from Girard. It has a voice box, but it cannot sit.

50cm (20in) walking doll with a head marked "*Déposé S.F.B.J. 6.*"

Poupées et Bébés en Tissu ou Feutre Bourré
Dolls and *Bébés* made of woven fabrics or felt

The trend for dolls made of stuffed materials made a comeback in 1920 at the Leipzig Fair where they had a great deal of success, particularly Lenci's model. Calmettes gives a fairly clear analysis of this model in his book *Les Joujoux* which came out in 1924:

> "Ultra-modern dolls made of a knitted fabric have amusing heads which are more lifelike than the porcelain ones. These are made of masks of a silky material, manufactured in the same way as papier-mâché ones, by using hollow casts. Once they have been molded, they are dried, hardened, painted, and then placed on the torso.
>
> However, these are only the faces, and a large hairpiece must be used to conceal the joint between the doll's mask and body. To avoid this problem, manufacturers have had the idea of molding the head in one piece and it would thus be complete and presentable even without any hair.
>
> Whether the head is a full or half model, the faces are individually and painstakingly painted and each one has different features from the others. The eyes have a delightful saucy expression, and these dolls are far superior to their predecessors: the heads are works of art and are really unbreakable."

In 1914 Emile Lang had started making stuffed felt toys in France. Lang was a hat-maker and manufacturer of fashion accessories. Following this, he patented a method of gluing fabrics in 1911, and on May 12, 1915, he patented a method of making fabric dolls' heads and animals by the hot-molding method. In the same year he launched his boudoir doll. On November 19, 1919, he took out a new manufacturing patent, this time for bodies made of stuffed fabrics.

On January 1, 1920, together with Pierre Guillemaut, an engineer of Arts and Manufactures, he founded the *Manufacture Française de Jouets en Tissue* (the French manufacturers of fabric toys). This new development opened up whole new markets and was of great interest to the S.F.B.J., since in 1923 they offered a partnership to Lang, bought up his business, and set up the *Société des Bébés Jumeaux* or Society of Twin Bébés. (The letter "X" is at the end of the word "Jumeaux" because in this case it means "twin" and is not a proper name. Jumeaux could give rise to confusion with the name of Emile Jumeau, who was not in any way involved in this transaction.)

Even in 1984, little is known about this business, but it seems that Lang kept a certain independence. In any case the association did not last long. In a report on the 1937 Paris Exhibition Gaston Decamps says that Lang was, "a dissident member of the *Société des Bébés*."

By entering into the society, Lang gave the S.F.B.J. access to designs which had previously been exclusive to him, such as the animals of Benjamin Rabier (a famous French artist) and Jean Ray's dolls. He was also responsible for the creation of other models within the society, such as dolls designed by Beatrice Mallet and Fratellini's clowns. Lang also created a stuffed doll department in the S.F.B.J., and was probably responsible for the fabric doll which was patented on April 7, 1924, and for Alfred's penguin (taken from Alain Saint Ogan's comic strip).

Emile Lang exhibited the toys and dolls he had produced in collaboration with the S.F.B.J. in *L'Exposition des Art Décoratifs et Industriels Modernes* (the Exhibition of Modern Decorative and Industrial Arts) in Paris in 1925.

In 1928, after the end of his association with the S.F.B.J., Lang would set up another *société* with his son, René, at 54 rue de Bondy in Paris. He kept to his specialities: boudoir dolls, pin cushion dolls, masks, dolls for boxes, felt, fabric or fluffy animals.

The famous designers' dolls and animals are easily recognized, but it is far more difficult to say which of the dolls made of stuffed materials, and felt dolls, were made by the S.F.B.J. because other manufacturers were producing the same articles. Pintel, in particular, was one of Lang's main rivals in the production of animals, as was Raynal in 1925 with his felt dolls; not to mention the many other less well-known French manufacturers.

An identification of these models must be based on an examination of the patents taken out by the S.F.B.J. of the movement or mounting of these dolls' eyes; or by looking at the company's catalogues and by examining the similarities between the faces of these dolls and those of some character *bébés*. When the body alone is made of stuffed fabric, the head (which may be either composition or bisque) often bears an S.F.B.J. mold number or one of their stamp-marks, "UNIS 301," for example. In such cases one can definitely identify it as an S.F.B.J. doll.

After Lang's departure the S.F.B.J. was to carry on making stuffed dolls, but in much smaller quantities; their principal products were unbreakable dolls and character *bébés*.

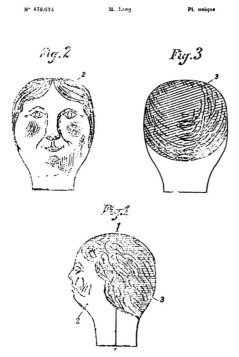

Patent drawing number 478,674 registered by Emile Lang on May 12, 1915.

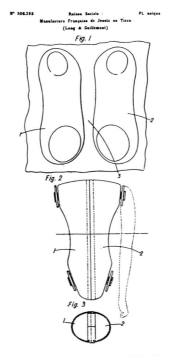

Patent drawing number 506,388 registered by Lang and Guillemaut on November 19, 1919.

NH. 218. Les
Fratellini. Albert,
Paul et François,
clowns articulés, habillage
fantaisiste très soigné.
Hauteur 0ᵐ35.
La pièce........... **22.75**

Advertisement in a 1925 Aux Trois Quarters department store catalog.
Musée des Arts Décoratifs.

N° 19108.
« **LA PARISIENNE** »
dessinée par Jean Ray,
poupée incassable⁣,
costume soie, très élégant.
Haut. 0ᵐ33 **45.**

Advertisement from a 1920 Au Bon Marché department store catalog.

N 603. - Les Poupées de " Béatrice Mallet ", en tissu bourré,
tête artistique incassable, habillage drap, se déshabillant, fille ou
garçon. Hauteur 0ᵐ35 .. .. **29.50**

An advertisement from the Aux Trois Quartiers department store catalog from 1922. *Musée des Arts Décoratif library*.

A 17-261. Poupée incassable, articulée,
tête drap moulé, fermant les yeux, chevelure
fine, bras et jambes en tissu bourré.
haut. 0ᵐ37 .. .. 51. »
haut. 0ᵐ48 .. .. 65. »

Au Printemps department store catalog for 1925 shows a doll with the S.F.B.J. patent number 590,016. This patent is for a moving eyelid and was registered on March 17, 1925.

F2811-

(11285)   Société Française de Fabrication de Bébés-Jouets.
                              8, rue Pastourelle. P A R I S.
           représentée par Monsieur F. Bricout, 17, boulevard de la Madeleine. PaR

                    -:-:-:-:-:-:-:- -:-:-:-:-:-:-:-:-:-:-:-:-:-:-:-:-:-

          Photographies representant un modèle de poupée en tissu.
          Modèle déposé le 7 Avril1924 au Secretariat du Conseil de Prud'hom
     Paris (Tissus) sous le N? 7440.
          La publicité a ete requise par le déposant le 7 Avril 1924.
          Le depôt a ete ouvert le 14 Avril 1924 pour être mis à la dispositi
     Public et du Tribunal s'il y a lieu.
          Les epreuves photographiques de ce modèle, ont ete exposées dans la
     le de Communication, à partir du 24 Avril 1924.

                         -:-:-:-:-:-:-:-:-:-:-:-

                                        Voir d'autre part les rep
     ductions photographiques de ces modèle, accompagnees d'une legende.

16.504   Société française de Fabrication de Bébés et Jouets
                         3, rue Pastourelle, Paris

                et M. PORTAL -SPADA, 30, rue Hamelin, Paris

           Représentée par Mme Perrier, 2 boulevard de Strasbourg, Paris

                    -:-:-:-:-:-:-:-:-:-:-:-

          Modèle de pingouin fétiche
          Modèle déposé le 22 Mars 1927 au Secrétariat du Conseil de Prud
     hommes de Paris (Métaux) sous le N? 20.485.
          La publicité a été requise le 20 Mars 1928 par Mme A. Gauguet,
     velle mandataire.
          Le dépôt a été ouvert le 26 Mars 1928 pour être mis à la disposition
     du public et du Tribunal s'il y a lieu.
          L'épreuve photographique de ce modèle, établie par les soins de
     l'Office National de la Propriété Industrielle, a été exposée dans la Salle
     Communication à partir du   17 AVRI 1928

Alfred, the penguin, designed by Alain St-Ogan the French comics artist. It was patented by the S.F.B.J. in 1928.

Matériaux modernes
Modern Materials

After World War I, a new material called *rhodoïd* was brought onto the market. It was similar to celluloid but much less flammable. Celluloid is a cellulose nitrate, and it is the presence of this nitro-compound, together with the camphor, that makes it flammable. Films (cinema, photographic and x-ray) used to be based on a cellulose nitrate, and among the dramatic fires for which this factor was responsible was that of the *Bazar de la Charité* in Paris. By putting this new acetate product on the market, scientists made its use much more widespread, and it was soon in use in many industries. *Rhodoïd* is the French name, derived from the Rhone factories where it was manufactured, for this cellulose acetate.

This substance was eminently suitable for children's toys, and, though they have never made celluloid *bébés*, the S.F.B.J. made some of them out of *rhodoïd*. But they were not well enough prepared to deal with this new material and were outdone by other manufacturers.

In 1947 another new material was made available, a polymer plastic, which was both rigid and flexible. It was much easier to work with than the cellulose derivatives, and has a finish similar to that of rubber.

Gradually the S.F.B.J. began to change over from the making of bisque heads and equipped themselves to mold and produce their *bébés* in this new substance. Their porcelain kilns were to be used first for the making of sanitary objects and then were abandoned. They began this project too late, however, and were overtaken by their rivals, such as Gégé among others. This was to be the S.F.B.J.'s last burst of creativity.

All of these later *bébés* are semi-articulated and very small, only 30cm (11¾in) to 40cm (15¾in) tall. They all look alike, with a commonplace child's face, devoid of personality. The mouth is small and closed with full lips; the eyes sleep and are large and round, with long eyelashes; the cheeks are chubby; the sides of the nose and the eyebrows have scarcely any modelling. The hairstyles followed the latest fashions: either a pony-tail, plaits, curls, or short hair which could be combed out.

The dolls had nylon underwear and either striped or tartan organdy dresses stitched in pastel colors. The clothes closely followed the fashions and activities of the little girls of the period: slacks, bathing suits, scarves, straw hats, and sports outfits.

Patou, the young baby doll made in 1951, wears a play-suit with baggy trousers and suspenders. In connection with these later products, the word *Bébé* disappeared definitively from the *Commercial Directory* in 1955. Here are the models of this later period of production:

1950
Annick: 45 (17¾in) and 50cm (19⅝in) high, either a little girl or boy.

1951
Patou: unbreakable, in flexible, washable plastic which feels like real skin; lifelike eyes; fully-articulated.

1952
Christine: 30cm (11⅞in) to 40cm (15¾in) high.
Viviane: a new head with sleeping eyes.
    All of these dolls came with a selection of clothes.

1954
Merveille: 35cm (13¾in) high, sleep eyes; light and elegant.
Véronique: a new series in four different sizes from 35cm (13¾in) to 52cm (20½in) in height; with natural hair and very pretty clothes.
Chérie: the head was made of a molded plastic substance and the body of cellular rubber which was soft to touch. The whole doll was supported by an internal metal frame and had no visible joints although she could adopt any position. 43cm (17in) high, she came with a wide variety of clothes and hairpieces.

In 1952, the year of Elizabeth II's accession to the English throne, the S.F.B.J. brought out a "coronation doll," notable for its dress. *Le Jouet Français* stated: "the manufacturer has taken every care to reproduce in minute detail the costume of the British Ambassador to Paris." Apparently this doll was the showpiece of the exhibition of French toys at New York City's Rockefeller Center.

S.F.B.J. advertisement in the magazine *Le Jouet Français* in 1956.

A 1952 advertisement in *Le Jouet Français*.

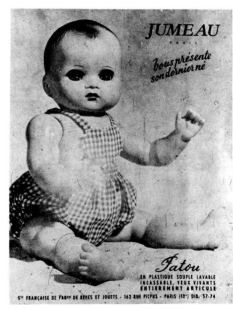

Patou, created in 1951, is made of a soft plastic which looks like skin. This was a 1951 advertisement in *Le Jouet Français*.

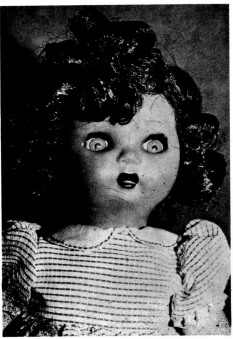

Detail of *Christine*'s face. *Photo by Chauveau.*

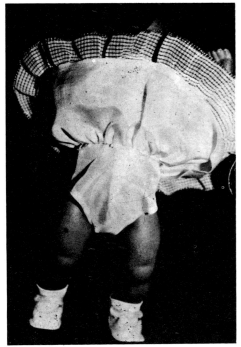

Christine is marked "*Jumeau*" and dated 1957. She is made of soft colored plastic and wears *Babybotte* plastic shoes made for S.F.B.J. *Photo by Chauveau.*

LA POUPÉE « CHÉRIE »

La grande famille des poupées JUMEAU est en pleine transformation! La collection 1954, complètement modifiée, comprend de nombreuses nouveautés dont une des plus remarquables est sans doute la nouvelle poupée « Chérie ».

Haute de 45 cm., cette poupée a une tête nouvelle en matière plastique injectée, aux yeux dormeurs, montée sur un corps en caoutchouc cellulaire souple, extrêmement léger. Ce corps est armé intérieurement d'un squelette qui permet de donner à la poupée toutes les positions les plus amusantes sans aucune articulation visible. Sa souplesse et sa légèreté exceptionnelles en font un article rêvé pour les « petits ».

Enfin, une grande variété d'habillages et des coiffures très originales en thibet, lui donnent un cachet d'élégance et de fantaisie qui sera particulièrement apprécié.

Advertisement in *Le Jouet Français* in 1954.

POUPÉES JUMEAU

La Société Française de Bébés et Jouets (Poupées JUMEAU), présente cette année aux Foires de Lyon et de Paris une collection renouvelée avec les nouveautés suivantes :

— La poupée « CHÉRIE » a une tête nouvelle, aux yeux dormeurs, en matière plastique injectée. Son corps, en caoutchouc cellulaire, armé intérieurement d'un squelette en métal flexible, peut prendre toutes les positions les plus amusantes. Il reste extrêmement léger et d'une douceur remarquable au toucher.

Haute de 43 cm., elle est présentée avec une grande variété d'habillages et

Poupée « Chérie »

de perruques allant des modèles classiques aux types les plus modernes.

— La poupée « MERVEILLE », entièrement en matière plastique injectée, dormeuse, hauteur 35 cm. Particulièrement élégante et légère.

— La nouvelle série « VÉRONIQUE » en quatre tailles allant de 35 à 52 cm., avec une gamme de têtes nouvelles coiffées en cheveux naturels, avec de très jolis habillages particulièrement réussis.

LE JOUET FRANÇAIS

1954 *Le Jouet Français* advertisement.

Ces quelques exemples illustrent la variété du costume adapté au bébé JUMEAU. *De gauche à droite :* « Viviane », raffinée, avec sa robe en taffetas écossais garnie de passementerie, sur un corsage lingerie et un jupon bordés dentelle, chaussettes et souliers en peau perforée et lacée; la coiffure à queue de cheval s'orne d'un ruban, et une gourmette dorée complète la toilette.

« Christine », porte une robe en cotonnade bleue à petits pois, empiècement blanc à manches volants, bloomer assorti, chaussettes blanches, et chaussures moulées en matière plastique injectée.

Viviane and *Christine* in a September 1953 advertisement in *Le Jouet Français.*

Malles, Trousseaux, Poupées Folkloriques
Wardrobes, Trunks and Regional Costume Dolls

Wardrobe-trunks were always one of the S.F.B.J.'s specialities, but unfortunately it is very rare to find a complete set these days. The dolls which came in these trunks or little suitcases were small in size, fully- or semi-articulated; they were rarely character *bébés*.

The S.F.B.J. produced regional costume dolls too, also very small, whose composition bodies were not always very well finished. The idea of these dolls, which were not intended to be undressed, was to show the regional costumes of France's provinces and colonies. They were sold to tourists and travelers. They were therefore for collections, and were appreciated more by foreigners than by the French themselves.

Another tradition, taken from Emile Jumeau, retained by the S.F.B.J. until the end of their period of production, was the manufacture of little costume dolls wearing historical outfits; for example, the *Marquise de Pompadour*, the *Empress Marie-Louise* and the *Empress Eugénie*. This collection, too, was most appreciated by foreigners.

Dresses for *Bébés Jumeau* from the Grand Magasins de la Samaritaine department store in 1912.

Doll, dresses and trunk marked *"S.F.B.J." Masayo Collection.*

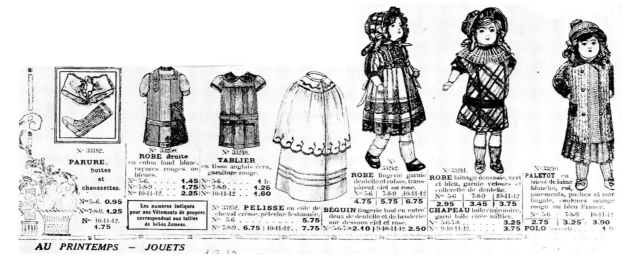

AU PRINTEMPS — JOUETS

Advertisement for small dolls from the May 1949 magazine *Le Jouet Français*.

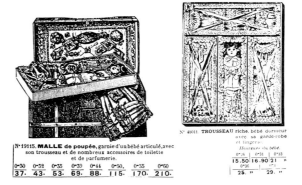

Small 15cm (6in) doll marked "*UNIS FRANCE*" outfitted in a Bretagne dress.

Small dolls dressed in historical costume and marked "*UNIS FRANCE*."

Small 12cm (5in) mignonnettes in French regional costumes. They are marked "*UNIS-FRANCE.*"

Les Jouets de la S.F.B.J.
S.F.B.J. Toys

This is an area not very well known to collectors, even though the S.F.B.J. produced a lot of toys. They were mainly made of *pâte* or pasteboard and plush. It is difficult to identify them because they were unmarked, and other manufacturers made similar products. Advertisements from the *Commercial Almanac* or that of the Chamber of Trade Unions give some information about them. Copies of S.F.B.J. catalogs may exist, but are not available to research workers.

Small papier-mâché dolls can sometimes be found in their original boxes with the manufacturer's name on them. Using these as models, department store catalogs can be searched to find the same boxes and thus find the manufacturing date.

As for little soldiers found in their original boxes, they have been made since the beginning of the century. They are called *soldats en carton incassables* or "unbreakable cardboard soldiers" and are listed in the *Commercial Almanac* until 1950.

The S.F.B.J. also made animals, circuses and pastoral settings of the same style, in pasteborad or composition.

In 1923 and 1924, with Lang's arrival and the creation of the *Société des Bébés Jumeaux*, the S.F.B.J. started making horses, animals with bellows, stuffed plush toys, and bears and animals on wheels.

They also made *poupards*, talking and non-talking. In 1924, the S.F.B.J. patented a talking mechanism for its *poupards*.

Lang not only brought the S.F.B.J. his way of making dolls from felt and other fabrics, but also his original idea of making animals from plush or cloth, inspired by the drawings of Benjamin Rabier and others. They were: the dog, cat, duck, elephant, horse, and these same animals dressed like people: the cook, schoolboy, gardener, and so on. They generally measured 31cm (12¼in) high.

Jean Ray's *Parisiennes* and Beatrice Mallet's dolls were also made.

In 1925, the S.F.B.J. added the Fratellini clowns, three brothers: Albert, Paul, and François. All are 33cm (13in) or 35cm (13¾in) tall.

And, in 1927, the penguin taken from the picture book, *Zig et Puce*, by Alain St. Ogan was manufactured. This penguin is a registered trademark.

It is difficult to give the S.F.B.J. credit for animals on wheels, because the *Manufacture de Jouets en Etoffe*-P.F. (Pintel Fils) made them as well.

In 1950, stuffed toys were still mentioned and we know that teddy bears were made in different sizes until the end of the S.F.B.J. The Champigneulles factory specialized in the production of animal toys.

S.F.B.J. composition toy soldiers in their box. They date around 1910. *de Monneron Auction,* Drouot, Paris, 1983.

Paper label from a box of S.F.B.J. toy soldiers. *de Monneron Auction*, Drouot, Paris, 1983.

Detail of a rider soldier. *de Monneron Auction.*

Detail of soldiers. *de Monneron Auction.*

7 — 239. BOITE DE SOLDATS cartonnage incassable, • peints en couleurs inoffensives.
6.50, 4.50, 2.75, 1.60 et ».75

16037-P. FERME modèle. composée de *personnages* et *animaux* en bois *compressé* et *coloriés*, coloris *inoffensifs* 4 *tailles*. Prix . . . . . 5.90, 4.90, 3.90 et 2.45

16040-P. CIRQUE composé de *personnages* et *animaux* bois *compressé* et *coloriés*, articulés et *incassables*, 3 *tailles*. Prix . . . . 6.90, 4.75 et 2.45

An S.F.B.J. advertisement in an address book from *la Chambre Syndicale des Fabricants de Jouets*, 1929.

N 815. - Les Animaux Drôlatiques, de " Benjamin Rabier ", Clown, Cuisinier, Pierrot, Bébé, etc. Hauteur 0ᵐ29.

La pièce. **10.50**

Advertisement from the Aux Trois Quartiers department store catalog, 1923.

NH. 4025. " *Zig et Puce* ", les héros du Dimanche illustré. POUPÉES bourrées. Humoristique. Habillage fantaisie. Hauteur : " *Zig* ", 0ᵐ48. " *Puce* ", 0ᵐ45. La poupée .... **69.**

Advertisement from the Aux Trois Quartiers department store catalog, 1929.

AU BON MARCHÉ — PARIS

N° 19210.
LES ANIMAUX de La Fontaine, par Benjamin Rabier,
sujets en étoffe, habillés
corbeau, chien, renard, Jeannette. Haut. 0ᵐ32 . . . . **23-50**

N. 475. "LES ANIMAUX HUMORISTIQUES" de BENJAMIN RABIER. Clown, paysan, cuisinier, écolier, jardinier, soubrette. Hauteur 0ᵐ31 .... **15.50**

Ad for animal toys from the Aux Trois Quartiers department store catalog, 1922. *Musée des Arts Décoratifs.*

. 683. **FOX**, chien blanc de Benjamin Rabier, avec manteau, monture métallique sur roues.

Hauteurs : 0ᵐ35	0ᵐ38	0ᵐ43
22.50	**26.50**	**38.** »

N. 565.
Fox ou Flambeau ANIMAUX de Benjamin Rabier, tissu bourré. 17., 21 et **29.**

N. 684. **CHIEN** Bull de Benjamin Rabier, monture métallique sur roues.

Hauteurs : 0ᵐ33	0ᵐ37	0ᵐ47
22.50	**26.50**	**38.** »

C-17-P-251. RADIO-SELF. Jouet aimanté, fonctionnant à la fois **29** fr.

C-17-P-252.
JOUETS ARTISTIQUES en tissu bourré.
Pingouin Alfred. 39 fr., **19.90**
Autres modèles. **10 fr. et 16 fr.**
Chien, Chat, Canard, Éléphant.
Prix . . . . . . **27 fr. et 39 fr.**
Cheval. . . . . **13 fr. et 22 fr.**

"Artistic toys" advertised in the Au Printemps department store catalog in 1928.

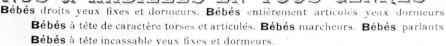

Exclusivites Commerciales
Commercial Exclusive Rights

France and Marianne

France and *Marianne* are two 80cm (31½in) dolls given to the two English princesses, Elizabeth and Margaret Rose, by the schoolchildren of France in 1938 on the occasion of a state visit of the King and Queen. Madame Georges Bonnet, wife of the French minister of foreign affairs, presented the gift in London, accompanied by three schoolchildren.

France and *Marianne* had been made especially for the occasion by the *Société Française de Fabrication de Bébés et Jouets.* The head had been designed by a company sculptor.

They had a well defined waist, slender legs and broad shoulders. They had moveable hands and eyes, as well as real eyelashes. *Marianne* was blonde with blue eyes; *France* was a brown-eyed brunette. Both had real hair. *Marianne's* was parted on the right while *France* had brown curls gather up in the back.

The April 1952 issue of *Le Jouet Français* gives the following description:

"They had a luxurious trousseau prepared by the *Haute Couture et la Mode Parisienne*. This extensive trousseau included magnificent furs and was worth almost one million francs. The trousseau consisted of a dozen little trunks covered with blue Morrocan leather.

The dolls were displayed in London and in the major cities of Great Britain, where they received well-deserved acclaim."

The winter 1983 issue of *Dolls: The Collectors' Magazine* carries an accurate description of the two dolls. This description notes that the blonde, with her light complexion, appears very English. The magazine also states that in April 1955 the two dolls were transferred from Buckingham Palace to Windsor Castle, where they were once again put on public display.

Finally, the author indicates that their eyes are typically Jumeau. Actually, the eyes were made at the request of S.F.B.J. by a Parisian oculist, M. Peigne, maker of artificial human eyes.

Coronation Doll

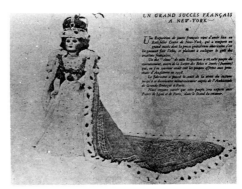

Doll dressed by S.F.B.J. in 1952 for the coronation of Queen Elizabeth II of England. The dress was an exact reproduction of the original. *Le Jouet Français* 1953.

In 1952 the year of the accession of Queen Elizabeth to the throne of England, S.F.B.J. brought out a "coronation doll," remarkable particularly for her outfit. According to *Le Jouet Francais*, "the designer was concerned with the accuracy of the dress to the point of verifying all details with the British Embassy in Paris."

This doll was apparently the center of the exposition of French toys at the Rockefeller Center in New York.

The doll *Marianne*, number 306, was made in 1938 to honor the British Princesses.

The doll *France* was made to honor the British Princesses in 1938. It is S.F.B.J. number 306.

France and *Marianne*.

Bleuette

Bleuette was "invented" by Editions Gautier (Languereau). She was originally created to launch a new weekly magazine for little girls: *la Semaine de Suzette*. A *Bleuette* doll was given to each new subscriber during the first year. *La Semaine de Suzette* then started printing dress patterns on a regular basis.

Other childrens' magazines had the idea of getting young readers interested in their publications by printing dress patterns for dolls long before *la Semaine de Suzette*. However, it was *la Semaine de Suzette* which had the original idea of selling the doll and actual clothes to go with her. *La Semaine de Suzette* was aiming to outsell the magazine *la Poupée Modèle*, which had been in existence 40 years longer, and *Mon Journal*, which was 20 years older. These magazines were both very successful with children.

The S.F.B.J. was put in charge of manufacturing *Bleuette*.

Bleuette remained popular for 60 years. This was due to the fact that a big part of playing with dolls involved dressing and undressing them, changing their clothes, and creating an "environment." *La Poupée Modèle* had already used the same idea in 1860, and it would return later with the *Barbie*® doll. Little girls have always liked having the latest fashions and nice furniture for their dolls. Dresses and furniture reflect the social and domestic life of an era.

To be assured of success, Mr. Gautier put great emphasis on quality. For that reason he approached a manufacturer in the Jumeau tradition, as well as one who could furnish the article in necessary quantities: S.F.B.J.

Bleuette is a small articulated, unbreakable *bébé*, measuring 27cm (10⅝in) tall. This is the perfect size for a little girl of five or six years. The doll's size places her between *la Poupée Modèle's mignonnette* and *Mon Journal's* doll which measured 50cm (19⅝in).

As the doll was originally given for free, the model had to be inexpensive. Also, in order for it to be easy to dress it was necessary to choose an articulated body. So, due to the money factor, an existing head mold was used: the Jumeau mold; and to further economize, it was a head with fixed blue eyes.

Bleuette's specifications, her place in the *bébé* series, pose complex problems since she was a *'hors de série*, a special model. It is important to know that the body, as well as the head, has changed over the years.

In the beginning the heads were not marked S.F.B.J. It was not until later that they were marked 301 or 60, and still later they had the Unis stamp.

The bodies were of the Jumeau type, always fully-articulated, with variations which were described for the S.F.B.J. fully-articulated, unbreakable *bébé*. *Bleuette* never had a stapled cardboard body, and always came with an open mouth.

According to the testimony of former little girls who used to play with *Bleuette*, other dolls could be bought and dressed like *Bleuette* using the *Semaine de Suzette* patterns. Anyway, as these dolls were very often played with, very few are found today with their original head.

Some chronological landmarks for *Bleuette*:
Starting in 1919, the heads had both moving and fixed eyes.
Starting in 1922, the heads had only movable eyes.
Starting in 1929, *Bleuette* had unbreakable or porcelain heads.
Starting in 1933, *Bleuette* measured 29cm (11½in).

The *Bambino* doll from 1930 and *Bleutte* from 1928.

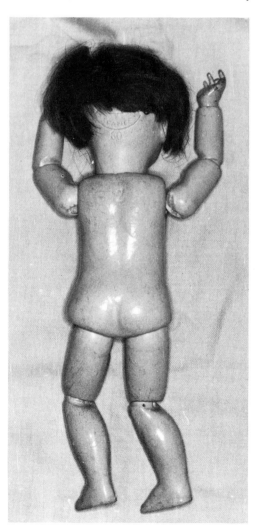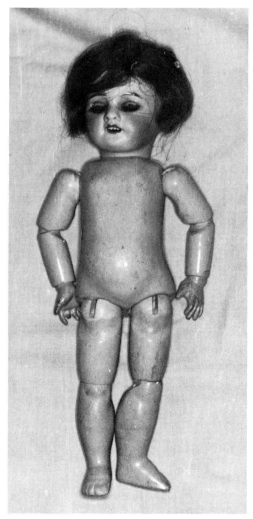

FAR LEFT: Back view of *Bleuette*.

LEFT: *Bleuette* from 1929, marked "*UNIS-FRANCE 60 8/0.*"

Bambino

The character *bébés* that the S.F.B.J. had produced with success since 1910, all represented small children, but it had not yet made newborn babies. This type of *bébé* appeared in Germany in the 1920s. The S.F.B.J. evidently did not come out with this kind of model before the years 1928 to 1930.

It was definitely *la Semaine de Suzette*, the little girls' journal, that made this type of *bébé* the vogue in France. *Bambino* was *Bleuette's* little brother.

In 1928 *la Semaine de Suzette* announced the arrival of *Bleuette's* little brother, *Bambino*, a beautiful character baby - *poupon*. This word, *poupon* was new; it meant a very small baby doll, a newborn.

But, curiously, this new *bébé* had no mark other than the number 1. According to its size, 25cm (9¾in), this number corresponded to German numbering. We have seen a *Bambino* from 1930, with all the characteristics of the baby number 351 made by Armand Marseille: a solid dome head with molded hair, small sleeping almond eyes, an open mouth with two lower teeth, and a flat nose. Besides, in its advertisement in *la Semaine de Suzette* which specified "French production" for *Bleuette*, made no such mention for *Bambino*.

The S.F.B.J. later came out with a baby identical to that of its German competitor. This may have happened in 1933 when *le Semaine de Suzette* announced a 26cm (10¼in) *Bambino*. We know that in 1936, this French *Bambino* existed, and that it was made by the S.F.B.J. with all its characteristics.

It resembled the first *Bambino* "like a brother," with a few exceptions. The semi-articulated composition body with bent limbs was perhaps a bit idealistic: it had a straight back and a prominent stomach. The mouth was more open, without teeth, but with a movable tongue like the system known to the S.F.B.J. and

found in the character baby number 251. This *Bambino* does not have any mark on the neck other than the number 3. This number corresponded to other S.F.B.J. *bébés* of this size. The eyes were more open and the brows more delineated than the previous *Bambino*.

Much later, in 1954/1955, *la Semaine de Suzette* announced another *Bambino* with an unbreakable head and sleeping eyes. This *Bambino* had a head made of *pâte* or molded heated cardboard, which when painted gave an appearance similar to that of bisque. The neck had the Jumeau number: "278 - 3," the last number being the size.

A fourth, and last, *Bambino* with a highly colored head, but the same face, came out later.

Some traits are common to all three *Bambino* varieties:
- a little hole at the base of the neck, in front, which probably served to pass a string that limited the counter-weight movements in the eyes.
- hip articulation of the "button" type.
- thighs with folds of fat on the inside.
- very shapely feet with turned-up big toe.

The assembly of the head was very special and characteristic: the rubber cord was held at the neck by a piece of metal bent into a reversed omega shape. The bottom opening of the head (like very young children, this baby had practically no neck) was wide, and had two side notches. It was an ingenious assembly that economized on the usual semi-spheric wooden piece; the lateral notches prevented the piece of metal from turning, which stopped the rubbing of metal against the porcelain, without preventing the head rotation.

Bambinos are rare today. They were less successful than *Bleuette*. Those found are still in good condition because, quoting their owners, they were not played with very often. The last ones, in particular, did not have very successful coloring.

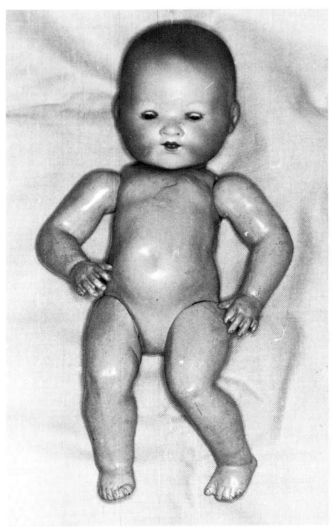

The first *Bambino* with the same face as mold 351 by Armand Marseille. It is 25cm (10in), has the S.F.B.J. assembly, and dates circa 1930.

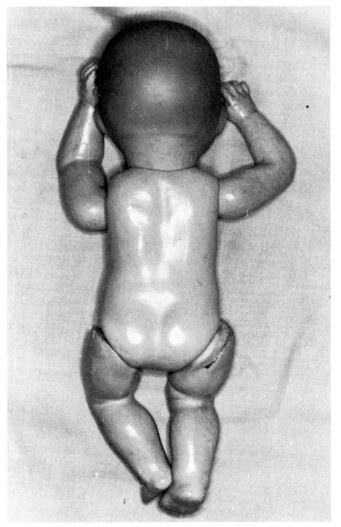

Back view of the first *Bambino*.

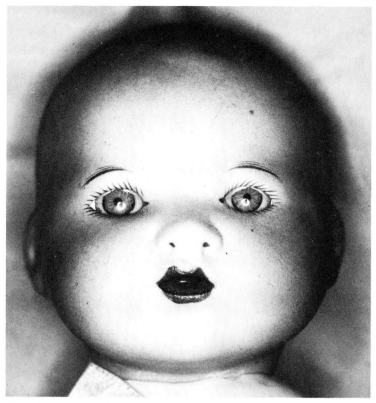

Detail of the face of the second *Bambino*. Notice the tongue. It is 26cm (10½in) and marked "*3*" on the neck. *Chovet Collection.*

26cm (10½in) second *Bambino* with a bisque head and sleeping eyes. *Galerie de Chartres*, 1980.

Bambino, circa 1940, with the original outfit made by Gautier-Languereau. *Chovet Collection.*

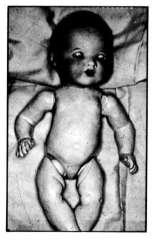

The second type of *Bambino* which looks like the first type. *Chovet Collection.*

Rosette

In 1955, *la Semaine de Suzette* introduced a 35cm (13¾in) tall *Bleuette* with the choice of a bisque head or an unbreakable head and with sleeping eyes and an articulated body. She had curly hair made of rayon, or braids made of natural hair. She was given the name *Rosette* and was presented the following year as *Bleuette's* big sister. *La Semaine de Suzette* outfitted her with a complete set of minutely detailed clothing, like they did her sister *Bleuette* and her brother *Bambino.*

Les bébés réservés aux Grands Magasins Parisiens

Baby dolls reserved for Parisian department stores

From 1899 onwards, all "undressed" *bébés* were sold wearing shoes and a chemise. The S.F.B.J. kept up this tradition producing not only the typical *Maison Jumeau* chemises but also those which were exclusively designed for individual shops. This factor will help the collector to recognize these chemises and sometimes to put a date on the *bébé*. In fact, there were several chronological variants of these chemises.

La Chemise Jumeau

Emile Jumeau had designed a chemise model at the end of the 19th century which the S.F.B.J. adopted and used until about 1925. This chemise was commonly known as the *robe Jumeau* and was made of flowered pink or blue cotton with a white background. It had a box pleat at the front and was edged at the bottom with a pleated flounce trimmed with lace. The neckline was edged by another pleated flounce which formed the collar. The sleeves were mid-length, puffed, and edged with lace. A belt edged with the same lace completed the outfit and had a label marked "*Bébé Jumeau.*"

This well-known model was depicted on the Jumeau boxes which were adopted by the S.F.B.J. All the *fabrication Jumeau bébés* wore this chemise; that is, fully-articulate dolls, with bisque heads, natural hair, open mouth showing the teeth, fixed or sleeping eyes, and painted fingernails. They came in all sizes from 38cm (15in) to 85cm (33½in), and size numbers 5 to 16. Some of these, from size 7, 47cm or 18½in, onwards, were talking dolls.

BÉBÉ Jumeau complètement articulé, tête biscuit, chevelure naturelle.
Hauteurs :

0·38	0·41	0·45	0·49
7.50	8.50	10.50	12.50
0m53	0·58	0·63	0·68
15.50	18.50	22 fr.	27 fr.

Le même parlant, yeux mobiles.

0·45	0m49	0·53
13.50	16.50	19.50
0·58	0·63	0·68
22 fr.	27 fr.	32 fr.

A *Bébé Jumeau* advertised in La Samaritaine department store catalog, 1906.

Nº 19129. **BÉBÉ** jumeau, fabrication extra-supérieure, cheveux naturels, articulé et chaussé, ongles peints

Numéros	5	6	7	8	9	10	11	12
Hauteurs	0m36	0m41	0m45	0m49	0m53	0m58	0m63	0m68
Muet, dormeur	14.75	17.	20.50	23.25	30.	34.	42.	51.
Parlant, dormeur			24.50	28.	35.	40.	49.	58.

A Jumeau doll advertised in the 1915 Au Bon Marché department store catalog.

87cm (35in) S.F.B.J. doll
marked "*Tête Jumeau 16.*"
*R.B. Collection, photo by
Doumic.*

Size	5	6	7	8	9	10	11	12	13	14 & 15
Years 1899 to 1920	38	41	45	49	53	58	63	68	72	76 & 81
Year 1920	36	41	44 or 45	49	53	57 or 55	62	67 or 66		

Chart showing size equivalents in centimeters for the S.F.B.J. dolls.

Size 16 = 85cm in 1913.

N° 48003. BÉBÉ Jumeau, fabrication extra-supérieure, cheveux naturels, articulé et chaussé, ongles peints. N° 5, haut. 0ᵐ38.... **9.90**

Muets, dormeurs à cils.

N°ˢ	6	7	8	9	10	11	12	13	14	15	16
Hᵗ	0ᵐ41	0ᵐ45	0ᵐ49	0ᵐ53	0ᵐ5\	0ᵐ63	0ᵐ6\	0ᵐ7?	0ᵐ76	0ᵐ81	0ᵐ85
	11,50	13,50	15,50	19,50	22,50	28.»	34.»	40.»	47.»	59.»	70.»

Parlants, dormeurs à cils.

N°ˢ	7	8	9	10	11	12	13	14	15	16
Haut.	0ᵐ45	0ᵐ49	0ᵐ53	0ᵐ58	0ᵐ63	0ᵐ68	0ᵐ72	0ᵐ76	0ᵐ81	0ᵐ85
	16,50	19	23,50	27.»	33.»	39.»	45.»	53.»	66.»	78.»

A *Bébé Jumeau* ad in the Galerie Layfayette department store catalog in 1913.

La chemise Eden Bébé

There were also chemises marked *Eden Bébé*. Generally speaking, these chemises would vary according to whether the dolls wearing them had a fine-quality bisque head or a washable, unbreakable one. However, a group of pleats were always at the front, and the bottom was always lace-edged. The top could have a wide-open collar over a buttoned lower part, edged with lace at the neckline, and could also have tapered or straight lace with a pleated flounce on the shoulders. The sleeves were short, gathered and edged with lace.

Z — 157. BÉBÉ
articulé, tête fine,
chemise
lingerie et dentelle.

0ᵐ51	0ᵐ45
3.25	1.60

Les mêmes,
fermant les yeux.

0ᵐ48	0ᵐ41
3.25	1.60

La Maison du Petit St-Thomas department store catalog showed the *Eden Bébé* in 1901.

BÉBÉ ARTICULÉ, *tête fine incassable* bouche à dents, chevelure flottante, chemise lingerie et ruban fabrication très soignée.

Hauteurs :	0ᵐ40	0ᵐ45	0ᵐ48
Prix......	3.25	4.50	5.50

An *Eden Bébé* ad in La Ville St-Denis department store catalog in 1914.

16019-P. BÉBÉ articulé *lavable et incassable*, chemise lingerie *dentelle*, bouche à *dents* et *chaussé*.

Hauteurs	0ᵐ53	0ᵐ46
Prix.	5.90	3.90
Hauteurs	0ᵐ40	0ᵐ36
Prix.	2.95	1.95

The dress used for *Eden Bébé* dolls was shown in the Aux Classes Laborieuses department store catalog for 1913.

Z — 156. BÉBÉ articulé, tête absolument incassable et lavable, chemise lingerie fine.

Haut.	0ᵐ57	0ᵐ47	0ᵐ37
Prix.	5.90	3.50	1.60

The *Eden Bébé* advertisement in La Ville St-Denis department store catalog in 1914.

Z — 160. BÉBÉ entièrement articulé, tête absolument incassable et lavable, chemise lingerie ornée ruban et dentelle, article très soigné. Hauteurs :

0ᵐ47	0ᵐ41	0ᵐ32
7.90	5.50	3.90

A La Ville St-Denis department store catalog ad for the *Eden Bébé* in 1914.

151

Le Printemps

The peculiarity of the Printemps *bébé* was that, like that of the Galeries Lafayette, the first size was 31cm (12¼in), but the largest size was 86cm (33⅞in) until 1910. After that date the sizes were the same as those of all the other shops.

The Printemps *bébé* wore a chemise similar to the Jumeau doll. The front had a large pleat edged at the bottom with a large lace border. The belt was also made of lace and was stamped "*Bébé Printemps*" on a label at the front. The top of the chemise had a yoke made of a fancy material, which tapered to the chest. It was edged with a border of pleated or gathered lace like that at the hem. The neckline was also edged with lace. The sleeves were short, gathered and edged with a large lace border.

This model was produced until the time of World War I. In the 1920s the design was altered until it became so similar to the Samaritaine that the two models can easily be confused.

No 17175. BÉBÉ-PRINTEMPS complètement articulé, tête fine porcelaine, yeux mobiles à cils, perruque cheveux naturels, chemise façonnée lingerie, chaussé.

Nos	1	2	3	4	5	6
Haut.	0m,31	0m,34	0m,37	0m,40	0m,45	0m,48
Prix	4.90	5.90	7.50	8.75	9.75	11.50
Nos	7	8	9	10	11	12
Haut.	0m,53	0m,58	0m,62	0m,70	0m,76	0m,86
Prix	13.75	16.75	19.75	25. »	34. »	43. »

A 1912 ad for *Bébé Printemps*.

Dress from Samaritaine, 1924. The 31cm (12½in) doll is marked "*S.F.B.J. 3*" on the head.

17332. Bébé-Printemps complètement articulé, tête biscuit, avec dents, yeux mobiles à cils, chaussé, perruque cheveux naturels, chemise fine.

Nos	Hauteurs	Prix	Nos	Hauteurs	Prix
1	0m,31	4.90	7	0m,53	13.75
2	0m,34	5.90	8	0m,58	16.75
3	0m,37	7.50	9	0m,62	19.75
4	0m,40	8.75	10	0m,70	25. »
5	0m,45	9.75	11	0m,76	34. »
6	0m,48	11.50	12	0m,86	43. »

A 1908 advertisement for *Bébé Printemps*.

Le Bon Marché

Bon Marché was a customer of Emile Jumeau and reserved a typical, unsigned chemise. After the formation of the S.F.B.J. it kept this model until the start of the war in 1914.

This white cotton chemise was pleated at the front and edged at the bottom with a red flounce of *broderie anglaise*, English embroidery. The top had a tapered yoke at the front, edged with the same *broderie anglaise*. The gathered sleeves were edged with the same flat flounce. After World War I, the same model was produced until 1924 when the *broderie anglaise* was replaced by a lace edge.

In 1917 the Bon Marché *bébé* wore a completely different chemise: the pleated front was bordered at the bottom and half-way up by colored braiding; a large colored collar was open over a yoke. Across the yoke was a double line of braiding; the sleeves were gathered and finished in a band.

Nᵒ 1903.
BÉBÉ
du Bon Marché,
complètement
articulé,
et chaussé,
de fabrication
supérieure, tête
fine en biscuit,

1901   1902

jolie chevelure flottante. *Propriété exclusive du « Bon Marché ».*

1	2	3	4	5	6	7	8	9	10	11	12
0ᵐ26	0ᵐ28	0ᵐ31	0ᵐ33	0ᵐ37	0ᵐ41	0ᵐ45	0ᵐ49	0ᵐ53	0ᵐ58	0ᵐ63	0ᵐ68
2·45	3·25	4·25	5·25	6·25	7·25	8·25	9·75	11·50	14·50	17·50	21 »

Le même, parlant, bouche à dents, yeux mouvants.

						11·50	13·50	16 »	19 »	22·50	26 »

A *Bébé du Bon Marché* advertisement from 1901-1902.

Dress from Au Bon Marché, 1900 to
1905.

N°
19133.

BÉBÉ
du **Bon Marché**,
complètement
articulé, chaussé,
fabrication supérieure.

1 0ᵐ26	2 0ᵐ28	3 0ᵐ31	4 0ᵐ35	5 0ᵐ39	6 0ᵐ40	7 0ᵐ47	8 0ᵐ49	9 0ᵐ53	10 0ᵐ58	11 0ᵐ66	12 0ᵐ70
5.25	6.90	8.25	9.90	12.75	14.50	17.50	19.50	22.50	27.	33.	42.
Parlant, yeux dormeurs. . . .						21.	25.	28.	33.	39.	47.

Au Bon Marché department store catalog from 1914.

N°   19329.

BÉBÉ
du *Bon Marché*,
fabrication jumeau, tout
articulé, dormeur à cils.

Nᵒˢ. .	1	2	3	4	5
Haut.	0ᵐ25	0ᵐ29	0ᵐ32	0ᵐ36	0ᵐ40
	4.90	**6.50**	**7.90**	**9.50**	**11.50**
6	7	8	9	10	11	12
0ᵐ43	0ᵐ47	0ᵐ51	0ᵐ56	0ᵐ59	0ᵐ64	0ᵐ70
13.50	**15.50**	**19.50**	**23.**	**28.50**	**33.50**	**40.**

A 1917 *Bébé du Bon Marché* advertisement.

154

Les Galeries Lafayette

The *Bébé Lafayette* wore a fairly fancy chemise. The bottom was lace-edged and there was a group of pleats at the front; the top was trimmed with double insertion between which there was a tapered yoke. A large flat collar surrounded the yoke and was edged by the same lace, set off by the same insertion. The sleeves were short and finished in a flat lace flounce.

The Lafayette *bébés* came in twelve sizes, but only started at size 3, 31cm (12¼in) and went up to 79cm (31⅛in).

Galeries Layfayette department store catalog ad, 1913 to 1914.

Bébé Layfayette ad from 1911-1912.

A la Place Clichy

The *bébés* reserved for this shop were also marked *Bébé Moncey*, and the chemise was a variant of the Printemps model.

The A la Place Clichy department store advertised their *Bébé Moncey* in 1903.

Le Samaritaine

The *Bébé Samaritaine* came in the same style of *chemise garnie dentelle*, or lace-trimmed shirt, until the end of World War I, a style which was very different from that of the other shops. This was the only chemise with a belt that tapered to a point at the front and which kept a double box pleat in place. The bottom edge had a heavy lace border. At the top the front pleats were edged with two strips of lace which formed the yoke and tapered to a point at the waist. The neckline was edged with lace. The mid-length sleeves were gathered and edged with the same lace.

The design of the chemise was simplified in the mid-1920s. The front was still pleated but the top consisted of a yoke of fancy material, tapering to a point and edged with a flounce trimmed with braid. The collar was high and straight, the sleeves short and slightly gathered. Both chemise and belt were edged with a double line of pink or blue braiding. This chemise was similar to the Printemps shirt of the same era.

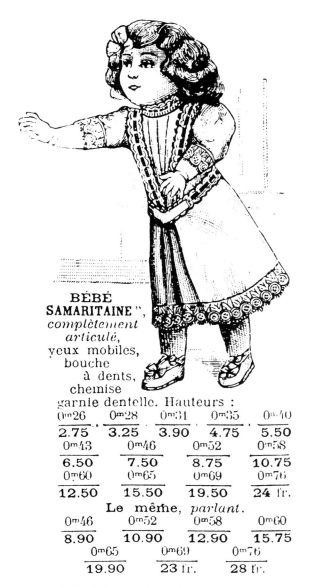

BÉBÉ
SAMARITAINE",
*complètement
articulé*,
yeux mobiles,
bouche
à dents,
chemise
garnie dentelle. Hauteurs :

0ᵐ26	0ᵐ28	0ᵐ31	0ᵐ35	0ᵐ40
2.75	3.25	3.90	4.75	5.50

0ᵐ43	0ᵐ46	0ᵐ52	0ᵐ58
6.50	7.50	8.75	10.75

0ᵐ60	0ᵐ65	0ᵐ69	0ᵐ76
12.50	15.50	19.50	24 fr.

Le même, *parlant.*

0ᵐ46	0ᵐ52	0ᵐ58	0ᵐ60
8.90	10.90	12.90	15.75

0ᵐ65	0ᵐ69	0ᵐ76
19.90	23 fr.	28 fr.

A *Bébé Samaritaine* ad from 1913.

BÉBÉ
" Samaritalne ",
complètement articulé,
yeux mobiles.

0ᵐ26	0ᵐ28	0ᵐ31	0ᵐ35	0ᵐ40	0ᵐ43	0ᵐ46	0ᵐ52
2.75	3.25	3.90	4.75	5.50	6.50	7.50	8.75

0ᵐ58	0ᵐ61	0ᵐ65	0ᵐ69	0ᵐ76
10.75	12.50	15.50	19.50	24fr.

Le même, *parlant.*

0ᵐ46	0ᵐ52	0ᵐ58	0ᵐ61	0ᵐ65
8.90	10.90	12.90	15.75	19.90

0ᵐ69	0ᵐ76
23 fr.	28 fr.

A 1914 *Bébé Samaritaine* advertisement.

BI 54465.
BÉBÉ
"SAMARITAINE",
*entièrement
articulé,*
perruque cheveux
naturels, tête fine,
yeux mobiles Haut. :

0ᵐ25.13.75	0ᵐ51. 45 fr.
0ᵐ28.15.50	0ᵐ57. 54 fr.
0ᵐ31.17.90	0ᵐ64. 65 fr.
0ᵐ35.20.75	0ᵐ64. 75 fr.
0ᵐ40.24.75	0ᵐ69. 87 fr.
0ᵐ43.29.50	0ᵐ75.105 fr.
0ᵐ46.34 fr.	0ᵐ78.120 fr.

Le même, parlant. Hᵗˢ :

0ᵐ43.39 fr.	0ᵐ57. 60 fr.
0ᵐ46.45 fr.	0ᵐ64. 70 fr.
0ᵐ52.51 fr.	0ᵐ64. 82 fr.
0ᵐ60 . . . 95 fr.	

A 1924 ad for *Bébé Samaritaine.*

A la Ville de Saint-Denis

Until 1914 the special chemise made for this shop was the same as that of Printemps and the Trois Quartiers except that the yoke was square.

In 1914 the chemise became visibly shorter, pleated at the front and edged with lace at the bottom. A large pair of suspenders made of lace and fancy material crossed the shoulders and met at the chest. The lace belt was worn at the same level. The neckline had a fine lace border. The sleeves were short, gathered and ended in a band of the same lace.

The *bébés* came in sizes 5 to 12.

BÉBÉ "Ville de St-Denis", fabrication Jumeau, complètement articulé, bouche à dents, chemise lingerie fine avec dentelle. Hauteurs :

0m52	0m46	0m43	0m40
7.25	6.25	5.25	4.75

0m76	0m69	0m65	0m60	0m58
19.50	15.50	12.50	9.90	8.25

Le même, parlant, dormeur.

Haut.	0m58	0m52	0m46
Prix	12.50	10.50	8.75
Haut.	0m69	0m65	0m60
Prix	20.50	18.50	14.50

A 1910 ad for the *Bébé Ville St-Denis*.

1903

6-114. BÉBÉ "Ville de Saint-Denis", complètement articulé, bouche à dents, chemise fine, garnie dentelle, fabrication "Jumeau".

Haut.	0m25	0m31	0m38	0m45	0m49
Prix	2.45	4 25	6.25	8.25	9.75
Haut.	0m53	0m58	0m63	0m68	
Prix	11.50	14.50	17.50	21. »	

A 1903 *Bébé Ville St-Denis* advertisement.

3009. BÉBÉ " *Ville-Saint-Denis*", fabrication Jumeau, complètement articulé, bouche à dents, chemise lingerie fine avec dentelle.

Haut.	0m76	0m69	0m65	0m60	0m58	0m52	0m46	0m43	0m40
Prix	19.50	15.50	12.50	9.90	8.25	7.25	6.25	5.25	4.75

Le même, parlant dormeur.

Haut.	0m69	0m65	0m60	0m58	0m52	0m46
Prix	20.50	18.50	14.50	12.50	10.50	8.75

The *Bébé Ville St-Denis* was advertised as "made by Jumeau" in 1911.

Z — 161.

BÉBÉ "Ville Saint-Denis", fabrication Jumeau, complètement articulé, bouche à dent, perruque fine, chemise lingerie, garnie dentelle.

Nos.	12	11	10	9
Haut.	0m69	0m65	0m60	0m58
Prix.	19.75	16.90	13.90	11.90
Nos.	8	7	6	5
Haut.	0m52	0m46	0m43	0m40
Prix.	8.90	7.50	6.50	5.50

Les mêmes, parlant, dormant.

Nos.	12	11	10	9
Prix.	25. »	23.50	19.50	15.50
	8		7	
	12.90		10.75	

The 1914 *Bébé Ville St-Denis* was described as made by Jumeau, completely articulated, had an open mouth with teeth and was dressed in a chemise.

Les Trois Quartiers

This *bébé* was also called *Bébé Madeleine* (because the Trois Quartiers shop was very close to the Madeleine church). She wore a chemise with a round or square yoke of fancy material edged with a large, pleated, lace flounce. At the front of the chemise were two flat pleats separated by a lace insertion. The bottom edge had a lace flounce. The sleeves were short, gathered and ended in a lace band.

This model was made until the 1920s.

These *bébés* could be found with a belt marked *Paris Bébé*.

In 1906 the first size of the Trois Quartiers *bébé* was 27cm (10⅝in).

Le Louvre

The *Bébé Louvre* wore a chemise of a simple design. At the front were two flat pleats and the bottom had a thin lace edging. The top of the yoke stopped at the level of the chest and was followed by a horizontal line of lace and by three insertions of lace spaced out vertically across the front. The neckline was lace-edged. The short sleeves were gathered and edged with a little lace border.

The chemise would stay the same until about 1925.

BÉBÉ TROIS QUARTIERS
entièrement articulé, chemise fine, yeux mobiles.
Haut. 0ᵐ27 . . . . **2·75**
0ᵐ40 **4·25** 0ᵐ46 **6·50**
0ᵐ55 **9** » 0ᵐ65 **15** >

A 1906 ad for the *Bébé Trois Quartiers*.

BÉBÉ MADELEINE
fabrication Jumeau
yeux mobiles à cils, tête fine, entièrement
articulé.
Haut. 0ᵐ28   0ᵐ40   0ᵐ43   0ᵐ57   0ᵐ5

| 3·90 | 6·90 | 9·50 | 14·50 | 21 » |

Le même, parlant. *Haut.* 0ᵐ43 . **11·75**
0ᵐ57 . . . . **15·75** *Emballage* » 25 et » 30

A 1906 ad for *Bébé Madeleine* from Les Trois Quartiers.

371·
Le "BÉBÉ DU LOUVRE"
dormeur à cils fabrication
supérieure, articulations
complètes.

1	2	3	4
0ᵐ25	0ᵐ29	0ᵐ32	0ᵐ36
10.50	12.75	14.50	17.75
5	6	7	8
0ᵐ40	0ᵐ43	0ᵐ47	0ᵐ52
21.50	25.50	29.90	39.90
9	10	11	12
0ᵐ57	0ᵐ60	0ᵐ64	0ᵐ69
48.»	57.»	69.»	81.»

An ad for *Bébé du Louvre* from 1922.

3714   LE BÉBÉ DU LOU
dormeur à cils, fabrication supérie
articulations complètes.

Nº 1	2	3	4	5
0ᵐ25	0ᵐ29	0ᵐ32	0ᵐ36	0ᵐ40
14.	**17.**	**20.50**	**25.**	**29.50**
Nº 7	8	9	10	11
0ᵐ47	0ᵐ52	0ᵐ57	0ᵐ61	0ᵐ65
46.	**55.**	**64.50**	**79.**	**95.**

A 1921 ad from the Le Louvre department store.

Most of the chemises reserved by the S.F.B.J. for the *bébés* of specific shops continued until about 1925. The arrival of semi-articulated, cloth and felt dolls between 1920 and 1925 brought with it a great variety of cloth, felt, organdy and artificial silk clothes to replace the chemises. Thus after this time there were more fully-dressed dolls and fewer *bébés* dressed in chemises alone. Then the chemises themselves were varied and simplified, and each shop followed the latest fashions rather than having its own model.

A study of the catalogs show that from the early 1920s onwards the *bébés* no longer came in all sizes, as the following table shows:

Sizes	1	2	3	4	5	6	7	8	9	10	11	12	13
Years from 1900 to 1923/25	25/26 cm	28/29 cm	31/32 cm	35/36 cm	38/40 cm	41/43 cm	45/47 cm	49/52 cm	53/58 cm	58/60 cm	63/65 cm	68/70 cm	76/79 cm

In 1934 only the even numbers (2, 4, 6, 8, 10, 12) were manufactured.

Marques
Trademarks

Annexes
Appendix

Les Marques Déposées de la S.F.B.J.
Trademarks Registered
by the S.F.B.J.

BEBE PRODIGE

131042

BÉBÉ JUMEAU

131043

BÉBÉ FRANÇAIS

131044

131045

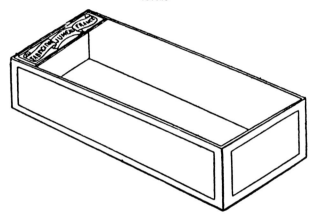

131041 à 131045. — M. p. désigner des bébés et poupées, déposées le 12 septembre 1911, à 1 h. 15, au greffe du tribunal de commerce de la Seine, par la *Société Française de fabrication de Bébés-Jouets*, 8, rue Pastourelle, à Paris.
Ces marques sont de couleurs variables.

CL. XLIV. — JEUX ET JOUETS
"BÉBÉ PARISIANA"
75122. — M. p. désigner des bébés, poupées et tous accessoires, déposée le 13 juin 1902, à 3 h., au greffe du tribunal de commerce de la Seine, par la *Société française de fabrication de bébés-jouets*, à Paris.

BÉBÉ PARFAIT
86638. — M. p. désigner des bébés et poupées, déposée le 24 septembre 1904, à 1 h., au greffe du tribunal de commerce de la Seine, par la *Société Française de fabrication de Bébés-jouets*, à Paris.

CL. XLIV. — JEUX ET JOUETS
EDEN-BÉBÉ
88618. — M. p. désigner des bébés et poupées, déposée le 16 février 1905, à 1 h. 15, au greffe du tribunal de commerce de la Seine, par la *Société française de fabrication de Bébés-Jouets*, à Paris.
(*Renouvellement de dépôt*)

BÉBÉ TRIOMPHE
143317. — M. p. désigner des bébés-jouets, déposée le 12 février 1913, 2 h., au greffe du tribunal de commerce de la Seine, par la *Société française de Fabrication de bébés et jouets*, 8, rue Pastourelle, à Paris.
(*Renouvellement de dépôt*. — Déclaration du déposant)

The S.F.B.J. had various registered trademarks at their disposal according to the agreements made between the various partners and defined by the company's statutes.

The marks which were used most often and renewed most frequently were:
— first Jumeau's own:
    Bébé Jumeau in 1911, 1926, 1941 and 1956
    Paris Bébé in 1911, 1926 and 1941
    Bébé Français in 1911 and 1926
    Bébé Prodige in 1911 and 1926
    The bee design for the shoes in 1906 and 1921.
— then the S.F.B.J.'s own:
    Bébé Parisiana in 1902, 1920 and 1935
    Bébé Parfait in 1904, 1920 and 1935
    Bébé Moderne in 1903, 1908 and 1920
— finally, Fleischmann and Bloedel's:
    Eden Bébé in 1905, 1938 and 1953
    Bébé Triomphe in 1913
— Although Bouchet had numerous marks, the S.F.B.J. only kept his:
    Le Séduisant in 1903, 1908 and 1920
    Curiously enough, the mark *Bébé Bru* was renewed very late on, only in 1938 and 1953.

This throws new light on some of the heads marked Bru Jne, whose face, though conforming to the Bru style of the end of the nineteenth century, has a closed, painted mouth which is, like the rest of the face, in the style of the dolls of the 1930s and 1940s.

There is still some doubt about the *Parisiana* doll, because this same mark was registered on April 20, 1905, by the *Comptoir General de la Bimbeloterie* (a company of toysellers, 6 and 8, rue des Haudriettes, Paris). Given that these trademarks, once registered, were protected for fifteen years, it is difficult to understand how it happened that this company could have registered the name only three years after the S.F.B.J. had registered it.

It is possible that the *Bébé Parisiana* was registered by the S.F.B.J. for the *Comptoir de la Bimbeloterie*, who were, as the name indicates, not manufacturers but retailers. In fact this doll was shown by the *Comptoir* at the Franco-British Exhibition in London in 1908, where J. du Serre Telmon was chairman and member of the panel. Neither the S.F.B.J. nor, for that matter, any other French manufacturer, took part in this exhibition.

The S.F.B.J. did not use the marks of some of its partners:
— of Remignard, *le Petit Chérubin*
— of Bouchet, *Bébé Géant, Gentil Bébé, L'Indestructible* and *Bébé Tête Mobile*
— of Rabery, whose successor and son-in-law was Genty, *Bébé de Paris*
— of Gobert, *Bébé Colosse*
Some of these were trade names and were not registered.

Nor did the S.F.B.J. confirm the registration of marks belonging to partners who joined the society later than 1899 (as if they were trying to get rid of their rivals):
— for the "Société Parisienne des Bébés": *Etoile Bébé* and *Bébé Mondain*
— for "La Parisienne": *la Parisienne, Euréka, Bébé le Reve, Bébé Eureka, Paradis Bébé, Bébé Stella, Bébé Lux*

— for the "Société Damerval et Lafranchy": *Bébé Mignon* and *Joli Bébé*

Some of the S.F.B.J.'s own trademarks will never be found together on the head and body of a *bébé*, for example, *Bébé Moderne* and *Bébé Parfait*. These names were only used for the boxes. On the other hand, some marks were used on the head, body and clothing right up until the end of the S.F.B.J.'s production; as in the case of *Bébé Jumeau*. This fact has given rise to much confusion among collectors who think they own or have bought a real "Jumeau," when in fact, what they have is an S.F.B.J. product. It should be said that the S.F.B.J. was largely responsible for this ambiguity. Counting on Emile Jumeau's international reputation for high quality goods, it even went so far as to call its factory, *Usine du Bébé Jumeau* (factory of *Bébé Jumeau*)! One could almost say that it was the S.F.B.J. which made the greatest contribution to the growth and use of Jumeau's name! This habit is so well established in France that it is difficult, even for the old ladies who were little girls at the turn of the century, to admit that their "Jumeau" *bébés* were, in fact, made by various manufacturers within the S.F.B.J. This is certainly the reason why so many studies of Jumeau's career include an examination of the S.F.B.J.'s products. In any discussion of Emile Jumeau's own work, which was neither influenced nor adapted by his rivals, then one must stop at the date 1899. All products manufactured after this, even if they bear the prestigious name of Emile Jumeau, were made by the S.F.B.J.

Finally, other trademarks, used by the S.F.B.J. but apparently not registered, are:
Bébé Bob, which should correspond to a character *bébé* and:
Bébé Vrai Modèle, found on the pink ticket stuck to the back of an S.F.B.J. *bébé*.

CL. XLIV. — JEUX ET JOUETS
79963
BÉBÉ MODERNE
79964
LE SÉDUISANT

79964. — M. p. désigner des bébés et poupées, déposées le 1903, à 1 h., au greffe du tribunal de commerce de la Seine, par Société Française de fabrication de bébés-jouets, à Paris

97596. — M. p. désigner des poupées, chaussures et semelles de chaussures pour poupées, déposée le 24 août 1906, à 1 h., au greffe du tribunal de commerce de la Seine, par la *Société Française de Fabrication de Bébés et Jouets*, à Paris.
Cette marque, de couleurs variables, s'appose de toutes manières convenables sur les produits. Elle est, de préférence, poinçonnée à froid sur les semelles et elle peut être reproduite sur tous emballages, etc.
(Renouvellement de dépôt)

PARIS-BÉBÉ

128025. — M. p. désigner des bébés et poupées, déposée le 13 avril 1911, à 1 h., au greffe du tribunal de commerce de la Seine, par la *Société Française de Fabrication de Bébés-Jouets*, 8, rue Pastourelle. à Paris.

Marques S.F.B.J.
S.F.B.J. Trademarks

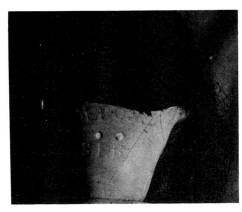

Several marks with the initials of the S.F.B.J. are to be found on their *bébés* heads:

1.   SFBJ, stamped in a hollow in a horizontal line. The letters are spaced out and quite large. This stamp is usually to be found on the heads of *bébés* who have a patented walking mechanism, and can be dated at around 1905.

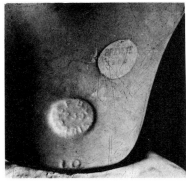

2.   SFBJ, written in a hollow circle, of which the four letters are placed one in each quarter. This mark was registered in England, and is to be found on *bébés* made at the turn of the century.

3.   SFBJ PARIS, incised in an elliptical hollow with a number in the middle. This number corresponds to the *bébés* mold number. Another number lower down on the nape of the neck indicates the size. Another number, near the cut-out, (usually to be found on models made after the 1920's), may also be present, giving the year of manufacture. It was characteristic of French and German manufacturers to mark their *bébés* and dolls' heads with the date. The name FRANCE may also be engraved above S.F.B.J.

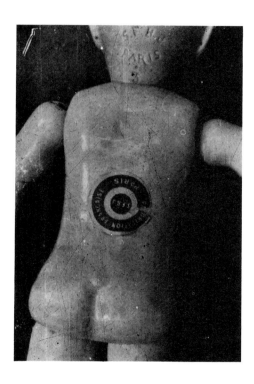

4. UNIS FRANCE. According to the Commercial Director, the S.F.B.J. would only have used the mark Unis France after 1924 This is to be found on some character *bébés*, especially those with carton-pâte heads, and on those numbered 60 and 301. Unis stands for *Union Nationale Inter Syndicale* (National Union of Trade Syndicates), a collective stamp which guaranteed that the product was of French origin, and was made under the auspices of the *Chambres Syndicales*. The *Union Nationale Inter Syndicale* was founded by the Parisian Chamber of Commerce on December 9, 1915, to protect and promote French products. This mark was accompanied by three numbers. The one on the left being that of the trade union; for example, *La Chambre Syndicale des Jeux et Jouets Français* had the number 71. The number on the right side was that which the Chambre Syndicale gave to its members. Curiously enough, the S.F.B.J. had number 149 which had been Girard's. Underneath the mark was a conventional number; in this example, it corresponds to the *bébés* mold number. The S.F.B.J. always used its own personal mark on character *bébés* heads, and it is this which confirms our present belief that this was the company's main production, and that of which they were proudest.

5. The S.F.B.J. Tri-color Cockade. This round tri-color ticket in the red, white and blue of the French flag, was stuck onto the backs of some toys and *bébés* and was used by the S.F.B.J. before and during World War I. It is a symbol of the fight against foreign competition, above all, that against the Germans. It would eventually be replaced by the stamp Unis France which was also the symbol of French production.

6. Finally, the S.F.B.J. mark used for the boxes and wrappings for the *bébés* and toys.

91052. — M. p. désigner des articles tels que : bébés, poupées, jouets, etc., déposée le 17 juillet 1905, à 1 h., au greffe du tribunal de commerce de la Seine, par la *Société française de fabrication de bébés-jouets*, à Paris.

Cette marque s'appose par tous moyens appropriés et en toutes couleurs sur les produits, ainsi que sur leurs étuis, boîtes et emballages, etc.

131186. — M. p. désigner des bébés et jouets, déposée le 22 septembre 1911, à 10 h., au greffe du tribunal de commerce de la Seine, par la *Société française de fabrication de bébés et jouets*, 8, rue Pastourelle, à Paris.

Cette marque est de couleurs variables.

Head

Mold Number	Bisque	Other Materials	Solid Head	Head With Open Pate	Set Eyes	Moving Eyes	Closed Mouth	Open-Closed Mouth	Open Mouth Showing Teeth, Tongue
226	226		226		226			226	
227	227		227		227				upper teeth
228	228							228	
229	229			229	229				6 upper teeth
230	230			230	230	230			6 upper teeth
231									
232									
233	233		233		233		dents inf & sup.		
234	234			234		234			without teeth moving tongue
235	235		235		235			upper teeth	
236	236			236		236			2 upper teeth
237	237		237		237				4 upper teeth
238	238			238	238				6 upper teeth
239	239			239	239		239		
240									
241									
242	242		242			242		nursing	
243									
244									
245	245			245		245		245	4 upper teeth
246						246		246	
247	247	cardboard & felt		247	painted	247	247	2 upper teeth	
248	248			248	248		248		
249									
250	250			250		250			4 upper teeth
251	251	cardboard		251		251			2 upper teeth moving tongue
252	252			252		252	252		
253			253		253		253		
254									
255	255			255		255			
256									
257	257							257	
258									
259								2 teeth	
260									
261									
262									4 upper teeth
263		cardboard	263			263			2 upper teeth moving tongue

271	271		271		painted	271			without teeth moving tongue
272	272		272			272			moving tongue

278		celluloid	278			278			without teeth

284		cardboard		284		284	284		

287		cardboard		287		287			2 upper teeth moving tongue
288		composition	288			288			tongue
290	290			290		290			tongue & 2 upper teeth
298		composition	298			298			
301	301	cardboard		301	301	301			4 upper teeth

306	306					306	306		

316		cardboard				316	316		

318		plastic				318	318		

Marks   Bodies

Without Mark	S.F.B.J.	Jumeau	Unis	Wood, Cardboard and/or Composition	Composition or Plastic	Stuffed Fabric		Sizes
226	226			226	composition			4 to 8
227	227			227	composition			0 to 10
				229				4
	230	230		230				4 to 15
	233			233				4 to 10
	234			234	composition			0 to 6
235	235			235	composition			0 to 6
	236			236	composition			0 to 12
237	237			237	composition			4 to 6
	238			238				4 to 10
	239				composition		Poulbot	4
	242			242			nursing (téteur)	4 to 6
	245			245			Googlie	2 to 4
247	247		247	247	composition	247		4/0 to 11
	250			250				6 to 10
	251		251	251	composition			2 to 12
	252				composition			0 to 10
							Pierrot	
	255						clown	30cm (11⅞in)
	263							11
			271		composition			0 to 3
			272			272		2
		278			composition		Bambino	3
			284		composition	fabric		60cm (23⅝in)
				287				60cm (23⅝in)
			288		composition			40cm (15¾in)
			290		composition			
					composition	298		
	301	301	301	301	301			4/0 to 16
	306	306			306		1938	45cm (17¾in) and 90cm (35½in)
	316				composition			4
			318		plastic			4

Tableaux Synoptiques
Table of Brands, Models, and Patents

Production Brands, Patents, and Registered Models

Year	Date	Patent	Brands and Models	Objects
1899				
1900				
1901	April 9	309,788		Improvements to talking *bébés*
1902	June 13		75,122	*Bébé Parisiana* (*bébé* and all accessories)
1903	June 5		7,963	*Bébé Moderne*
			7,964	*Bébé le Séduisant* (*bébés* and *poupées*)
	June 6	332,857		Improvement to animated objects (doll which talks and waves from her carriage)
1904	March 10	341,108		Improvements to *bébés* with sleep eyes
	June 3	3,318 addition to 341,108		Improvements to *bébés* with sleep eyes
	August 11	3,601 addition to 341,108		Improvements to *bébés* with sleep eyes
	September 7	346,106		Walking toy (animal harnessed to a wagon)
	September 24		86,638	*Bébé Parfait*
1905	February 10	351,422		Staple to attach cords (semi-articulated *bébé*)
		351,423		Device for elastic assembly of articulated toys
		352,382		Machine to produce articulated toys
	February 11	351,452		Mechanical *bébé* (walker without a key)
	February 16		88,618	*Eden Bébé* (Registered renewal) *bébés* and *poupées*
	April 5	4,674 addition to 352,382		Machine to produce articulated toys
	April 8	4,688 addition to 351,452		Walking mechanical *bébé* (without key)
	April 13	353,622		Talking bellows for toy *bébés* (outside controls)
	May 16	354,337		Articulated *bébé*
	June 9	4,904 addition to 352,382		Machine to produce articulated toys
	July 17		91,052	S.F.B.J. shield (*bébés, poupées,* toys etc.) in all colors on products, boxes, packaging)
	December 5	360,100		Toy-*bébé* head with sleep eyes (cardboard head)
1906	August 24		97,596	Register renewal of "bee" brand for dolls, shoes, doll shoe soles, applied with perforator, various colors)
1907	April 29	377,268		Toy with bellows (duck)
1908	June 5		79,968	*Bébé Moderne*
			79,969	*Bébé le Séduisant*
1909	February 24	399,883		Talking doll (phonograph)
1910	March 11	413,524		Phonograph for talking doll
	October 8	432,650		Nursing *bébé* (*Bébé têteur*)
1911	April 13		128,025	*Paris Bébé* (*bébés* and *poupées*)
	May 5	440,520		Plastic composition to make toys (mixed dough)
	May 24	441,459		Device to fix dolls' heads
		441,460		Machine to cast small objects
	July 12	443,389		Specially applied varnish for dolls and other objects
	September 12		131,041	*Bébé Prodige*
			131,042	*Bébé Jumeau*
			131,043	*Bébé Français*
			131,044	Fabrication Jumeau
			131,045	Jumeau box
	September 22		131,186	Drawing of *bébé* holding hot-air balloon (*bébés*, toys, different colors)

Year	Date	Patent	Brands and Models	Objects
1912	May 23	15,978 addition to 441,460		Machine to cast small objects
	September 6	16,459 addition to 432,650		Nursing *bébé* (smoker)
1913	February 12		143,317	*Bébé Triomphe* (register renewal)
	April 8	456,447		Improvements to *bébés* (talking and walking with key)
	April 26	457,184		Improvements to doll heads (sleeping eyes in cardboard heads)
1914				
1915	September 21	479,798		Improvements to doll heads in porcelain
1916	January 17	480,695		Improvements in the production of doll heads and other papier-mâché objects
1917				
1918	April 25	528,243		Composition for fixing sleep eyes in doll heads
	September 16	515,600		Procedure and device to mold dough with water or other volatile liquid with heat
1919	April 7	522,945		Improvements to artificial blown eyes
	December 4	507,074		Improvements to sleep-eye doll heads
1920	January 14		180,036	*Bébé Parisiana*
			180,037	*Bébé Moderne*
			180,038	*Le Séduisant*
			180,039	*Bébé Parfait*
	August 3	23,399 addition to 479,798		Improvements to porcelain doll heads
1921	April 2		8,624	*le Papillon* (dolls)
	September 22		17,140	bee drawing (renewal)
1922	March 3	549,556		Procedure and apparatus for compression molding of hollow pieces
	November 28	559,197		Improvements to sleeping *bébés*
1923	December 27	575,058		Machine to stuff cloth
1924	March 15	578,765		Improvements in production of dolls and other toys (felt or cloth)
	April 7		7,440	Registered model of cloth doll
	September 29	586,685		Talking baby (legless *poupard* with talking bellows)
	December 4	590,016		Device for moving of sleeping *bébés* eyelashes (immobile or painted eyes on felt, cloth, or cardboard heads)
1925	April 11	596,574		Procedure to mount mobile eyes in sleepy *bébés*
1926	February 9		93,492	*Paris Bébé* (register renewal)
	February 20	613,014		Improvements to *bébé* assembly (stuffed heads)
	August 24		102,338	*Bébé Prodige* ⎫
			102,339	*Bébé Français* ⎬ (register renewal)
			102,340	*Bébé Jumeau* ⎭
1927	March 22		20,485	penguin model
	June 3	635,471		Sleeping *bébé*
1928				
1929				
1930	December 2	706,823		Sleeping *bébé* (eyes move in all directions)
1931				
1932				
1933				
1934				

Year	Date	Patent	Brands and Models	Objects
1935	February 28	798,847		Improvements to doll heads (sleep eyes)
	June 2		234,979	*Bébé Parisiana*
			234,980	*Bébé Parfait*
1936				
1937	March 4	48,193 addition to 706,823		Sleeping *bébé* toy
1938	July 15		292,459	*Eden Bébé* ⎱ (register renewal)
			252,460	*Bébé Bru* ⎰
1939	January 27	849,560		Stuffed toys, improvements in the production of unbreakable toys
	February 8		298,885	Latiss - dolls and washable toys
1940				
1941	February 15		316,608	*Paris Bébé* ⎫
			316,609	*Bébé Jumeau* ⎬ (register renewal)
			316,610	*Bebé Français* ⎭
1942				
1943				
1944				
1945				
1946				
1947				
1948				
1949				
1950				
1951				
1952				
1953	April 30		10,240	*Éden Bébé* (register renewal)
			10,241	*Bébé Bru*
1954				
1955				
1956	June 15		69,072	*Bébé Jumeau* (register renewal)
	September 20	1,157,571		System for "walking" figurines
1957				

Les Brevets
Patents

309,788

MÉMOIRE DESCRIPTIF
déposé à l'appui d'une demande de

Brevet d'Invention de quinze Ans

Pour Perfectionnements aux bébés parleurs.

Par la Société Française de fabrication
de bébés & jouets.

by Jacques Porot

The knowledge of a manufacturer and his products, even when one cannot visit him and question him because he lived in another period, is nonetheless accessible, by his products when these exist, by his sale catalogs which are perfectly identifiable, or by resellers' catalogs (especially department stores for toys) where they are rarely identified, by the commercial directory where each producer, according to his means, mentioned in more or less detail the elements of his production, and finally by going through invention patents.

In these patents, the most original elements concerning the creator's personality, are listed.

A manufacturer-merchant is always conditioned by two tendencies, two contrary requirements: keep producing the well-known product that "works" and sells well, and at the same time find a new product which will draw the attention of the buyer and maintain competition.

Let us specify that at the time these acts and documents were drawn up, they used the term "merchant" to designate the professionals who invented, made, and sold dolls and toys.

The patent is the expression of creative activity, but it would be better to say of the creative impulse. There are many inventions that were never actually made. In the exhaustive list of S.F.B.J. patents, it is not surprising to find some discoveries futile, others completely unrealistic, as well as drawings which are the faithful and exact representation of a doll in his collection. This is the case with the S.F.B.J. as for other creators.

The creative impulse reveals the dynamism of a company.

The first striking thing in the study of S.F.B.J. patents is the disparity. Some patents which present devices for eye suspension, for example, or motor transmission, reveal the engineer. Others, revealing a knack for putting things together, seem to be the fruit of reflection and the experiment of a modest executor. The disparity is probably the result of collective work.

Some patents aim at economizing, others reveal a tendency to produce the luxury toy. These two tendencies confronted each other before 1899, before the communal French-German concept that took the name of the S.F.B.J.: the trashy, the cheap, which according to Du Maroussem represented Fleischmann and Pintel, against the quality and prestige maintained by Jumeau and Bru (Girard). The S.F.B.J. may have found a reasonable solution to maintain both quality and profitability. It seems that Fleischmann had a modest triumph, and Jumeau, a reasonable conquest. Thanks to which, the S.F.B.J. was able to cover the entire market, quality and low price together. Besides, the 58 years during which the S.F.B.J. lasted, during two wars, and a between war period troubled with a grave economic crisis, shows the solidity of this venture.

A total overview and some statistics give an idea of the S.F.B.J.'s preoccupations.

A total of 52 patents or additions were registered from 1901 to 1956.

RÉPUBLIQUE FRANÇAISE.

OFFICE NATIONAL DE LA PROPRIÉTÉ INDUSTRIELLE.

1ʳᵉ ADDITION

AU BREVET D'INVENTION

N° 432.650

XX. — Articles de Paris et industries diverses.   N° 16.459
1. — Jeux, jouets, théâtres, courses.

Bébé téteur.

SOCIÉTÉ FRANÇAISE DE FABRICATION DE BÉBÉS ET JOUETS résidant en France (Seine).

RÉPUBLIQUE FRANÇAISE.

OFFICE NATIONAL DE LA PROPRIÉTÉ INDUSTRIELLE.

BREVET D'INVENTION

du 6 juin 1903.

XX. — Articles de Paris et petites industries.   N° 332.857
1. — Bimbeloterie.

RÉPUBLIQUE FRANÇAISE.

MINISTÈRE DU COMMERCE ET DE L'INDUSTRIE.

DIRECTION DE LA PROPRIÉTÉ INDUSTRIELLE.

BREVET D'INVENTION.

Gr. XX. — Cl. 1.   N° 613.014

Perfectionnement au montage des bébés en tissus bourrés.

SOCIÉTÉ FRANÇAISE DE FABRICATION DE BÉBÉS ET JOUETS résidant en France (Rhône).

Demandé le 20 février 1926, à 11ʰ 30ᵐ, à Lyon.
Délivré le 13 août 1926. — Publié le 6 novembre 1926.

Périodes Inventives (tableau A)
Inventive Periods (chart A)

Ten patents were registered for the first year. In 1905, six years after the creation of S.F.B.J. a record was set. 15 patents were registered for the 1903-1905 period.

There was a calm between 1906 and 1909, and a steady recovery from 1909 to 1913: 11 patents, averaging two a year. The war (1914-1920) did not prevent average creative activity. From 1922 to 1930 there was steady activity averaging more than one patent per year.

From 1930 on, requests for patents become sporadic: five patents in 26 years. The market became uniform, the models became standard and more importance was placed on the outside presentation (character *bébés*, rag dolls), than on complicated inside mechanisms.

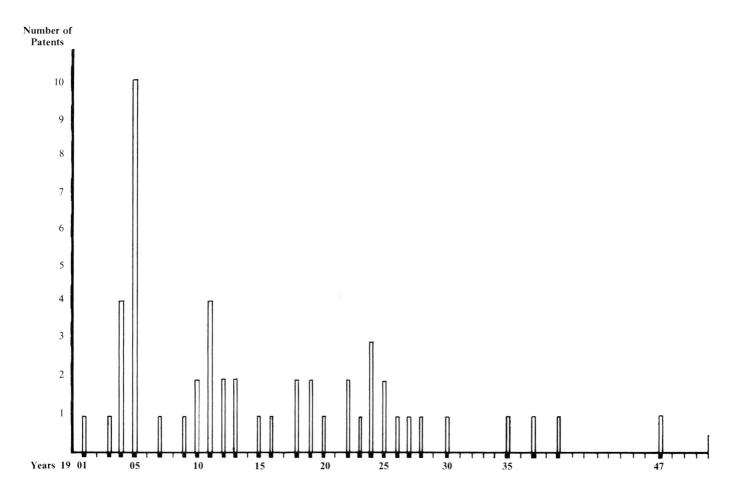

Domaines Explorés (tableau B)
Explored Areas (chart B)

A completely surprising statement of fact: for 52 patents registered between 1901 and 1956, 17 were taken out for eyes. The problem of eye production, attachment, and movement, was a dominant preoccupation, and not only for the S.F.B.J. Imagined solutions were never completely satisfying. Talking mechanisms were tried six times (twice by a phonograph). Walking mechanisms or complex mechanisms (walking, kissing, and talking), were recorded six times. Procedures for assembly (articulation and joints), were registered three times; almost always to simplify and economize rubber bands. Once a nursing doll was created, in 1910. As for the rest, eighteen patents cover the choice of materials or production apparatuses (molding and assembly).

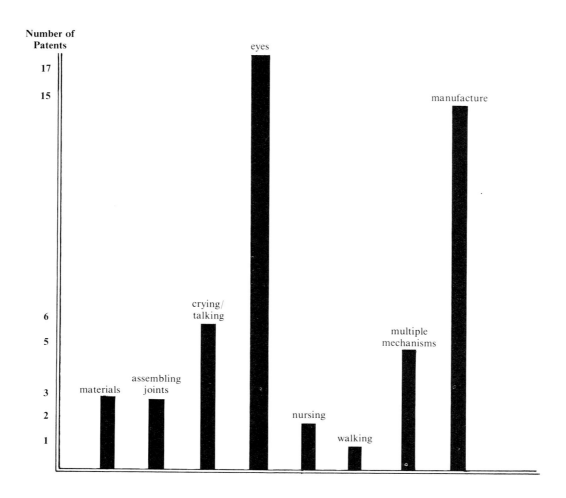

La Date des Brevets
Patent Dates

The official documents carry three dates: that of the handing in of the claim (giving the time down to the minute), that of the delivery, and that of the publication. There are sometimes considerable lapses between these dates, especially between that of the handing in of the claim and that of its delivery; this is due to the length of the investigation into the novelty of the invention. But, legally, it is the date and the hour of the handing in which stands in case of dispute. It is this date that must be given in any publication (newspaper, review or book) briefly referring to patents. But, included here are the three dates, because their gaps could suggest a particular fact, and thus further research.

No. 443,389

XIV — Chemical Arts

Demand made July 12, 1911.
Delivered July 13, 1912 — Published September 23, 1912.

Varnish specially applicable on dolls and other objects

This patent is a treatment for the surface of objects, not unlike the glaze in ceramics:
soaking in a silicate bath. But, a cold glaze.

The present invention is a varnish specially applicable in the industry of *bébés*-toys and other figurines.

Until today one used an alcohol-based varnish, applied with a brush. Its finish on dolls or other figurines was always rather crude. Bits of paint were spread in a way by the brush; and finally, the toy covered was neither washable, nor resistant to changes in temperature.

Contrary to this, the present varnish gives the material greater solidity, and a uniform film covering on the object; it can be used according to the case, matt or glossy: it is not altered by temperature changes, and is completely washable. Besides, being applied through soaking and not by brush, one avoids the irregularities of brushstrokes, as well as a great loss of time.

The present varnish is obtained by simply immersing the object in a bath of water-glass or glass-wort. It should be allowed to dry on the peg on which it was immersed. This varnish is brillant; a dull finish can be obtained by adding barium oxide.

Materials

No. 440,520

XX — Paris Articles and Various Industries.
1.   Games, Toys, Theaters, Races.

Request made May 5, 1911.
Delivered May 6, 1912 — Published July 12, 1912.

Plastic composition for the production of toys

One of the innumerable recipes for making "pâte" or "composition."
This one's originality is that it contains scories or cinders, residue after the combustion of coal.

One obtains this composition in the following way: one takes bits of paper and one puts them in a fiber separating machine that breaks them up into fibers.

One also crushes the cinders, particularly the slags, using a pebble crusher, in order to obtain a fine cindery powder.

One also takes sifted sawdust from pitch-pine, mahogany, pine, or other preferably resinous wood.

Finally, one mixes paste glue with another glue, preferably vegetable, which will give a bit of strength.

One adds to this mix of glue, just the paper fibers, then the pulverized slag and finally the sifted sawdust and mixing continually without heating. The paste thus obtained is next pressed into blocks of all desired shapes; these blocks just dried in open air, then the drying room, can be finally painted, assembled and formed in various manners using the usual procedures for toy production.

The composition thus described has the advantage of being stronger than that generally used, and turns out of the mold in a cleaner and easier fashion.

This advantage is greatly due to the presence of the scoria powder in the mix. Experience shows that, without this powder, the mix tends to stick to the mold's sides so that the blocks taken out, present a grainy or wrinkled surface, on the contrary, with the crushed scoria, the paste comes out easily and the objects have a smooth unified surface, which can be easily painted. Consequently, one gets solider toys with a better appeal than those molded using the current compositions.

No. 849,560

GR. 20 — Cl. 1

Demand January 27, 1939 at 2.51 p.m. in Paris.
Delivered August 21, 1939 — Published November 27, 1939.

Improvements in the production of unbreakable toys.

This patent is for a production process: coating stuffed cloth dolls with latex.
Concern over protecting the surface arises again twenty-eight years after patent number 443,389 of 1911!

The present invention consists of making these toys, in whole or in part, by an envelope of cloth stuffed with a fibrous or supple matter such as kapok, bits of cotton, cork powder and so on, and by a latex covering applied to this envelope after stuffing and forming.

This covering can be applied to the entire toy, or on certain parts before or after their assembly, by dunking in a latex bath, or spraying pulverized latex, or any other appropriate manner.

This covering, once dry, is vulcanized. Desired coloring can be obtained either by adding latex pigments or appropriate coloring material, or by a later application of color through any procedure.

Toys thus made unite the advantages of "stuffed" toys and rubber ones, without their inconveniences.

They are unbreakable, untearable, cannot be smashed, or lose their form; they are light and soft to touch, their physical aspect resembling that of natural skin, is agreeable; they notably have the advantage of being washable with soap and water, and consequently offer qualities of hygiene, while "stuffed" toys whose coverings become dirty and do not lend themselves to washing, are nests for germs, and often became dangerous for children's health.

Non-clothed toys, representing for example, animals, will be preferably completely covered with latex, while *bébés*-toys, and dolls could carry parts covered in latex, assembled to a stuffed body with covering and a plaster or other head.

Assembly

No. 354,337

XX — Articles from Paris and various industries.
 1. Games, Toys, Theaters, Races.

Petitioned on May 16, 1905.
Delivered on July 24, 1905 — Published on October 4, 1905.

Articulated *bébé*

In this patent an original concept combines short cross linking-through the thighs
with possible knee joint articulation.

In the present baby, the legs are articulated at the knees, with the components held in position by traction of a cross-link placed as it would be in semi-articulated dolls; the lower part of the leg is attached to this cross-link by an inextensible lengthwise link such as a metallic wire; the elasticity of the cross-link is used to hold the upper leg parts tight against the body, and to push upwards the lower leg part against the corresponding upper part at the same time.

In regards to existing dolls with knee joints, a great deal of labor could be simplified, a considerable reduction in elastic links used and consequently an important saving made in manufacturing.

Elastic string h goes through the legs and the body, tightly stretched, with the ends fixed on the thigh's external surface, around the hips; wires i are hung below, to knee-caps f, and above, to string h as shown in the drawing. Of course the construction of the legs and the body could be varied without straying away from the invention. For example, for the hip joints, a socket could be formed in part d and the knee cap in the body; at the knee, the knee-cap could be formed on part d and the socket in corresponding part e.

The knee-cap joint sockets could be more or less complete or even reduced to simple circular or almost circular flanges etc. All means of linkage could be used to fix the ends of string h to parts d of the legs as described. For example, wires i could be directly attached to parts c or replaced by strings, tin strips or any other appropriate inextensible linkage.

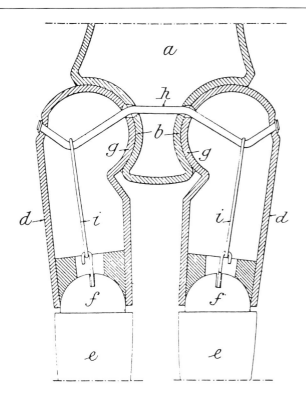

Figure 1

No. 441,459

XX — Articles from Paris and various industries.
1. Games, Toys, Theaters, Races.

Petitioned on May 24, 1911.
Delivered on May 25, 1912 — Published on August 7, 1912.

(Delivery was postponed on patent by the execution of article 11 S 7
of the July 5, 1844, law modified by the April 7, 1902, law.)

Device to fix dolls' heads

This patent is a detail in the head mounting.

The present invention aims for a device used in fixing dolls' heads more conveniently than with the existing devices.

Up to now, a rubber string is used, passing through a spiral-shaped metal ring with a diameter bigger than the lower hole of the head. The fitting of the ring in the head and that of the rubber string in the ring are particularly difficult when dealing with heads with a closed top. On top of the great fitting difficulty, the device inconveniently causes head-breakage due to the ring being caught between the neck walls or bottom of the head. Moreover, as the ring could hang more or less high within the head a relatively important loss of rubber results.

According to the present invention this inconvenience could be avoided by using a particular attachment part replacing the ring mentioned above, made of metallic thread folded in the V shape with a loop on top; the width of the V is greater than the loop diameter so that the ends of its prongs lean against the internal surface of the bottom of the head, while the loop could easily slip through the lower hole at the bottom of the head. Thanks to the V shape, the loop used in introducing the rubber string, is lowered as much as possible, so that the required length of rubber string can be minimized. The fitting becomes extremely convenient and quick, even when the top of the head is closed up, because the linkage can be inserted directly into the hole at the bottom of the head, and even after the rubber string has gone through the loop. Not only that this operation is convenient and quick, it does not involve any danger of breaking heads.

The loop has the shape of a spiral with a gap where the prongs begin to part, allowing the rubber string to pass easily.

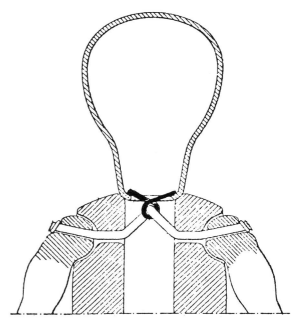

Figure 1

Assembly

No. 613,014

Gr XX — Cl 1.

Petitioned on February 20, 1926 at 11:30 a.m. in Lyon.
Delivered on August 13, 1916 — Published on November 6, 1926.

Improvements on the assembling of stuffed *bébés*

This document helps to date *bébés* assembled in this manner.

In the current manufacturing of stuffed dolls, the head is articulated by a swivel axle, on a plate located in the upper part of the casing of material that shapes the body. The shoulders end with a plane surface at their upper part, giving the doll an ugly angular shape.

The present invention aims to remedy this inconvenience. It involves the mounting of the head on a hollow part bulging out according to the shape of the shoulders and located in the upper part of the body.

As shown in the partial section of the drawing, the upper part of the doll body is limited by part a, molded or embossed in any appropriate material.

Part a, located in the material casing b, gives the exact shape of shoulders to the upper part of the doll's body.

The assembling of head c to piece a is insured by pivot axle d and shock absorbing discs e.

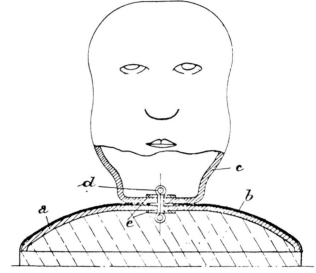

Figure 1

No. 309,788

How to perfect talking *bébés*

This patent adds a supplementary lever which holds back the valve to the little speaking mechanism.

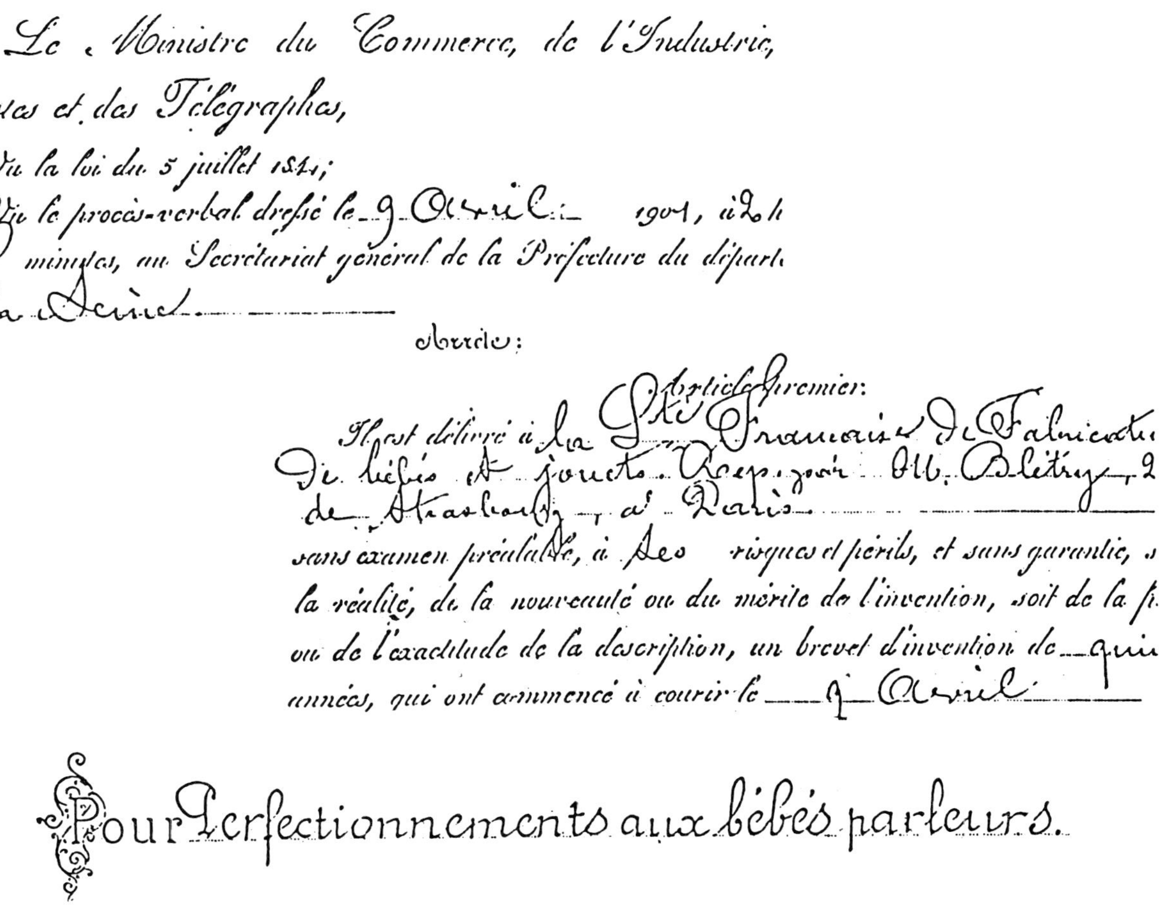

Figure 1

Our invention aims to perfect that which we have already produced in the phonetic mechanisms of talking *bébés* which say "Daddy," "Mommy," or other analagous sounds. The aim is now to produce a crying sound, without it being necessary to lie the doll down, as has been the case up till now.

The attached illustrations represent, as an example, a walking and talking *bébé*, equipped with our perfected phonetic apparatus, which is so arranged as to work automatically, so that while the doll walks, it says "Daddy," "Mommy" in a clear, distinct voice and then, the same utterances, but in a voice badly articulated or crying.

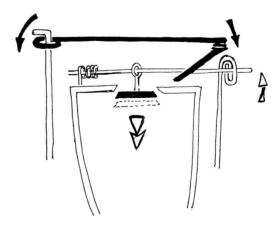

Figure 2

Sound Mechanisms

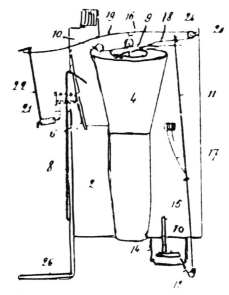

Figure 4

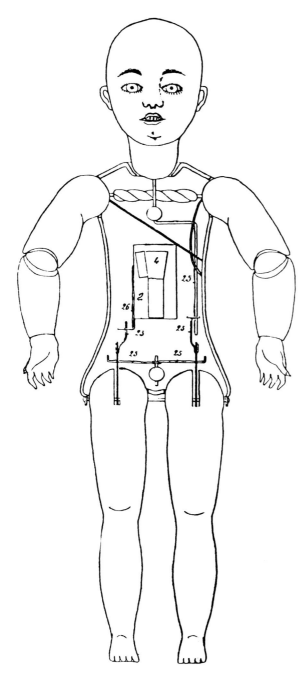

Figure 3

Drawings for patent No. 309,788, a talking *bébé*.

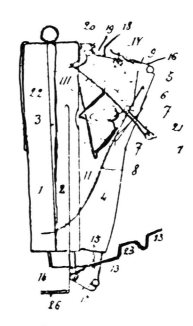

Figure 5

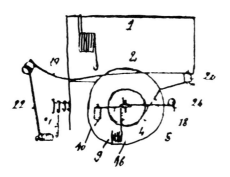

Figure 6

No. 353,622

XX — Articles of Paris and Diverse Industries
1. Games, Toys, Theaters, Races.

Requested April 13, 1905.
Issued July 3, 1905 — Published September 15, 1905.

Talking-Bellows for *bébés*

This patent is for a talking and crying bellows mechanism, combined with a flexible,
exterior control column.

The placement of these organs is such that when the *bébé* is placed on its back, the pressure exerted by the weight of the doll on the control column, fills the bellows, so that the doll cries spontaneously when it is placed upright again.

When the doll is being carried, the same control column can be maneuvered to make it talk or cry; it can also be bent back along the length of the body, so as not to be in the way.

The same bellows-mechanism, can be equipped with a counter-weight acting automatically to modify the opening and closing of the valve and, consequently, the articulation of the sounds emitted by the doll when it is lying down or upright.

Attached to the mobile flask-boards (3) is a metal column (6), bent double (figures 1 and 3), the furthermost end of which passes through an opening in the back of the doll, where it is attached to an articulated column (8). One end of this is in the form of a fork and in this way is connected to the column (6) by an axle (9); the other end is equipped with a cross-bar (10), which functions as a fulcrum, either for the doll when lying flat on a table, or for direct manual maneuvering of the bellows.

The movement around the axis (9) allows the column (8) to be aligned along the length of the body of the doll, as indicated in figure 2. If, after the column (8) has been thus straightened, pressure is applied to the crossbar (10), the flaskboards (3) will become compressed and the bellows distended inside the doll. The same effect is produced when the column (8) is pushed back manually, or when the baby-doll is placed in a lying position on a table.

In this last position, the crossbar (10) provides a fulcrum which is sufficiently stable for the doll to remain on its back. As soon as pressure is released from the column (8), or the doll is picked up again, the flaskboards of the bellows may close, with a springing-back action.

The bellows represented also include a counter-weight (14), mounted on an oscillating column (15), which pivots on the flaskboards (3), the oscillations being limited by a sort of stirrup (6).

This counterweight is connected, by a flexible wire, to the lever which controls the air-valve (5); when the doll is placed lying down, the counterweight stretches the wire, preventing the lever from springing back, until the moment it is freed, by the normal pulling action on the column.

This results in the production of a sound which is continuous and crying. On the contrary, when the *bébé* is upright, the sounds produced, such as "Daddy," "Mommy," are clearly articulated.

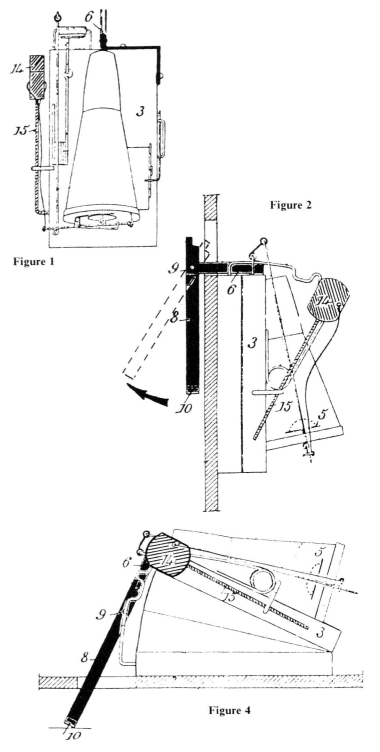

Figure 1

Figure 2

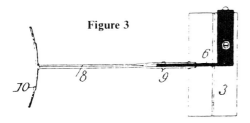

Figure 3

Figure 4

Sound Mechanisms

No. 377, 268

XX — Articles of Paris and diverse industries
1.   Games, Toys, Theaters, Races

Requested April 29, 1907.
Issued July 5, 1907 — Published September 3, 1907.

Toy with Bellows

This patent features an animal whose sound mechanism is placed inside the body:
something which is not new with regard to dolls!

Following the current invention, the bellows function by pressing on the back of the animal, but the bellows are placed within the body, the fixed part being supported by the legs and the mobile part being connected to the back or body. As a consequence of this placement, the legs are not rigidly fixed to the body, as is the case with similar known toys, but they are able to re-enter the body, to a certain extent, when pressure is exerted on the back. The bellows is thus concealed and protected in the interior of the body, instead of forming an ugly and illogical base to the toy. Furthermore, this placement permits the use of the bellows with a soundbox or speaking mechanism, and also allows the bellows to be combined with various accessory mechanisms, none of which are visible on the exterior of the animal; this last result was not able to be achieved with the sort of placement known hitherto, because of the difficulties involved in having the mechanical workings pass across the legs, which are generally thin and sometimes made of iron wire.

When the duck's back is pressed, the pressure is transmitted by the pegs (5) to the flaskboards (3) and this then moves, with the body, around the hinge of the bellows. The bellows then produces a sound simultaneously with the duck's movement.

So as to make the toy even more entertaining, the duck's movement is accompanied by an opening and closing of the beak. To achieve this effect, the bottom part of the beak is articulated on an axis and is extended, at the back, into a tail, attached to this is a string (10), which passes around the two steering pins and is fixed to one of the branches of a lever (12), the middle section of which is articulated on the mobile flask, and the other branch of which is a channel, which leads to a fixed point (14) on the fixed flaskboard. When the bellows close, the lever is forced to oscillate and pull the string, which then activates the beak; this part is then raised by the action of a metal or rubber spring, when the bellows slacken.

The action of the bellows, or more generally, the movement of the body in relation to the legs, may also be combined with several other mechanisms, with a view to activating the wings or the tail or some other part of the toy, regardless of the type of animal it may represent.

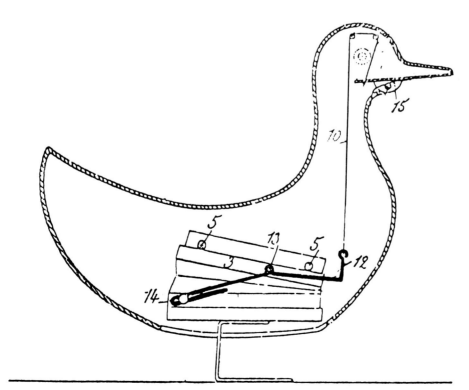

Figure 1

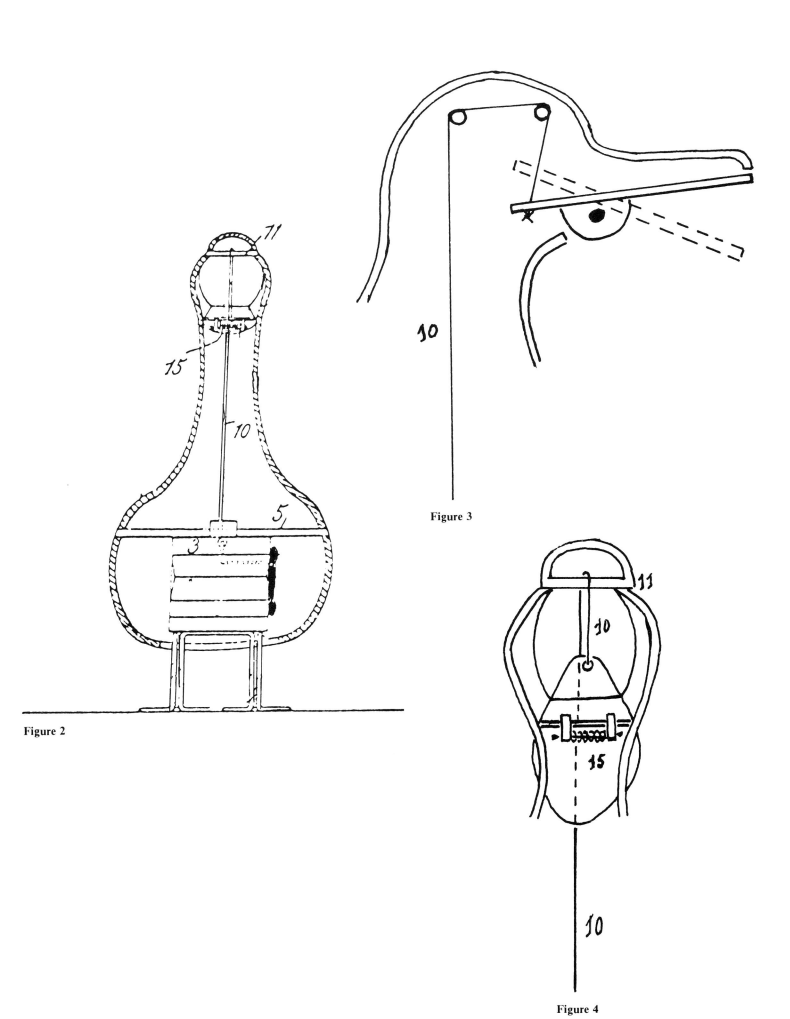

Figure 2

Figure 3

Figure 4

Sound Mechanisms

No. 399,883

XX — Paris Articles and diverse industries.
1.   Games, Toys, Theaters, Races.

Requested February 24, 1909.
Issued May 7, 1909 — Published July 9, 1909.

Speaking Doll

A patent which will interest lovers of mechanical music.
Its theoretical interest lies in its complexity, being one of the best examples of the excess of technicality in doll-making,
but at the same time, a good specimen of miniaturization.

The aim of the present invention is a speaking doll, with a phonograph, the placement of which permits the doll to speak clearly in all positions.

To date, the dolls equipped with a phonograph have had the sound-reproducer resting on the striated surface of the cylinder or of the record, in the same way as in gramophones and other speaking machines. The result is that if the doll is turned in certained directions, the reproducer deviates from the striated surface, under the influence of the weight, and thus all production of sound ceases.

This invention obviates this disadvantage, in the sense that the reproducer is guided, such that it always remains at an invariable distance from the striated surface, the surface of the cylinder, for example.

It cannot deviate from this surface, even if the apparatus is turned upside down. Nevertheless, it is essential to be able to move the sapphire, or the needle, without touching the surface of the cylinder; this result is obtained by connecting the arm of the needle to the turntable, by means of some sort of articulated system. Preferably this system should be suitably balanced, so as to be unaffected by the weight, regardless of the position. It should also be able to be moved at will, at the same time as the drivescrew deviates the sapphire, or needle, from the striated surface, before guiding the sound-reproducer back to its position of rest.

The attached illustration, by way of an example, shows a way of putting into practice the aim of the invention.

Figure 1 is a partial vertical cross-section of a speaking doll.

Figure 2 is a vertical cross-section of the sound-reproducing device.

Figure 3 is a plan of this device, as seen from underneath.

Inside the body of the doll is fixed a turntable, complete with all the workings of a phonograph which, in this example, consists of a cylinder and a sound-reproducing device with sapphire (5).

On one side, the sound-reproducer is guided, parallel to the cylinder, by a sliding-block (6) which is fixed to the turn-table and which connects to the sound box by means of a sliding-bolt. The opposite side of the sound-reproducer is guided by a column (8), which is connected to the sides of the turntable, and along which glide the flanges (9), which are fixed to the sound-box.

Thus guided, the aforementioned box remains always at an invariable distance from the cylinder, even if the apparatus is turned upside down.

The sapphire (5) is connected to the turntable (10), by means of a lever or arm (11) and a small connecting-rod (13); this lever (11) is articulated on the large arm of a cranked-lever (13), the axis of oscillation of which is carried by a rigid arm, fixed to the sound box; activated by a spring attached to the arm, the lever (13) extends to move the pivot of the lever (11) towards the cylinder, so that the sapphire remains pressed against the cylinder and the connecting-rod (12) remains extended. The vibrations of the sapphire, when the cylinder turns, produce variations in the tension of the connecting-rod and, consequently, corresponding vibrations of the turntable (10). This functions independently of the position of the doll.

The sound-reproducing mechanism works by means of a transferred movement from a screw, the rotation of which is connected to that of the cylinder, and from a screw-nut, or part thereof, which is fixed by means of a hinge, to the sound-box and is pressed against the screw by springs.

Parallel to the screw is an off-center shaft, one end of which passes across the side of the doll, and which is equipped with a button, by means of which it may be turned. In the position of rest, shown in the illustration, the shaft exerts no pressure on the screw-nut; but if it is turned, about half a revolution, it pushes the end of the screw-nut, displacing it away from the screw, so that the transferred movement of the sound-reproducing mechanism ceases; at the same time, the screw-nut pushes against the small arm of the cranked-lever (13) and, as a consequence, raises the sapphire-arm (11), which then displaces the sapphire of the cylinder. It is thus possible to move the sound-reproducer and all the workings which are attached to it, without the sapphire making contact with the

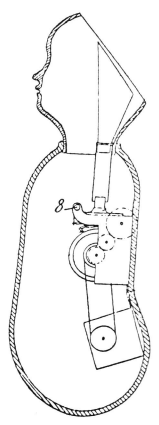

Figure 1

cylinder; this displacement may be obtained, for example, with the help of a type of pulley, attached to the sound-box.

So as to direct the emitted sounds into the head of the doll, it would be advantageous to unblock the central tube of the sound-reproducer, by means of an oblong speaker, fixed in the body of the doll, the narrow orifice of this speaker, placed in the doll's neck, being joined to a second speaker, the opening of which is placed in the doll's head. The two speakers may be connected by means of a socket-joint, which allows the doll's head to rotate in all directions.

Summary

The principal characteristics of the present invention are as follows:

1. The direction of the sound-reproducing mechanism by means of some type of sliding-block, which maintain it fixed, at an invariable distance from the striated surface;

2. The connecting of the needle (or sapphire) to the turntable by means of an articulated system, permitting it to deviate from the striated surface, without touching the sound-reproducer;

3. The device connecting the sapphire to the turntable comprising a lever-arm which is articulated, in part, to a small connecting-rod, attached to the turntable, and also, in part, articulated to another lever for maneuvering;

4. The mechanism allowing the sapphire and the turntable to come together at the same time as the drive-nuts of the sound-reproducer is caused to deviate from its screw.

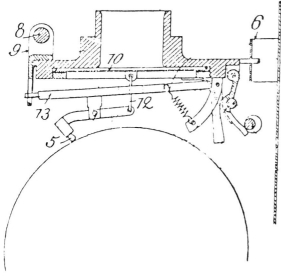

Figure 2

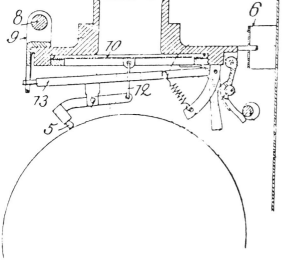

Figure 3

Sound Mechanisms

No. 413,524

XII — Precision instruments, electricity.
2. Mechanisms of Physics and Chemistry,
   Optical and Acoustic Devices

Requested March 11, 1910.
Issued May 28, 1910 — Published August 11, 1910.

Phonograph for a speaking doll

This concerns a study of record gramophone technique which is of a very high level.
Like the previous patent, it may be of interest to lovers of mechanical music.
This patent is reproduced in its entirety, without amendment or editing,
because its precision and complexity permit no simplification.

The characteristic arrangement of the workings of this mechanism assure functioning in all positions, automatic return of the sliding-carriage to the center of the record, when it has reached the periphery and its automatic arrest in this position — ready to recommence when the mechanism is once again set in motion; furthermore, the mechanism is arranged so as to permit the changing of the record very easily.

The accompanying illustrations, by way of example, explain the essential features of the invention.

Figure 1 is a side-view of the phonograph

Figure 2 is a front-view of the same, the speaker having been removed.

Figure 3 is a partial cross-section, along the line AA in figure 2.

This apparatus comprises a large turntable (1) and a small turntable (2), connected one to the other by cross-bars and, between them, creating the sort of movement which is characteristic of a clock-mechanism; (3) denotes the barrel, (4) the receiving shaft and (5) the regulator, which controls the speed of rotation in the manner already familiar.

On the extremity of the shaft (4) which crosses the turntable (1) is fixed a flange (6), which serves as a support for the record (7). The record is kept fast against the flange by means of a sprocket (8) screwed to the end of the shaft and by a washer (9) interposed between this sprocket and the record. Attached is the upper part of turntable (1), by means of a hinge (10), is a mobile framework (11), which supports the sound-reproducer (12) and the instruments which are attached to it; this framework can lie parallel to the record and be maintained in this position, by means of a spring-latch (14), against a stop (13). By lowering the latch, the framework (11) is freed and raised at the hinge (10), completely releasing the record (7), so that it may be easily changed.

By means of two flanges (15), the framework (11) supports the screw (16), which serves to move the sound-reproducing device; fixed to this screw is a cog (17), which engages with the sprocket (8), when the framework is in the position of functioning shown in the illustration.

Also attached to the framework (11) are two columns (18 and 19), which are parallel to the screw (16); one of these columns (18) serves to direct the sound box (12), which, to this effect, supports a pipe (20) the sliding motion of which exerts a gentle friction on this column. Column (19) serves to guide a piece called the carriage (21), which slides easily along the column. At the back part of the box (12) is fixed a short column (22), which is fixed into a cleft (23) at the cranked end of the carriage (21). This results in the sound-reproducer and the carriage being thus obliged to move, together, along the columns (18 and 19), even though they may oscillate around these columns, independently of each other.

The movement of the carriage and the sound-reproducer is obtained by means of a portion of a wing-nut (24) which is fixed to the carriage (21) and which may engage with the screw (16). To maintain this engagement of the wing-nut and screw the framework (11) supports a narrow steering-shaft (25), against which slides the end of the carriage which is opposed to the column (19).

Also attached to the framework (11) is a cranked lever (26), the arm of which ends in a rounded tip (28), and which also has a projection (29) which is placed so as to make contact with the carriage (21); the arm of the lever (27) extends a short distance away from the brake-disc (30) of the speed-regulator and is activated by a spring (31), which pushes it against the edge of this disc, thereby stopping all clock-movement. The lever (26) is normally prevented from obeying the action of the spring (31) by a prop (32), one end of which is articulated (33) on to the framework (11) and the other end of which is engaged under the round tip (28) as indicated in the illustration. A column (34) fixed on to the prop

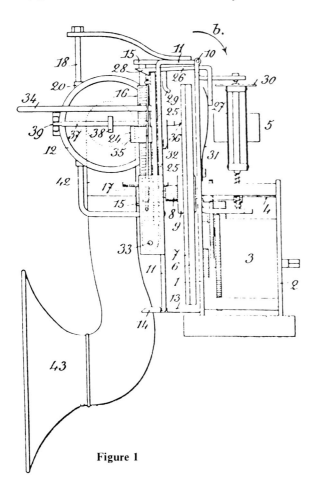

Figure 1

(32), makes a projection on the outside of the doll's body (not shown). This allows the prop to be pushed back under the round tip (28) when it has escaped, as will be seen further on, under the action of a return spring (35).

The sapphire of needle (36) is carried by a column (37), which passes freely through a ring (38), which is fixed at the center of the diaphragm and which is articulated (39) on the box (12). So as to maintain the contact between the sapphire and the record (7) and between the ring (38) and the column (37), a spring (40) is attached to the shaft connected with the sound-reproducer (22) on one side, and on the opposite side, to the shaft connected with the carriage (41). The traction of this spring turns the sound-reproducer around the column (18), in the direction of the arrow (a) and, consequently, maintains the desired contact on (38) and (7). The megaphone (42), to which the detachable speaker (43) is fixed, is attached to the sound box (12).

This apparatus functions as follows: The prop (32) being interlocked with the round tip (28) and maintaining the lever (26, 27) well away from the brake-disc (30), the clock movement makes the record turn at the same time as the screw (16); thus the carriage (21) is drawn upwards by the screw (16), which is engaged with the wing-nut (24), the end of the carriage being so guided as to slide against posterior face of the narrow steering-shaft (25).

The carriage draws with it the sound-reproducer with speaker, the sapphire being maintained pressed against the record (7), by the action of the spring (40) in such a way as to ensure the reproduction of the voice recorded on the record. When the extremity of the carriage arrives at the end of the steering-shaft (25), the projection (29) meets the carriage, so that the arm of the cranked lever (26) is raised and the rounded tip (28) releases the prop (32), under the action of the return spring (35). As soon as the prop is released the lever (26, 27) oscillates in the direction of the arrow (6), under the action of the spring (31); this oscillation results in the arm (27) pushing against the disc (30), thereby immediately stopping all clock movement; furthermore, the projection (29) pushes the carriage (21), thanks to an appropriately inclined plane, either on the projection or on the carriage, such that the extremity of the carriage passes over the steering-shaft (25), and the wing-nut (24) is kept apart from the screw (16). The result is that the carriage, no longer being raised by the screw, lowers to its point of departure, sliding along the length of the column (19) and of the anterior face of the shaft (25) until it is below the shaft.

To set the apparatus in motion again, it suffices simply to push the column (34), so that it causes the prop (32) to slide underneath the tip (28) and the arm (26). Thus the carriage will be pushed by the prop behind the shaft (25) and the wing-nut (24) will consequently engage with the screw (16) at the same time as the arm (27) frees the disc (30), permitting the clock movement to once again, activate the screw (16).

Without deviating from this invention, the forms and positions of the various parts of the mechanism may be varied, just as the non-essential details of construction specified above, may also be altered, without affecting the functioning.

Summary

The principal features of the present phonograph for speaking dolls are as follows:

1. The placement of the motor and the speed regulator on a fixed stage and the placement of the sound-reproducing device and its drive-screw on a mobile framework, permitting the changing of the record easily;
2. The fitting of the record to the motor-shaft, by means of a sprocket which constitutes a screw-nut, screwed to the end of the shaft;
3. The engaging of this screw-nut with the cog-wheel fixed to the control-screw of the sound-reproducer;
4. The steering-device of the carriage drawing with it the sound-reproducer;
5. The brake-lever being maintained inactive, during the functioning of the mechanism, by an oscillating prop and freed from this prop by the arrival of the carriage at the end-point, all movement ceasing under the action of a spring;
6. The action of this lever on the carriage disengaging it from the control-screw, at the same time as the cessation of movement;
7. The arrangement of the sound-reproducing device, the shaft supporting the sapphire-case and the mobile megaphone.

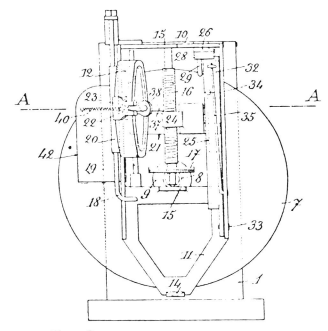

Figure 2

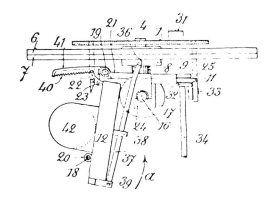

Figure 3

Sound Mechanisms

No. 586,685

XX — Articles of Paris and diverse industries.
1. Games, Toys, Theaters, Races.

Requested September 29, 1924 at 17 minutes past 4 o'clock, in Paris.
Issued January 8, 1925 — Published April 1, 1925.

Speaking *Bébé*

This "invention" is not highly original and is very little different from that of patent 377,268.
Nevertheless, the dating of the object is assured by this patent.

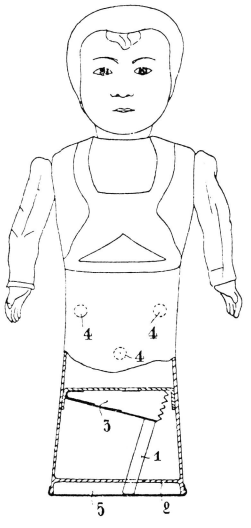

Figure 1

The aim of the present invention is the production of a *bébé* or any other speaking-toy, which is characterized by a mechanism which may be placed in any suitable position in the body of the doll, the emitted sounds being reinforced by the aid of orifices also placed suitably, and covered by elastic membranes.

The accompanying illustration represents, by way of example, a form of the speaking *bébé*:

This particular doll is fashioned in a rigid form, but, obviously, it need not necessarily be so. A rigid column (1) is positioned in the lower part of the doll. This column passes through an opening in the inner lining (2) and is fixed at its other extremity, to a bellows (3), equipped with all the devices which usually accompany such a mechanism — valve, tongue etc. In another part of the doll's body, the orifice (4), covered by an elastic skin, permit a stronger resonance of the sounds emitted by the bellows. The extremity of the column is housed in its compartment (5) covered by a skin or a gauze, which allows a certain pressure to be exerted on the said extremity, which as a consequence then activates the bellows (3).

No. 432,650

XX — Articles from Paris and various industries.
1.   Games, Toys, Theaters, Races.

Petitioned October 8, 1910.
Delivered October 9, 1911 — Published December 11, 1911.

(Patent, the delivery of which was postponed in execution of article 11 S 7
of the law of July 5, 1844, modified by the April 7, 1902, law.)

Nursing *Bébé* (*Bébé têteur*)

This is a nursing *bébé* whose suction bulb is within the body and not in the head.
Note that this device refers to the great concern for assembling eyes.

The current invention aims for a nursing *bébé* whose nursing device is arranged in a special way in order to clear the interior of the head-area, which facilitates the installment of the mobile eye system, in case the *bébé* has to be sleeping as well as nursing.

Another advantage is to leave an ample space in the doll abdomen to install the talking system, in case the *bébé* has to be talking as well.

Moreover, the device is arranged in such a way that no nozzle should be permanently fixed in protrusion on the *bébé* mouth in order to accommodate the bottle tube; thus the *bébé* is rid of the bottle and consequently resembles any other baby without being disfigured by a nozzle coming out of its mouth.

Other characteristics of this invention are in the use of a hollow-block to lodge the pear-shaped suction bulb and to install the device within the toy body, and in the use of a stop component suited for limiting the head rotation in order to prevent the over-twisting and the cutting of the suction intake tube.

The nursing device requires a rubber tube, of which one end leads to the *bébé* mouth, and the other to the rubber pear-shaped bulb which is placed in the back, facing an opening, that allows squeezing it with a finger.

According to this invention, the tube goes through the neck easily and rises inside the head, to go back down to the mouth, forming a loop that is fixed to either side of the head, roughly around the ear area; with a certain amount of glue. This laterally-placed loop does not obstruct either the installation nor the functioning of the sleeper's eyes.

The end or the tube adjacent to the mouth is fitted with a ring made of rubber or other material, which is attached to the mouth inner surface with some glue.

On the other hand, the rubber bottle tube is fitted with a nozzle made of wood or some other hard material which can be easily inserted in the mouth opening.

A wood block is attached to the inside of the doll, allowing one reduced area and one large area 10; the latter, being hollow in order to lodge the pear-shaped bulb, is cut with an opening to allow the tube through. A vertical rod passes through the reduced area; the upper part of this rod is attached to a hoop that is sealed inside the doll neck, and the lower end is bent under part 10 of the block. This extremity can swing between two bearings 14, made of cork or other, is attached under the block in such a way that the rod cannot rise and that its rotation is limited. The doll head, rigidly attached to this rod, is thus rested on the body and cannot be twisted in such a way that would damage the suction intake tube.

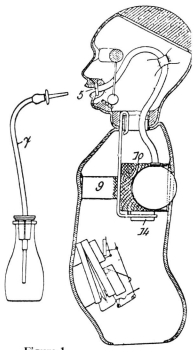

Figure 1

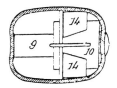

Figure 2

Nursing and Smoking Mechanisms

No. 16,459

1st Addition
to the Patent

No. 432,650

XX — Articles from Paris and various industries.
1. Games, Toys, Theaters, Races.

(Main patent taken on October 8, 1910)

Petitioned September 6, 1912.
Delivered November 22, 1912 — Published February 6, 1913.

Nursing *Bébé (Bébé têteur)*

This patent is for a smoking *bébé* without any originality from the nursing doll of the main patent.

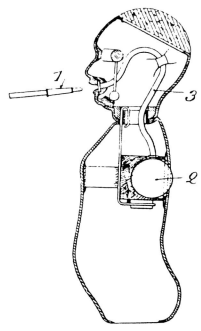

Figure 1

This addition aims for a modification brought to the nursing *bébé* described in the main patent, modification which consists mainly of substituting a cigarette-holder or another smoker's article whose mouthpiece could be inserted in the doll's mouth in place of the bottle mouthpiece.

The functioning of the pear-shaped rubber bulb, placed in the toy's body and connected to the mouth by a flexible tube, allows maintaining the burning of a cigarette placed in the cigarette-holder, with the effect of drafts inhaled and compressed by means of this bulb, so that the doll appears to be smoking.

There will not be any modification necessary in the construction of either the doll body or the organs that it contains.

It is understood that instead of representing a *bébé*, the toy could represent any individual.

No. 332,857

XX — Articles from Paris and small industries.
1. Toy business.

Patent for fifteen years petitioned June 6, 1903.
Delivered September 5, 1903 — Published November 10, 1903.

Improvements of animated objects

This is about an intricate toy, almost an automaton, combining a mechanical doll,
talking and gesticulating, with a car.
Its originality is that the doll could be separated from the car.

The present invention aims for improvements of animated toys and consists in greater detail in the combination of a mechanical doll, talking or making gestures, with a car available to support this doll and to activate it by the wheel-motion when the car rolls along on the ground, this combination being accomplished in such a way that the doll could easily be removed from the car and still be activated by hand as an ordinary mechanical doll.

Here, doll means not only a small human shape made of wood, cardboard or other material, but any animated object with human or animal shape as well.

Likewise, the shape and the lay-out of the car bear no significance on this present invention.

By virtue of examples, two ways of carrying out the invention object are going to be described, in which the car is a type of "dog-cart" and the doll, a type of "*bébé*" blowing kisses and turning its head."

Figure 1. is a vertical cut-section of the first-stage of the improved toy

Figure 2. is a drawing of the same object viewed from below.

Figures 3 to 5 show variants of the gear mechanism.

Figure 6 is a vertical section of another stage of the toy.

Figure 7. is a cross section made, following line AB of Figure 6.

The doll was represented naked for more clarity, but in practice it could be dressed without interfering with its functioning.

In Figures 1 and 2, (a) designates a mechanical doll whose head and arms are jointed in a known way in order to blow kisses with both arms; (b) designates a dog-cart built in a known way, to which a particular device was adapted to accommodate and activate the doll. This device requires a support cross-piece, attached to the car, and on top of which a swivelling pendulum is mounted 2, of which one end is connected by a small driving-rod 3, to a starting-handle 4 formed on the axle 5, and the opposite end is connected to the starting-handle by a small driving-rod 6 - attached to a vertical rod 8 which is driven below, in the cross piece 1 and above, in the car seat 9. By this lay-out, the axle rotation 5, rigidly locked with the wheels 10, is intended to transmit the oscillation motion to the beam 2 and consequently to the starting-handle 7, as well as to the rod 8.

The upper end of this rod is flattened and could be fitted in the hole of a similar shape perforated in the clutch 11, mounted in the lower part of the doll trunk so that it could turn.

The clutch 11 is fixed to a vertical shaft 12, which is equipped with a cross-member 14 inside the doll body. On the other hand another vertical shaft, or almost vertical 13, is connected to the doll head at the top, and to the arms and forearms at the bottom, by a starting-handle 16 and by strings 17; the shaft 15 is supported by a cross member 18 and the starting-handle 16 is extended by a groove 19 in which the starting-handle 13 is inserted, in such a way that upon oscillating the clutch 11 with the shaft 12, shaft 15 must oscillate equally with the doll head, while the arms are being alternately bent and extended. Consequently, making the car roll is sufficient to produce these head and arm motions when clutch 11 is engaged on rod 8; the doll is then seated in the car and turns its head while it blows kisses, right and left, as it moves forward. When the doll is removed from the car, clutch 11 is naturally disengaged from rod 8; the head and arm motions could then be manually produced as with other known mechanical dolls.

The described driving-gear device transmits a double oscillation to the driving-shaft 12 at each wheel revolution 10. In certain cases, it is better to use a reduced speed transmission, in order to send out the doll's kisses at wider intervals. For example, Figures 3 and 4 show such a device, in elevation and in vertical section; this device requires a pinion 20 fixed on the motor axle 5, and meshing with a toothed wheel 21 of which the axle 22 is mounted in a box 23 fixed to the car; an eccentric gear 24 is fixed on this axle and engaged in a groove of an oscillating lever 25, mounted on the box 23; finally, the lever 25 is connected to the handle 7 of a vertical rod 8 by a small connecting-rod 26, the vertical turning in a sleeve 27 fixed on the box cover 23. When the axle 5 turns, the wheel 21 spins at a reduced speed, and at each wheel revolution, the eccentric gear transmits an oscillating motion to the lever 25, and consequently to the rod 8 which transmits this motion to the doll as it was described before.

Another simpler device (Figure 5) includes a small pulley 28 wedged up on motor axle 5, a bigger pulley 29 connected to the previously mentioned by a belt 30, and by a small driving-rod 31 which connects pulley 29 to a starting-handle 7 fixed to rod 8: at each revolution of the big pulley, that is for example every two or three revolutions of axle 5, starting-handle 7 and rod 8 undergo a double oscillation which they transmit to the doll.

Figures 6 and 7 show a lay-out of how the doll turns its head, greets with one arm and talks while the car is rolling along. For this purpose, the car carries a box for support 23 in which axle 33 is mounted, the axle equipped with a toothed wheel 21, an eccentric gear 24 and a starting-handle 34. Wheel 21 meshes with a pinion 20 fixed on the engine axle: eccentric gear 24 is inserted in a groove 35 of an oscillating lever 25 which activates starting-handle 7 of rod 8 by push-rod 26, as in display indicated in Figure 1 and 2; finally starting-handle 34 activates, by means of push-rod 36, a slide 37 vertically guided by box 23 and by permanent slide 38.

Slide 37 ends with a nose (spout) 39 supposedly to engage with the corresponding nose 40 of a mobile rod 41, which is guided in a fixed support 42 located against the back of the car seat 43. Rod 41 can move vertically and crosswise, with springs 44 and 45 pulling it, the first spring upwards, and the second to the left (Figure 7): this rod carrying in its upper part a clasp 46, in which a ring 47 is inserted, the ring being connected to a string 48 which goes through two holes in the doll body.

One end of above mentioned string is attached to a pair of bellows 49 fixed on the front part of the body and equipped with a

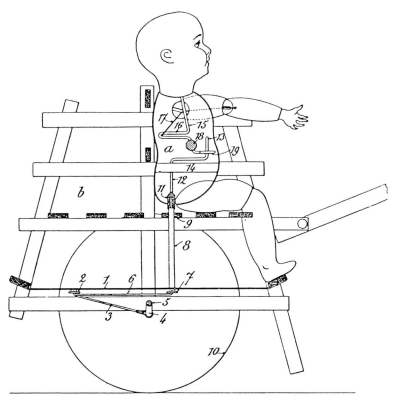

Figure 1

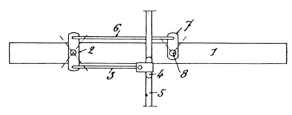

Figure 2

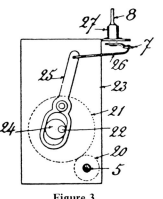

Figure 3

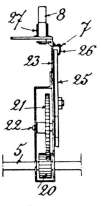

Figure 4

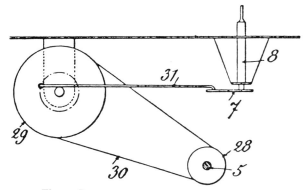

Figure 5

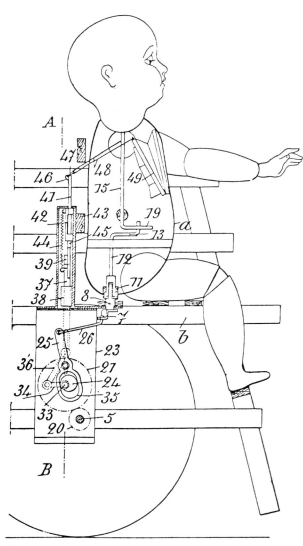

Figure 6

Patent drawings for No. 332,857.

known appropriate sound producing device; the other end of the string is attached to one of the doll's arms in such a way that it could bend upon pulling on the string.

It is understood that while the car rolls along, pinion 20 turns wheel 21 and axle 33: the eccentric gear thus oscillates lever 25 and starting-handle 7, rod 8 with clutch 11, shaft 12 and starting-handle 13, handle with slide 19, shaft 15 and the doll's head. At the same time, starting-handle 34 raises and lowers slide 37: upon lowering, nose (spout) 39 drives rod 41 downwards until inclined plane 50 of nose 40 meets a fixed stud 51 which requires it to move aside, so that rod 41 misses slide 37 and rises abruptly under the action of spring 44; through this mean, string 48 being attached to rod 41 is pulled gently downwards and suddenly released, thus it is appropriate for good functioning of bellows 49; the doll's moving arm is activated by the same string 48.

When slide 37 is brought back to point of origin, nose 39 separates nose 40 to the right and engages above it in order to pull it down again.

The doll can be removed easily after opening clasp 46 and disengaging ring 47; clutch 11 is out of gear with rod 8 as in displays described previously. The doll is then operated manually on ring 47 to talk or to salute.

Without straying from the present invention, mechanical displays of the execution procedures above mentioned could certainly be modified, by all means appropriate to the fitting-up of the car and the doll, and in the nature of the gestures, etc...that the doll makes.

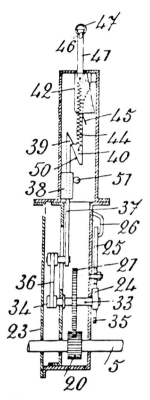

Figure 7

Walking and Multiple Functions

No. 346,106

XX — Articles of Paris and diverse industries.
1. Games, Toys, Theater, Races.

Requested September 7, 1904.
Issued November 11, 1904 — Published January 5, 1905.

Walking toy

This patent is for a walking toy comprised of an animal harnessed to a vehicle,
the legs of this animal being contrived with a known mechanism.

This mechanism consists, essentially, of a crankshaft (on the handles of which the legs are articulated) and a narrow steering shaft, which crosses the channels formed at the top of the legs.

The invention consists in the first place, in the application of this type of mechanism, which until now was reserved for cheap toys made exclusively of tin, to high quality toys, of greater dimensions and made of various different materials, so as to give the animals a much more life-like appearance.

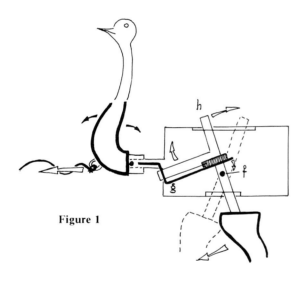

Figure 1

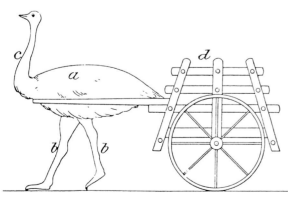

Figure 2

Another characteristic of the invention is that the animal's walking is determined not by the pushing, from the back to the front, of a vehicle equipped with some sort of motor, but instead by a traction exerted manually on the body of the animal or better still, by the control of a motor placed inside the body, causing the crankshaft to turn.

The invention also consists in using the movement of the crankshaft or the legs of the animal, to move the head, making it oscillate from front to back, right to left and so on.

To detail the body of an animal, for example an ostrich, mounted on feet or legs and equipped with an oscillating neck: the body is harnessed to a vehicle, in which, for example, a doll may be placed.

The body, the neck and the legs of the animal are made of heavy cardboard and then covered with feathers, painted and worked on, so as to reproduce, as far as possible, the appearance of the real animal.

A metal cage, supporting a crankshaft f and a steering column g, is fixed inside the body of the animal.

In the top part of each leg a metal T-shape h is fixed, the vertical part of which is guided smoothly into the grooves at the top and bottom of the cage while the horizontal part is pierced by a groove which smoothly crosses the steering column g. Furthermore, the metal T-pieces h are crossed by the crankshaft f so that the legs are joined to one another and are thereby forced to make elliptical movements when they are activated.

The neck is mounted on an axle which is borne by the supports of the cage, in such a way that the head and neck can rock backwards and forwards; in addition, inside the body there is an extension bearing a counterweight, which presses on the crankshaft and is raised, alternatively by it. This results in the oscillating movement of the neck.

To make the toy move, it is necessary only to pull it, with the aid of a string attached to a ring at the neck.

When the control is mechanical, it is easy enough to include, within the cage, a cylinder containing a spring-motor, which can be connected to the crankshaft by suitable cogs.

The details of construction of this particular toy may, of course, be modified; for example, the movement of the neck could be controlled by the top ends of the metal pieces h, the neck being placed higher up than is indicated in Figure 2. Instead of making the animal a biped, it could be equipped with four legs, or paws, which could be controlled, in pairs, in the same way as outlined previously; two or more animals could even be harnessed to the same vehicle.

No. 351,452

XX — Articles from Paris and various industries.
1. Games, Toys, Theaters, Races.

Petitioned February 11, 1905.
Delivered May 6, 1905 — Published July 18, 1905.

Mechanical *Bébé*

A mechanical *bébé* that walks, turns its head, kisses and talks is not a new idea.
The originality of this patent is in the assembly with hard friction of thighs on the trunk.

The present invention aims for a mechanical *bébé* that could make complicated motions when starting to walk, such as turning its head, blowing kisses, and talking.

As an example, the attached drawing shows a production procedure of the invention object:

Figures 1 and 2 are vertical sections of a mechanical *bébé*.

Figures 3 and 4 show the details of a connection part on a greater scale.

The doll's legs are jointed on a common cross-axle 3 which is fixed to the hollow body by metallic parts, so that the legs can swing back and forth.

To activate the interior mechanism of the doll, each leg is equipped with a lever 6 jointed on axle 3 and arranged so that it could act upon a pendulum 7 which moves around a fixed vertical axle 8; this lever is driven forward around axle 3, when the leg

bends backwards around the same axle, by means of a pin 9 that goes through slit 10 through which passes lever 6. This slit allows the leg to be raised forward in relation to lever 6 and consequently to give the doll the sitting position.

In order to avoid the over-swinging of the leg in relation to lever 6, an elastic friction between that lever and the inner surface of the slit 10 is produced. To the effect, lever 6 is made up by a metallic thread, folded and bent according to the shape represented in Figures 3 and 4, in order to form a loop 11 and in arm 12 the loop surround loosely axle 3 and constitutes an articulation eye of lever 6.

Parts 6, 11 and 12 form an awkward set that has to be warped in order to fit in slit 10, so that it would rub elastically against the flat parallel inner surface of that slit when the set is being rotated around axle 3. The doll's legs can thus remain steady in all assigned

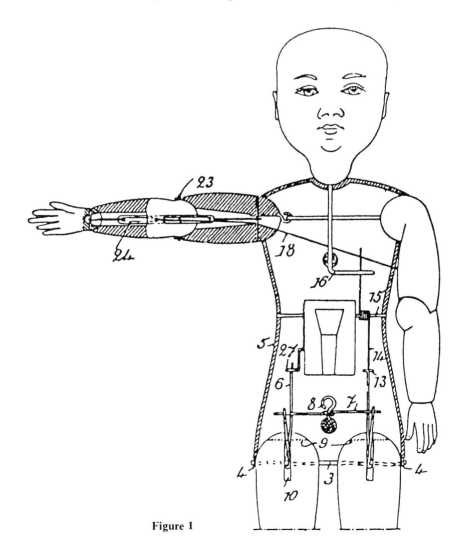

Figure 1

positions instead of collapsing under their weight as soon as it is left alone.

When one of the levers 6 is pushed forward by pin 9 of the corresponding leg, pendulum 7 is in turn pushed by the lever mentioned and forces the other lever 6 to move backwards, acting on pin 9 of the opposite leg. The result is that the bending of one leg backwards determines automatically the bending of the other leg forward, which appropriately assures the doll's walking motion.

The upper part of lever 6 mounted on the left leg is bent a lot more in order to form a cross-eye 13 in which one end of a pendulum 14 is inserted, the pendulum oscillates on a fixed horizontal axle 15 whose opposite end acts on lever 16 inter-independent with the doll's head. This lever is equipped with one eye in which pendulum 14 is inserted so that the handle has to follow the forward and backward motion of the pendulum, and thus turns the doll's head right and then left at each step.

The same pendulum 14 acts on a thread 18 of which one end is fixed to the doll's body and the opposite goes through a hole in the right arm, to be attached to the forearm 22, passing in front of joint 23. When the top of the pendulum 14 is moved forward, it pushes the thread 18 again in front of it and forces it to extend the forearm 22 forward, to meet the action of an elastic string 24 that passes behind joint 23 and is attached to the shoulder by one end, and the forearm by the other; that way, the doll makes the gesture of a kiss.

At the same time, lever 6 mounted on the right leg can activate the bellows 25 of a speaker 26 saying "Mommy," "Daddy"; to that effect, the upper end is engaged in an eye 27 fixed on a moving flap of the bellows and thus forcing the flap to move in coordination with the legs, while making the doll talk.

The construction of levers 6 that can produce these various effects by the walking motion transmitted to the doll is extremely simple, solid, and costs little. It can be modified according to the arrangement of the mechanism that these levers have to activate, but in all cases the awkward shape of each lever set 6, which has to produce an elastic friction on the joint inner-face as was described above, will be characteristic element of the invention.

Of course, the invention is applicable to all kinds of mechanical dolls, disregarding the number and the nature of motions that animate them.

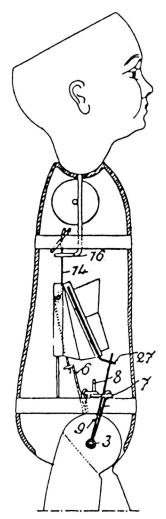

Figure 2

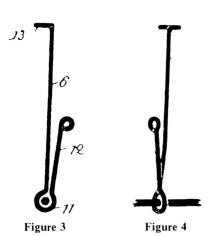

Figure 3   Figure 4

No. 351,452   Add 4,688

Main Patent taken out February 11, 1905.
Petitioned April 8, 1905.
Delivered June 30, 1905. — Published September 16, 1905.

Mechanical *Bébé*

This device for assembling thighs with heavy friction, the main patent, could be used at all other joints to save rubber, a matter of great concern at the beginning of the 20th century.

As an example the attached drawing shows a production stage of the device applied to the knee joint.

The leg ends on top with a knee-cap which is inserted in a cavity made in the lower end of the thigh. This knee-cap is equipped with a slit or vertical mortise joint, bent from back to front, and through which passes axle 5.

The leg and the thigh are connected together by a metallic rod 6 that consists of threaded part 6a screwed in the thigh, and of a hook-shaped part 6b that surrounds axle 5.

Hook 6b is bent in such a way that it would produce an awkward shape, when disengaged, and that would then undergo a certain elastic warping when being inserted in the slit. The friction that occurs at the inner surface of the slit could be varied accordingly in intensity by deviating the tip of the hook more or less sharply. The leg consequently experiences certain difficulty moving around axle 5 in relation to rod 6a, in other words to thigh 3 which is inter-independant of it.

When the assembled parts must be able to turn, one in relation to the other around their longitudinal axle, this motion is possible due to the rotation independence of rod 6 in the thigh. It is the case of elbow joints and head joints etc. As far as knee joints, on the other hand, it is better to prevent this rotation, for example by means of a peg 7 which is fixed in the thigh, the head of the peg being inserted in the slit at some distance in front or behind rod 6.

In the general execution procedure, the thigh is solid, but it can also be hollow; in the latter case, it is better to fit, at the base, a massive plug through which rod 6a passes. Of course, the rod can be fixed or somehow held in place within the thigh, for example by a hook, stiff or elastic, formed at the internal end, or by a nut, a pin, a bolt, and so on.

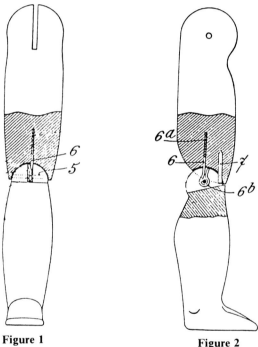

Figure 1   Figure 2

No. 456,447

XX — Articles from Paris and various industries.
1. Games, Toys, Theaters, Races.

Petitioned April 8, 1913.
Delivered June 18, 1913 — Published August 26, 1913.

Improvements on dolls and toys

This patent has two aims:
a friction joint system (again saving rubber), and
an independent leg device allowing the walking doll to sit down.

The present invention aims for improvements in the walking and talking dolls and toys whose head and arms are being moved simultaneously with the legs.

One of the improvements relates to the fitting of the arms in order to modify voluntarily the relative position: each arm is inter-independant on a stud placed in the shoulder, and fitted with lubrication in a socket or hollow axle which is placed across the body and which could be moved by the motor system swivelling around its axle. The friction of the studs within the socket is sufficient to engage the arms in the swivelling of the socket, but still allows easy rotation of each arm in relation to the socket in any desired position. This arrangement eliminates at the same time the well known inconvenience in the fitting up of the arms by means of elastic strings.

The studs could be replaced by sockets fixed to the arms and fitted by friction to the axle ends, solid or hollow that go through the body.

Another improvement is in the use of particular linking organs to link the legs to the eccentric gears moving them, organs which could be shortened, as we already know, to allow the doll to sit down; each of these organs is made up by two parts of metallic string, one part tightly rolled up in spiral to form a tubular guide through which the right hand side of the other part could slip in easily.

An execution procedure of a toy doll according to the present invention is illustrated in the drawings attached hereby as examples.

1 designates the motor with clock-motion, which has winding and escape devices of some sort, and which activates an eccentric gear-shaft 2 that controls the arms, the head, the legs and the bellows of the talking device.

Across the top of the body a socket 4 is placed and supported at the ends in order to rotate around its axle. The socket receives from eccentric button 5 a swivel motion by means of a push-rod coupled to a starting-handle fixed on the socket.

To the shoulder of each arm, a solidly fixed stud goes in one end of socket 4 and is held by friction by pressure of spring 10 of metallic string, the spring appropriately fixed on one side of the stud. The arms can thus be rotated in relation to the socket, independantly from each other.

The head that can be turned to either side, is activated by a socket by way of arm 11 fixed to the socket and by way of arm 12 fixed to the head axle.

Eccentric gear 13 oppositely placed to gear 5 activates normally the bellows.

On the other hand, the other two eccentric gears 14 engage the legs in the walking motion by way of special push-rods, each made up by two parts 16 and 17 made of metallic string. Part 16 is twisted in spiral at one end in order to form a tubular guide 18 through which the rectilinear part of part 17 could slip in easily. The latter has, at one end a loop that surrounds eccentric gear 14, and at the other a hook that prevents it falling out of guide 18. When the doll is standing and when shaft 2 turns, eccentric gears 14 pull push-rods 16 and 17 alternately in order to engage the legs in the walking motion; this traction is transmitted from part 17 to part 16 by way of guide 18. On the other hand, upon lifting the legs forward to seat the doll, part 16 slides on to part 17. This construction of sliding push-rods is more economical and more solid than the construction of corresponding organs used up to now.

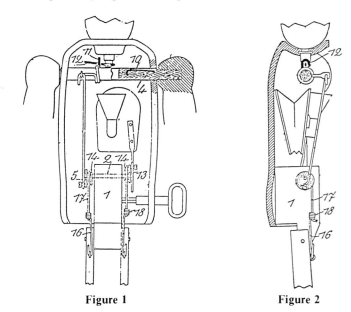

Figure 1   Figure 2

No. 1,157,571

Gr. 20 — Cl 1.
International classification: A 63 h.

Petitioned September 20, 1956 at 10:20 a.m. in Paris
Delivered December 30, 1957 — Published May 30, 1958.

System for so-called "walking" figurines

This patent is a system for walking figurines without motor, by alternate balancing of the legs.

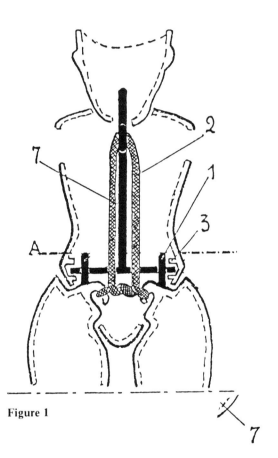

Figure 1

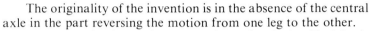

The originality of the invention is in the absence of the central axle in the part reversing the motion from one leg to the other.

The leg motion is obtained by the following device: Each leg is extended above its swivel-axle by handle 1.

The legs are attached to each other at swivel-axle height, by an elastic band or by spring 2 which could possibly support the head and the arms. The elastic band is arranged in such a way that the legs of the subject come back to the standing position when they are no longer pulled by an opposite force, e.g. the body weight upon the legs in the sitting position.

Within the body, the piston lugs 3 allow holding a part in place with the shape of a semi-disc, semi-circle, triangle etc. 4, having, if necessary, one or several notches or lugs 5 in order to limit the extent of the motion. The same result could equally be obtained by means of stops within body 6.

The semi-disc, or all other forms of part, is placed in the body front part, allowing free access to levers 1 in the back part, for the sitting position, for example.

A rod could be fixed on part 4, inter-independant from the head, making it swivel from right to left during the alternate motion of the legs.

Figure 4 is a section made between lines A and A' of figurines 1 and 2 of the same device, but using part 4 of a different shape, having notch 5 serving as a stop.

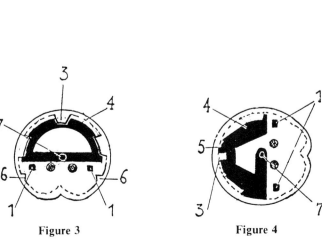

Figure 3 **Figure 4**

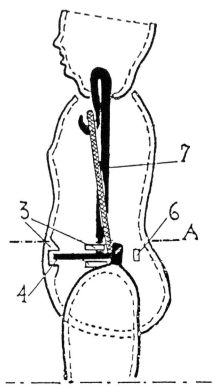

Figure 2

No. 341,108

XX — Items from Paris and various products.
1.   Games, Toys, Theaters, Races.

Petitioned March 10, 1904.
Delivered June 1, 1904 — Published July 30, 1904.

Improvement of eye movement in *bébés*

This patent inaugurates a long series of attempts and research for the improvement of eyes. An important preoccupation in technology at the beginning of the twentieth century was that eyes look realistic and that their expression be real. It was one of the most difficult problems for manufacturers to resolve. The reason for this passion for making beautiful eyes was to make the doll as life-like as possible. Eyes were supposed to express the brightness of beauty and the movement of life; today we are less demanding. The brightness of the eyes, the sparkle and the depth were obtained by clever use of materials, particularly the use of crystal. The detail in the design of the eye was also an important factor. To give the impression of life depended on being able to give the eye movement. Glass had to be combined with different materials, first of all porcelain, then paste and eventually cardboard. These materials had differing physical characteristics causing friction when they were used together, which in turn caused war and breakage. Dust collected in the hollow sections needed for the movement of the eyes and this too caused wear and stiffness. Despite the 17 patents taken out by the S.F.B.J., perfection was never attained. This is why the manufacturers finally gave up. This patent is a first study of the assembly of eyes through a technique of suspension which eliminated the friction of the glass against the plaster or the porcelain.

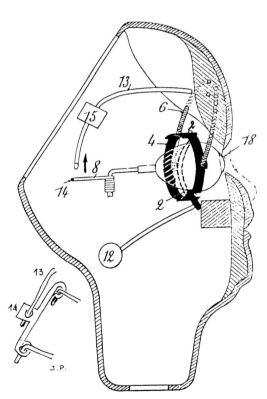

Figure 1

There are now different types of moving eyes in dolls' heads. Some only move round a horizontal axis, others called living eyes only move round vertical axes, and there are others which move in every direction.

In all these systems, the eyes are pear shaped and their bulging or spherical part fits into a plaster socket in the doll's head. The eyes and their sockets are only partly in contact so that there are spaces for dust and other foreign bodies. Friction is high and the play is irregular because the eye is not quite spherical. In short, the movement of the eyes most of the time is very slow and frequently gets blocked.

In addition, the movement of the eyes to the right or the left requires the use of specific techniques of suspension in order to release the mobile system from the action of the counterweights, and therefore the manufacture becomes even more complex.

The present invention solves these problems because the eyes are placed in position with metal pivots in metal revolving shells, which are also connected with metal pivots to props fixed in the doll's head. The axes of the eyes and of the shells are perpendicular as in a cardan suspension, so that the eyes can move in every direction on their metal pivots without any friction. Due to this new device, the eyes can move very easily and give the doll's face a much more real expression.

It is no longer necessary to make pear-shaped eyes with a perfectly spherical part for guiding, but the front part of the eye should be roughly spherical.

Moreover, with the head in its upright position, it is pointless to hold the eyes open with a specific device because the metal shells can themselves hold the eyes in the right direction when they make contact with the stop inside the head.

The drawing below gives some idea of the conception of the invention.

Diagram 1 is a vertical section of the doll's head and of its
   left eye.
Diagram 2 is a detailed description of the mechanism of the
   eyes seen from the back.
Diagram 3 represents the same mechanism.

Each eye has the shape of a globe, but only the front part has to be roughly spherical. This part is fixed to a vertical axis made of wire. It is fixed by giving the middle part of the axis 2 the shape of a loop. This loop is fixed with wax or cement etc.

Before it is fixed, the extremities of the axis 2 are introduced into diametrically opposed holes in the circular shell 4: this is assembled so that it moves round its horizontal diameter on the extreme parts of a forked support 6, which is embedded inside the head.

The two eyes are linked with a connecting rod 8 articulated with two stems which move with the eyes. 12 indicates counterweights necessary for the easy movement of the eyes already described. A forked wire 13 is fixed to the upper part of the head. It is used to guide a protruding part 14 of the connecting rod 8, and to maintain a stop mechanism 15, in cork for example.

Part 14 bumps into it when the head is back, so the closing of the eyes are relatively limited. The advantage of this device is that when it is being manufactured the position of the stop 15 can easily be adjusted by sliding it into the fork 13.

18 indicates the eyelashes stuck on each mobile eye.

Within the limits of the present invention, it is possible to a certain extent to modify the different parts of the mechanism described above; in particular, one can replace the two circular shells 4, by semi-circular or forked shells, but the vertical axis of the eyes will then jut out. Moreover, instead of assembling the shells 4 in two different frames, one can assemble them in one single frame.

The Figures 4 and 5 show the front part and the profile of a different prop articulated for an eye.

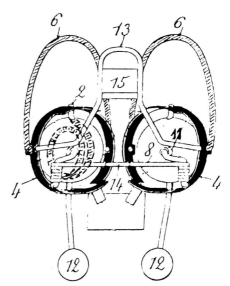

Figure 2

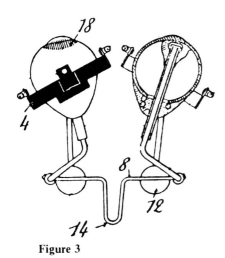

Figure 3

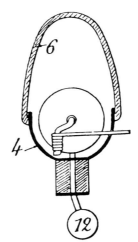

Figure 4

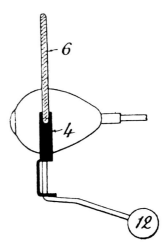

Figure 5

No. 3,318

1st Addition
to the Patent
No. 341,108

XX — Items from Paris and various products.
1. Games, Toys, Theaters, Races.

(Principal patent taken out March 10, 1904.)

Applied for June 3, 1904.
Granted August 19, 1904 — Published October 21, 1904.

Improvements in *bébé* eye movements

This patent is for a simplification of the principal patent for oscillating eyes.

The attached drawing gives various examples of eyes which are life-like, i.e. moving left and right. A similar system can be applied not only to eyes which can move at the same time round horizontal and vertical axes, but also to eyes moving in one single direction. In Figures 1 and 2, the eye, which is fixed on a rod 2, turns freely without the shell 6. This shell is fixed to the head with the stirrup 8 and the shell 9. In Figure 3, there is only one counterweight 12, which is fixed with a rod 13 to the doll's head. In both cases, Figures 1 and 2 and also in Figure 3, there is friction of metal against metal. In the versions, Figures 4 and 5, friction of glass against metal by valves is attached to props embedded in the head.

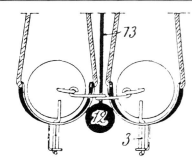

Figure 3

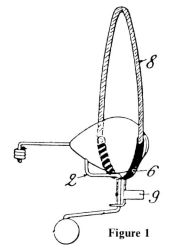

Figure 1

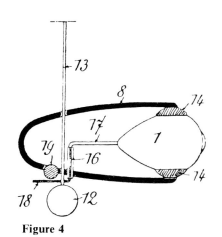

Figure 4

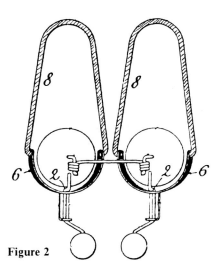

Figure 2

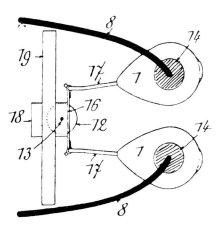

Figure 5

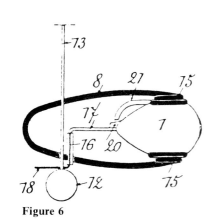

Figure 6

No. 3,601

2nd Addition
to the Patent
No. 341,108

XX — Items from Paris and various products.
1. Games, Toys, Theaters, Races.

1st addition No. 3,318.
(Principal patent taken out March 10, 1904.)

Applied for August 11, 1904.
Granted October 25, 1904 — Published December 7, 1904.

Improvements of eye movement in dolls

A simplification of the eye mechanisms previously described in that the suspension is obtained with just a bent wire.

In some examples described in the previous addition to the French patent of March 10, 1904, the eyes are maintained between caps or metal guides which enable them to oscillate in every direction. In one case, in particular, the guides are made of spiral wires whose shape corresponds to spherical caps. These guides can be fixed to stirrups or props which are embedded in the doll's head. They can also become part of the stirrups themselves.

The purpose of the present addition is to improve the guiding mechanism of the eyes: each eye is now held up behind the eye-opening of the porcelain face with a simple wire which is properly curved and embedded in the doll's head. The weight of the mobile eye is mostly supported by this wire, so that friction occurs almost exclusively between the smooth surfaces in glass and metal. Thus the resistance is reduced to the bare minimum. Moreover, there is not the problem of dust and foreign bodies blocking the eye movement, because the surfaces in contact are smooth and have a large area of contact.

The present modification simplifies to a great extent the making of toy dolls and ensures the easy and regular working of the mobile eyes, whichever way they move, horizontally, vertically or in both directions at the same time.

In Figures 1 and 2, one can see that each spherical eye is now placed behind its opening and it loosely correpsonds with a U shaped wire 3. The extremities of this wire are fixed in the head with plaster whereas the U loop holds up the eye under and behind its centre.

The lower part of this loop can be seen on the drawing, so that the base or the bases located under the eye jut out and support the weight of the eye almost completely. The spherical eye in glass can turn freely between these bases and the edges of the eye opening.

The two eyes are joined through a metal sheet 5, forming a small connecting rod, and through two bent wires. They are embedded in the eyes and form articulated levers at the extremities of the small connected rod.

The eyes are forced to move in relation to the head by a wire supporting a counterweight 8. This wire hangs freely in 9 at the top of the head and it goes through an ear 10, jutting out over the sheet. When you bend the head right or left, the counterweight tends to remain vertical, and thus it changes the relative position of the eye mechanism.

Plugs in cork or another elastic material, are fixed on the sides of the head in order to limit the oscillations of the mechanism.

Besides a rod 12, a wire is fixed across the head just in front of the ear 10, which is kept from bending by the counterweight and from rising by the rod 12. In consequence, the eyes can only move right or left.

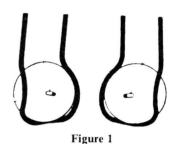

Figure 1

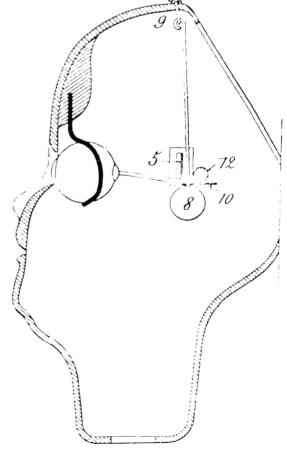

Figure 2

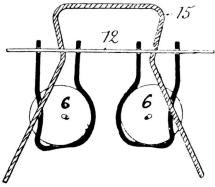

Figure 3

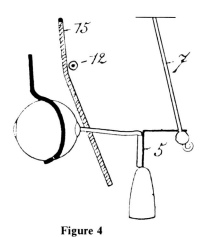

Figure 4

Drawings for patent No. 3,601.

In the model shown in Figures 3 and 4, the props or guides for the eyes are made as above, and the eyes are also joined by levers 6 and a small connecting rod 5. Two devices can be used to raise or lower the eyes: either a counterweight which is fixed to a small connecting rod 5 or two counterweights fixed to proper extensions of the levers.

7 indicates a wire hanging at the top of the head and going freely through a projecting part of the small connecting rod 5: a pearl is set on the lower extremity of this wire and holds up the projection when the head is up. When the doll is lying down, the counterweight keeps the eyes in their initial position so that they seem to close; their relative oscillation is limited by a wire 12 fixed across the head.

The drawing of the mechanism also includes a stirrup 15 in wire. It is embedded in the head and its halves meet the lever 6 laterally in order to limit the oscillation to the right and left.

In the examples above, the support of the eye has a U shape with an arch from the back to the front; however the invention is not limited to this model and includes others; but what is essential in any case is to surround the spherical part of the eye with a fixed wire previously bent in order to keep it from falling.

No. 360,100

XX — Items from Paris and various products.
1. Games, Toys, Theaters, Races.

Petitioned December 5, 1905.
Granted February 12, 1906 — Published April 12, 1906.

Doll's head with mobile eyes

This invention deals with how to avoid problems due to the deformation of cardboard heads,
either in keeping the distance between the sides with a metal frame
or in hanging the eyes in this frame itself with reference to previous patents.

This invention particularly concerns heads in cardboard or similar compositions of a more or less hygrometric nature. Under the influence of atmospheric variations, these heads contract or dilate in such a way that, when given mobile eyes, these latter become either too loose or so tight in their sockets that they cannot oscillate any more. In order to avoid the inconvenience of heads made of these so-called "unbreakable" materials, the invention consists of keeping a constant distance between the sockets through the combination of the proper metal frame with the cardboard head and mobile eyes.

The annexed drawing gives the example of two models.

Figure 1 is a vertical section of a head showing the inner side of the face.

Figure 2 is a similar view of another section.

Figure 3 is a cross section corresponding to the Figure 2.

On Figure 1 the eyes a are maintained by the plaster sockets b embedded in the interior sides of the unbreakable head. It is noticeable that the plaster itself is hygrometric and that, during the making of the head, it contains a lot of water which disappears very slowly; the use of this material increases the inconveniences mentioned above. With reference to the invention, the distance between the sockets b is made constant by a rectangular frame in solid metal, both of whose sides are embedded in the plaster sockets themselves.

d indicates the counterweight with a ball fixed to the eyes in the usual way.

Instead of being rectangular the frame c can become round, oval or anything, provided it is rigid and keeps a constant distance between the sockets, in order to avoid the problem of the hygrometric variations.

In the model shown in Figures 2 and 3, the frame itself f can be used as sockets; plaster then becomes useless to maintain the eyes, and this solves the problems mentioned above. In this case the frame is still made of metal but its legs have bent parts g corresponding to the external and back sections of the eyes so that the eyes have a steady position but can oscillate quite freely at the same time. The frame h is embedded in the head with wax h or with some other material. Thus, the sockets g are not linked with the possible contraction and dilatation movements of the head, and their distance is kept the same. This kind of frame also has the advantage of making the setting of the eyes easy and quick.

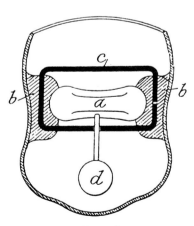

Figure 1

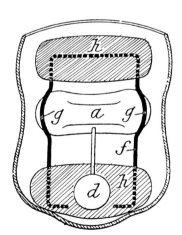

Figure 2

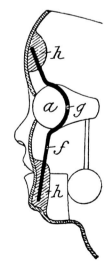

Figure 3

No. 457,184

XX — Paris articles and various industries.
1. Games, Toys, Theaters, Races.

Petitioned April 26, 1913.
Delivered July 5, 1913 — Published September 13, 1913.

Improvements to doll heads

The devices in the preceding patent do not appear to be sufficient to assure the rigidity of the cardboard: here an orientation is made towards an interior metallic box. This patent indirectly announces the event of the cardboard doll itself, which inaugurates the era of the plastic doll. In fact, the abandonment of those materials such as porcelain and composition, in favor of a common material and a lower price, was at first to the advantage of the consumer, then later to that of the manufacturer. This patent shows how imagination overcame the inconveniences of the new materials.

This invention is to perfect the production of doll heads in cardboard equipped with mobile or sleeping eyes.

Until now, one only succeeded in assembling mobile eyes in porcelain heads. With cardboard heads, the plaster supports for the eye bearings did not find the walls of the cardboard a rigid enough stronghold for the functioning of the eyes.

Following the present invention, one can, on the contrary, use mobile eyes in a practical, economic and durable way, on all types of cardboard or other soft-material heads. This result is obtained thanks to the use of a rigid metallic armor in which the mobile eyes are assembled, which is attached to the inside of the cardboard head.

The drawings, here annexed, as example, show the object of the invention.

The mobile eyes a pivot in the plaster bearings b, which are paired on the two cheeks of a metallic armature (shown here by continuous lines) attached to the interior of the cardboard head.

This armature consists, in this example, of a metal sheet cut in a crescent or horseshoe shape, and stamped or embossed more or less to the shape of the forehead and cheeks; the two sides of this armature are entertwined in such a way as to give the necessary rigidity, for example, by an iron stem whose two extremeties are sealed on the plaster, or welded or stapled to the armature. The attachment of the armature to the cardboard head can be obtained in any manner, preferably by using staples f which are placed in the part of the forehead later covered by hair.

g and h show two cork buffers designed to limit the eye oscillation in a known manner; one of these is attached for example, to the armor, and the other to the cardboard head.

It goes without saying that the form of the particular arrangement of the rigid structure, could vary without changing the character of the invention, the same as one could vary the particular construction of the eyes and their manner of assembly on the armature.

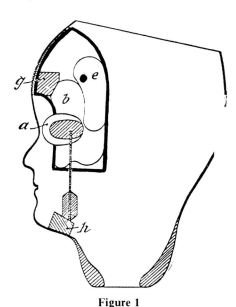

Figure 1

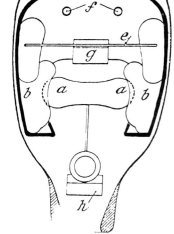

Figure 2

No. 528,243

XX — Paris articles and various industries.
1.   Games, Toys, Theaters, Races.

Petitioned April 25, 1918 at 3:53 p.m. in Paris
Delivered August 12, 1921 — Published November 8, 1921.

Composition for the attachment of mobile eyes in doll heads

This patent evokes again the difficult problem of attaching eyes, even in porcelain heads.

This invention entails a composition designed for affixing eyes in porcelain or heads of other types of material.

Until now, one used plaster mixed with water for this purpose. This product produces the following inconvenience: in humidity it swells slightly and the result is that the eyes, enclaved in their socket of plaster, no longer play freely, or lose all mobility.

The present invention is to prevent this inconvenience.

In this end, instead of water, a solution of skin glue, of animal or vegetable gelatin or other agglutinant is used to thin the plaster; additionally, one adds to the plaster, or substitutes for this latter, zinc powder, lime carbonate, pulverized cloth or paper and so on, to obtain a smooth paste, which shrinks in volume in solidifying and which thus gives the necessary play around the eyes for their movement, one can, besides, obtain a more or less important play, by modifying the fluidity of the composition. Besides the advantage already cited, the new composition sticks better to the wall of the head, whatever its substance.

As an example: the composition can be obtained by mising
50% glue and
50% solid materials (plaster, zinc white, lime carbonate).

No. 507,074

XX — Paris articles and various industries.
 1. Games, Toys, Theaters, Races.

Petitioned December 4, 1919 at 3:42 p.m. in Paris.
Delivered June 12, 1920 — Published September 4, 1920.

Improvements to doll heads with sleep eyes

This patent is a search for eye stability.
One must not only assure the attachment despite the deformations of the head (it probably is a question of cardboard)
but ward off the young user's tendancy to plunge her fingers into the doll's eye sockets.
The solution is to suspend the eye in a metal "shell."

The present invention's object is a device of simple and economical make, designed to maintain the eyes mobility in dolls' heads such as to easily assure a perfect attachment while allowing a complete liberty of movement. This device will preferably have joints and an elastic link (or tie) to avoid the harmful effect of variable head deformations or expansions, and to prevent the child from ruining the device by putting its fingers in the eyes. In the case of large heads, which generally have non-spherical or slightly flat eyes, this elastic and articulated device has the advantage of holding the eyes without rattling or excessive pressure in their various positions.

The annexed drawing represents, as an example, two doll heads assembled according to the invention.

Figure 1 is a vertical cut down the middle of a head.

Figure 2 is a vertical cut of the same head following the line A-A of Figure 1.

Figure 3 shows the development of an iron support used to hold the eyes in the head.

Figure 4 is a vertical cut down the middle of a head with larger dimensions.

Figure 5 is a vertical cut following line B-B of Figure 4.

Figure 6 shows a horizontal cut along line C-C of Figure 4.

Figure 7 shows the development of an attachment piece for the eyes.

Figures 8 and 9 are detail variants of the gripping suspension device of the eyeball.

In Figures 1, 2 and 3, the eyes are mounted on a fork 1 carrying a counterweight 2 which hits against a piece of cork 3 serving as a shock absorber: each eye is held by a piece of iron 4 (Figure 3) bent to square along a a, its extremity 5 being sealed against the wall of the head and its extremities 6 being appropriately bent to follow the shape of the eye. The eyes held between these pieces 4 and the walls of the head, can pivot freely, but are prevented from escaping in all directions. A brace 7 consolidates the head and serves to stop the rocking of the fork.

In Figures 4, 5, and 6 a head of larger dimensions is shown, in which the eye supports are articulated and tied elastically.

Each support is made of a piece 8 shown in Figure 7.

This piece is pulled back along line bb to form a hinge and joins a loop 9 sealed to the wall of the head.

The extremities 10 are appropriately bent to the form of the eye, and part 11 is bent or re-bent as indicated in Figure 6.

Part 11 is pierced with holes and a spring 12 stuck to each side in one of the holes to exert a traction on the two supports so that the eyes are applied with a ligth pressure against the wall of the cavities 13 arranged in the head.

The form and the dimensions can vary slightly due to changes in humidity or temperature without influencing the pressure of the eye supports, such that these latter can always move with the same facility once the spring tension is set, what's more, the elasticity of

the whole allows the use of eyes not quite spherical while avoiding jamming or shaking in any position.

The spring gives, and the eyes recede slightly until the extremities of parts 11 hit against the walls, without any deterioration.

This device also has the advantage of rendering the assembly easy and rapid. Naturally the form of the metal parts used as supports can be slightly modified, for example, so that these pieces envelope almost completely the socket, they could be made of metallic strings, bands and so on.

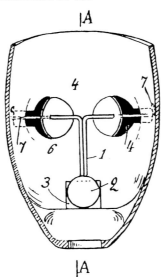

Figure 1

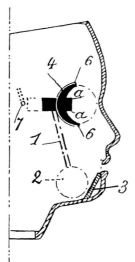

Figure 2

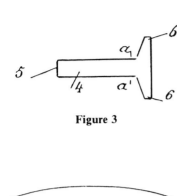

Figure 3

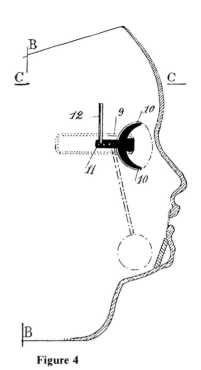

Figure 4

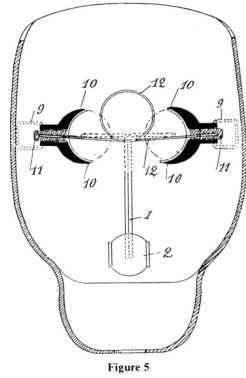

Figure 5

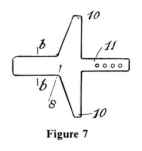

Figure 7

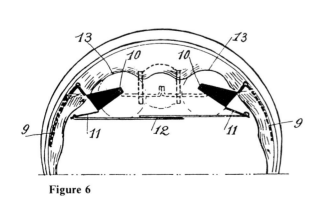

Figure 6

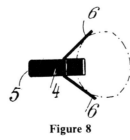

Figure 8

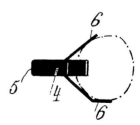

Figure 9

No. 522,945

XX — Articles of Paris and various industries
1.   Games, Toys, Theaters, Races.

Petitioned April 7, 1919 at 3:53 p.m. in Paris
Delivered April 11, 1921 — Published August 9, 1921.

Improvements to blown artificial eyes

This patent returns to the very interesting production technique for glass eyes
in which the search for realism was pushed to the extreme.
N.B. The accompanying diagram has been redrawn.

Figure 1

Figure 2

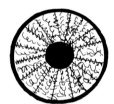

Figure 3

This invention is designed to improve the production of blown glass eyes in order to more perfectly imitate a living eye.

It has been observed that in the actual blown eye, the coloring of the iris' innermost part spreads uniformly to the edge of the pupil, while in a living eye, this coloring becomes darker around the edge, and forms a dark ring around the area of the fibrilla. This difference in coloration accounts for the dead look blown eyes actually present, despite the greatest care in their execution.

To perfectly imitate the living eye, this invention will modify the usual production procedure of blown glass eyes, in the following manner: Instead of directly applying on the white ocular globe the coat of glass with the iris coloring, one first applies a glass disk with a darker coloring, and one places on this disk, a second disk of lighter coloring than that around the edge of the pupil.

One next places, as usual, the variously colored or white enamel filaments, which imitate the iris fibrilla, then the black enamel round piece to form the pupil, and finally a transparent glass dome for the cornea, using a blowpipe to unite all these elements in a partial mixing.

The interposition between the white globe and the edge of iris, of an enamel disk of darker color, produces around the iris after a partial mixing and blowing, a circle that is flushed with the central lighter part, in a perfectly gradual range of color, due to the partial mixing of the different enamels at the place of contact, particularly at the periphery, which is brought to a higher temperature.

No. 559,197

XX — Articles of Paris and various industries
1.   Games, Toys, Theaters, Races.

Petitioned November 28, 1922 at 4:23 p.m. in Paris
Delivered June 9, 1923 — Published September 11, 1923

Improvements to *bébés* with sleep eyes

Here it is a question of a very interesting fitting together which allows eye oscillation and independant lid closure.
This avoids the cramming of the eyelashes in the socket during a sideways look.

In the mechanism of sleeping *bébés*, the lid, whether painted on the eye or made by a glaze, or any surface shaped to the form of the eye and carrying lashes, participates in all eye movements: vertical movement for closing the eye and lateral movements.

On this latter case, the lashes mass together in ugly bristles in the corner of the socket, to which the eye is directed.

The present invention is designed to remedy this inconvenience.

On this mechanism, the lid, independent of the eye, participates only in a vertical movement of the eye, and stays immobile in all other lateral movements. Under these conditions, the lashes are normally arranged in the socket whether the eyes are open or closed, and the device approaches reality. A frame is made of metal stems scaled at their furthest extremity and holding at a right angle arched pieces which play the role of bearer plates.

Each bearer plate is equipped with a tail 4 formed in the middle by folding the same piece of iron. A metal stem is established to pivot 5 between the tail 4 and the bearer plate 3, and in a piece 6 connecting the two stems of the mechanism. Each stem 5 carries an eye fixed on 5' on the stem by mastic or other procedure.

A metallic plaque or other material, stamped in the form of the eye, constitutes the lid which is hooked to the corresponding bearer plate. Cork shock absorbers 9 or other appropriate material placed laterally in the interior of the mask allow a certain motion of translation of piece 6, movement which leads to the rotation of the two globes around axes 5.

The bearer plates are not touched, and stay in contact with the shock absorbers 10 in cork or other material established to correspond to the normal position of the eye pupil in the socket. The eyes thus go to the right or left - according to whether piece 6 comes in contact with the absorber 9 to the left or the right without the lids, and necessarily the lashes, moving.

Piece 6 is equipped with a weight which when the *bébé* is vertical, tends to apply the end 4 against the absorber. If one inclines the baby as in Figure 3, the weight is affected by gravity and forces the whole, formed of the eyes, the rockers 3 and the lids to oscillate on axis x-y (Figure 1) which will correspond to the grudgeon pin axis, where the bearer plates are articulated. In this movement, the eyes close in their sockets, the pupils disappear as the movable lids, connected with the bearer plates, close to mask the white of the eyes.

The lashes close as well, but are not wrinkled, their movement being concentric with axis x-y.

For more realistic cares, the guides formed by stems 13 in the mask's interior, bring the pupils back to a direct position by obliging piece 6 to be placed in a median position when one inclines the baby. A transversal stem 19 which stems 5, 5', 5" meet in their movement, limits the amplitude of the eye oscillation.

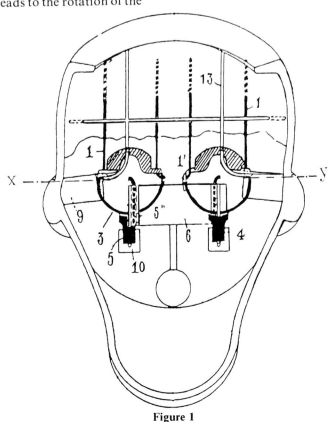

Figure 1

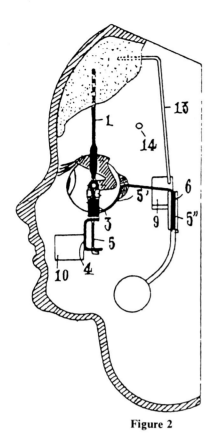

Figure 2

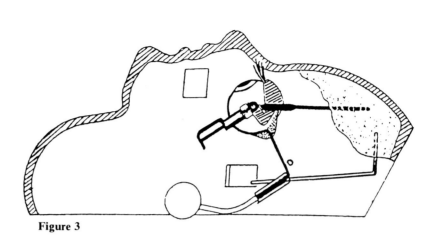

Figure 3

Illustrations for patent No. 559,197.

No. 590,016

XX — Articles from Paris and various industries.
1. Games, Toys, Theaters, Races.

Petitioned December 4, 1924 at 3:57 p.m. in Paris
Delivered March 7, 1925 — Published June 9, 1925.

**Device for the shifting of sleeping doll's eyelids,
involving fixed eyes or eyes painted on heads made of cloth felt,
cardboard or other material.**

This device has been designed for the installation of a rocking mechanism in a stuffed,
stiff, hollow head with the mechanism in a cardboard compartment.
It is surprising that the realistic "seesaw" eyelids did not appear until 1925.

The sleeping dolls' eyes are generally fixed to a device that automatically transmits a vertical shifting according to the position given to the sleeping doll.

The present invention aims for a device that automatically transmits a vertical shift to the doll's eyelids, the eyes remaining immobile or simply painted, on heads made of fabric, felt, or cardboard for stuffed dolls.

The attached drawing represents:

In Figure 1 a sectional view showing an eyelid in the up position

In Figure 2 a sectional view showing a lowered eyelid

In Figure 3 a rear view of the eyelid shifting device.

The sleeping doll automatic device for eyelid vertical shift comprises axle 1, supported at each end by supports 2 and 3, inside the head. On axle 1, eyelids 4 are mounted by means of part 5. Counterweight 6 suspended on rod 1, causes the eyelid shift according to the position given to the sleeping doll, the eyelids inserted through a slot that has been made above each eye. The vertical travel of the eyelids is obtained by means of stop 7 for the up position, Figure 1, and of stop 8 for the down position, Figure 2.

Partition 9 separates the compartment where the devise is located, in the back of the head, filled with some stuffing material.

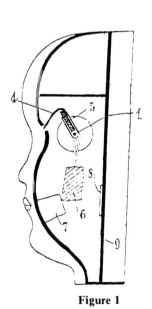

Figure 1

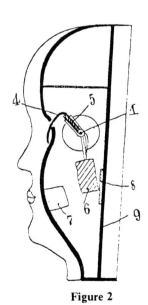

Figure 2

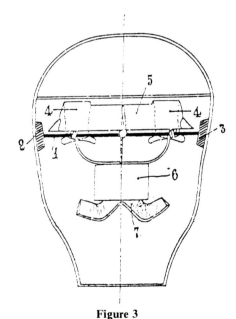

Figure 3

No. 30,243

1st Addition
of Patent
No. 590,016

XX — Articles from Paris and various industries
1. Games, Toys, Theaters, Races.

(Main patent taken December 4, 1924)

Petitioned March 17, 1925 at 4:31 p.m. in Paris
Delivered December 31, 1925 — Published March 30, 1926.

**Device for the shifting of sleeping doll's eyelids,
involving fixed eyes or eyes painted on heads made of fabric,
felt, cardboard or other material.**

The difference from the main patent is in the omission of the support cross-axle.
The support is provided by a plate fixed on the "inner back of the head."
This process would probably be interesting at the mounting stage.

The present addition aims for improvements in the mounting of the device that allows the automatic shift of a sleeping doll's eyelids, the new device forming a set that is fixed on the inner surface of the head, bearing the eyelids and all the organs required for their shifting.

The mobile eyelid device includes part a, somehow fixed on the material forming the inner back of the head. Part a bears in its upper section two flasks or attachments c, on which part e has been fixed by cut-up parts d; part e's upper part is rolled up to accommodate rod 1 whose ends swivel the eyelids.

Bent parts f, belonging to attachments c, support part e when the eyelids are raised. The counterweight, fixed on the lower end of part e, causes the shifting of eyelids 4 in the manner already described in the main patent, the eyelids travelling in the direction of arrow g being limited by the meeting of the rolled end of part e and the upper part h of part a.

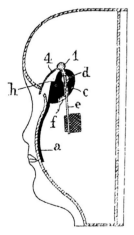

Figure 1

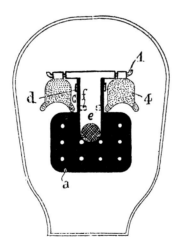

Figure 2

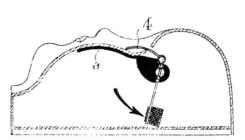

Figure 3

No. 596,574

XX — Articles from Paris and various industries
1.   Games, Toys, Theaters, Races.

Petitioned April 11, 1925 at 11:30 a.m. in Paris
Delivered August 11, 1925 — Published October 27, 1925.

Assembly process of sleeping doll's mobile eyes

This patent is for a simple and original system for eyes that "give another impression."

In the sleeping doll, a mounting process of mobile eyes, that connects the eyes, no matter what material they are made of, with a central axle swivelling on an inter-independent support of the head; an appropriate counterweight being fixed on the eyes to insure the orbit shifting, according to the position given to the doll.

According to the invention eyes A are preferably made of wood, but they could be made of any other material, metal, glass, porcelain etc, and painted, whether by hand or by imprinting thus giving the eye a look other than the one of glass eyes.

These eyes are connected by axle B made of metal or other, following a diameter.

This axle is mounted so that it could pivot on an appropriate support such as the one indicated in C, being inter-independent of the head and the body.

On the lower part of eyes A two rods are fixed, each equipped with a counterweight allowing the swivelling shift of the eyes in front of the orbits, according to the position given to the doll.

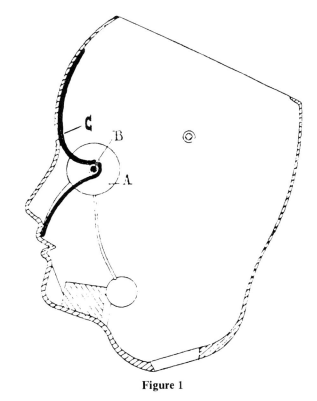

Figure 1

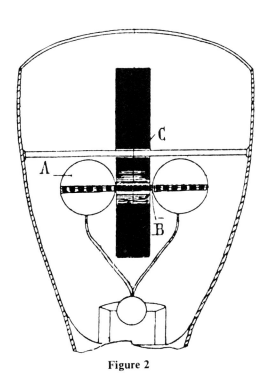

Figure 2

No. 635,471

Gr XX — Cl 1.

Petitioned June 3, 1927 at 1:52 p.m. in Paris
Delivered December 28, 1927 — Published March 16, 1928.

Sleeping *bébé*

This is a rather confusing patent because a process to represent the teeth is being introduced in the already complicated description of the eye assembly. It is interesting and includes interesting terminology: the word denture is used to designate all the teeth, and the term "light obscure" for the inside of the open mouth.

1. For the eyes, on one hand there is an original mounting on elastic suspension, with a sort of "shock absorber" that registers the volume variation of the head on finger pressure of the child; this mounting is for simple sleeping eyes.

2. A telescoping coupling of the eyeballs is added to the mounting with a small heavy mass that allows them to swivel (to roll). The whole thing could be mounted in the device on elastic suspension.

3. For the teeth, a simple, stamped, small plate is painted and glued to the back of the mouth.

The present invention aims for improvements in the manufacturing of sleeping *bébés* and in particular concerning the mounting of rolling eyes and dentures.

To that effect, the eyeballs are mounted so that they could slide laterally to adapt their opening to that of the orbits; moreover, in order to give to an external pressure, the eyes are preferably supported elastically in a support or an appropriate guide.

To facilitate the mounting of this support in the head, it is advantageous to construct this support so that it could elastically lean against the inner walls of the head; this mounting also allows for compensation of the differences in dimensions that could arise with the easily warped material (cardboard paste) that constitute the dolls' shatter-proof heads.

The setting of the eyes within their sockets is preferably limited by the stops mounted behind each eyeball and appropriately fixed inside the head.

The eyes are mounted on axle 3 on which they could be tightly fixed if the eye opening is strictly determined; in the case shown, the central portion of axle 3 is cylindrical, and its ends (Figure 3) have a section of a shape other than circular (square, rectangular, etc.) so that the eyes could slide on these ends without however, rotating in place; this mounting allows the eyes to fit into the socket openings that slightly vary from one head to the other, and even according to the hygrometrical variation, if the head material is sensitive to it.

Axle 3 is loosely supported in a support made of a metallic band 4, for example, with the profile shown and with one loose end, to which a spring 5 of metallic string is fixed in the shape of something like a U, whose prongs lean on either side of the support on axle 3 in order to support it elastically, pressed toward the sockets; therefore if the child wanted to poke at the doll's eyes, these eyes could move slightly without causing damage to the toy, then they could move back into a normal position under spring pressure; their shifting is limited by stops made of parts 6 of metallic string, located behind the eyes and fixed by the upper end on a rib that reinforces the head.

Clip 8 is fixed on axle 3 having at the base a counterweight that strikes an internal protrusion in the head with the interposition of a part made of a shock-absorbing material such as felt, leather, cork, rubber etc.

The whole thing is placed in the head by means of a small metallic bar 12, in the middle of which the end of band 4 has been soldered, across from the band bearing spring 5; this small bar, slightly arched to give some elasticity, is forced into the head and held in place by sharp claws that have been set in the head inner walls.

Each part 17 ends with a sheath 18 in which it nests with the sheath of the other part 17. This telescopic mounting allows the fitting of the eye opening to the socket opening; the entire works of parts 17, axle 16 and the eyes, is mounted in support 4 (not shown) in the same manner as the middle part of axle 3 (Figures 1 to 3).

Instead of having the shape shown, parts 17 could completely surround the eyeballs.

Behind each of the eyeballs a rod has been fixed, ending with a ring. Those two rods are joined by a small push-rod weighted down in the middle by a heavy mass 21; that way, when the head is tilted to the right or to the left, mass 21 engages the push-rod that pivots, by way of the rods, the eyeballs around their axles 16 so that the eyes could move simultaneously right or left; the motion is limited due to the fact that the rods are inserted in the loops carried by stop parts 6 mentioned above.

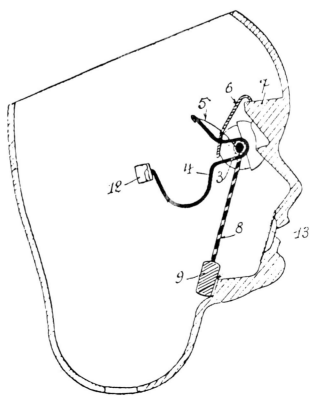

Figure 1

In case the eyes must be both sleeping and rolling, it would be better to use the mode of construction shown in Figures 6 and 7.

In this case, axle 16 goes through each eye, the axle being inclined and mounted in metal part 17 in front of form shown and in order to simulate the eyelid by its front upper part.

In the existing unbreakable heads for dolls, the teeth could be simulated by a line of white paint between the lips or, if the mouth is pierced, by a denture quickly cut out of celluloid or other substance, which, in both cases, produces a generally mediocre effect and leaves, in the second case, a slit through which the child has a tendency to insert things which may deteriorate the head interior and damage the teeth.

According to the invention an opening is kept in the head, and in front of that opening a small plate has been placed, a plate made of paper, bristleboard or other similar substance that would imprint in great detail, in order to allow the exact reproduction of the shape or aspect of the visible part of the teeth and gums and that, if necessary, could be embossed to bring out the teeth from a surrounding colored background.

That small plate shown in 13 (Figures 1 and 2) and shown in detail in Figures 4 and 5, bulges out in 14 so that it could fit the contour of the corresponding portion of the head, and in this bulging part, the teeth 15 are embossed so that they are in relief; the background colored in brownish-red, brings out perfectly the teeth that had been left in white.

The small plate cut out to the desired dimensions, is glued behind the opening simulating the mouth, and the illusion is more complete as the brownish-red background brings out the whiteness of the teeth, and the bright red of the lips seems to be the interior of the open mouth.

Small plates of the kind described could be manufactured economically in great volume, besides the fact that a small number of formats would fit all doll heads. The plates constitute a new industrial product at a low cost and of a very convenient use.

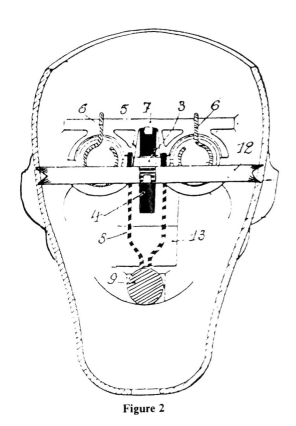

Figure 2

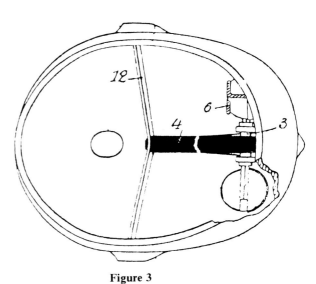

Figure 3

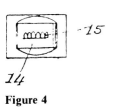

Figure 4

Figure 5

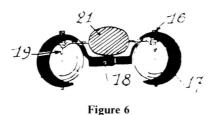

Figure 6

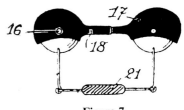

Figure 7

No. 35,010

1st Addition
to Patent
No. 635,471

Gr. 20 — Cl 1.

(Main patent taken out June 3, 1927)

Petitioned March 7, 1928 at 1:45 p.m. in Paris
Delivered June 11, 1929 — Published October 23, 1929.

Sleeping *bébé*

This is an odd addition to the main patent, and was delivered only after fifteen months of waiting:
the novelty probably seemed debatable.
In fact, the only major modification is in the shape of the part that provides elastic suspension.
It also seems to be a ridiculous, obsessional search for economy.

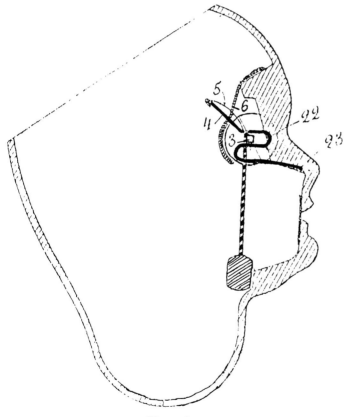

Figure 1

The present addition aims for different improvements in order to make the construction more economical.

Metallic blade 4, support of axle 3 is counterbent forwards and sealed in 22 e.g. in the nose indentation instead of leaning backwards on a small crossbar for support, while the bent part is sealed in 23; the latter part sliding, leaving axle 3 completely loose in forward motion. This device leads to a simpler assembly.

Instead of using expensive glass eyes which are often of irregular shape, we could use reproductions of eyes made by industrial imprinting on paper, cardboard, metal, celluloid or other substances. These prints will be cut up and contoured according to desired shape; in the case of fixed eyes, these prints could be glued on the outer surface of the head, at a normal place; if the openings have been made, the eye prints could be pasted under the eyelids, inside the head.

In the case of mobile eyes, the eye print will be fixed on ball 2 mounted on axle 3.

Instead of being contoured the small plate on which the teeth have been embossed could simply be flat.

No. 706,823

Gr 20 — Cl 1.

Requested December 2, 1930 at 2:02 p.m. in Paris
Delivered April 4, 1931 — Published June 30, 1931.

Sleeping doll

In this patent, the key-word is "bridge-eyelid" (*pont-paupière*).
We are heading for a simplification:
the eyes become simple balls, no more rods or axles puncturing them or crossing them.
However, the multiplicity of anticipated variants make this patent more an exercise of style than a practical solution.
But many of these various parts are found in existing dolls, and it is a help in dating them.

In the following toy, the bridge-eyelid 25 is made of two symmetrical parts; in each an eye is mounted, these two parts are then assembled, one extending the other by fixation on the counterweight rod that causes the opening and closing of the eyes.

Each part mentioned above is obtained simply by cutting and embossing sheet metal, and the production is much easier and less costly than that of similar parts usually used in toys of this type.

Moreover, the above operations are performed so that, on the outer surface of each eyelid-bridge, a spare protruding part fits into a socket made in the head wall at the time of mounting, and constitutes the swivel-pin of the bridge eyelids.

The making and the mounting of this swivel-pin are performed at the same time with those of the bridge-eyelids, which will notably simplify things.

Finally, the invention also foresees other particular arrangements relative to different ways of making the elastic support of bridge-eyelids that prevent the child from damaging the lids in case he tries to poke out the eyeballs from the sockets.

The attached drawing represents, only as an example, different ways to produce the invention object.

Figures 1 to 4 represent different phases of making bridge-eyelids.

Figures 5 to 7 pertain to a sleeping doll.

Figures 8 to 10 pertain to a sleeping and eye-rolling doll.

The bridge-eyelid of this toy is made up of two symmetrical parts 1 and 1a, respectively corresponding to the left eye and the right eye, each being produced from a mold cut out of sheet metal, according to the shape shown in Figure 1.

The mold is then embossed and bears a part 3 to cover the upper part of the eye, and semi-circle 4, these two parts being joined together by band 5 and bearing on each side and on their outer edge, clamps 6 and 7 (Figures 2 and 3).

Parts 3 and 4 are then pulled down, one toward the other, by folding band 5, so that the set takes shape of the spherical part simulating the eye the two clamps 6 coming together.

Folding band 5 is done in such a way that the band is shaped into a cylinder in order to form a hollow axle.

The eyeballs are then placed inside parts 1 so that parts 3 simulate the eyelids, and clamps 7 are folded back to hold them in place.

In the case of a sleeping doll, the eyeballs are glued to these parts (Figures 5 to 7).

In the case of a sleeping and eye-rolling doll, clamps 7 hold the eyeballs in place, and the eyeballs can pivot about easily.

The assembling of both parts making up the bridge-eyelids is insured by rod 9 that carries counterweight 10 making the eyelids open and close; the upper end of this rod is folded back and tightly squeezed on clamps 6. The whole works is ready to be mounted in the doll's head.

According to the procedure shown in Figures 5 to 7, this head

Figure 1

Figure 2

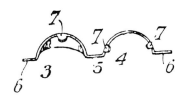

Figure 3

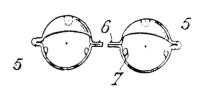

Figure 4

bears on the inside, two bosses in which grooves 13 were made, grooves that will lodge the bridge-eyelid axle.

The grooves ending up on the back faces of the bosses in order to allow the mounting of the axles, are then enclosed by small blocks 14, made of cork, or in any other appropriate material, glued to the head walls in such a way that the bridge-lid is now held in place, and can swivel around both axles under counterweight action, engaging the eyes in its rotation.

When the counterweight is in the lower position, it holds the eyelids open and the eye pupils in front of the sockets, and leans against a shock absorber made of felt or other supple material.

The grooves have a depth greater than the axle diameter (see Figure 7) so that the eyelid-bridge can move to the front or to the back of the head.

Spring 16, carried by blade 17 that is fixed to the head's front wall, leans on both ends, upon clamps 6 of both parts 1 and 1a, and pushes forward the eyelid-bridge.

The bridge can then give under external pressure and the spring brings it back to normal position.

The counterweight's upward pivoting is stopped in the position corresponding to the eyelid closing by way of rod 20, which strikes against rod 9.

In the case of a sleeping and eye-rolling doll (Figures 8 to 10), the eyeballs are mounted pivoting in parts 1.

The elastic fixation device of the eyelid-bridge could be analog to the one described below.

It could be replaced by two vertical rods 21 fixed on the internal wall and bent back at both ends, in the shape of loops in which the eyelid-bridge trunnion is engaged.

The elasticity of these rods will have the same function as that of spring 16; besides, the eyeball movement within their lodging allows them to give under external pressure without deforming the eyelid-bridge.

Each eyeball is inter-independent with rod 22 fixed on the back part and articulated by horizontal brace 23, placed halfway between the eyes. The set forms an articulated parallelogram that makes all the eye rolling motions inter-independent.

This rolling is caused by inertia of mass 24 hung on rod 25 that goes through brace 23 and supports it while the upward pivoting of rods 22 is stopped by rod 26 fixed above them.

Counterweight 10 is held still in the position corresponding to the eyelids closing, by rod 9 striking against the edge of stip 27 which is fixed to the front wall.

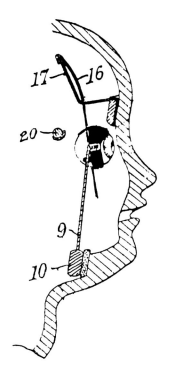

Figure 5

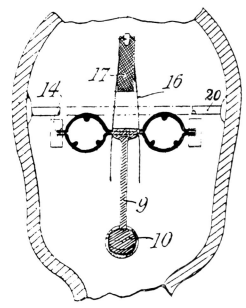

Figure 6

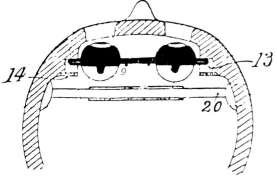

Figure 7

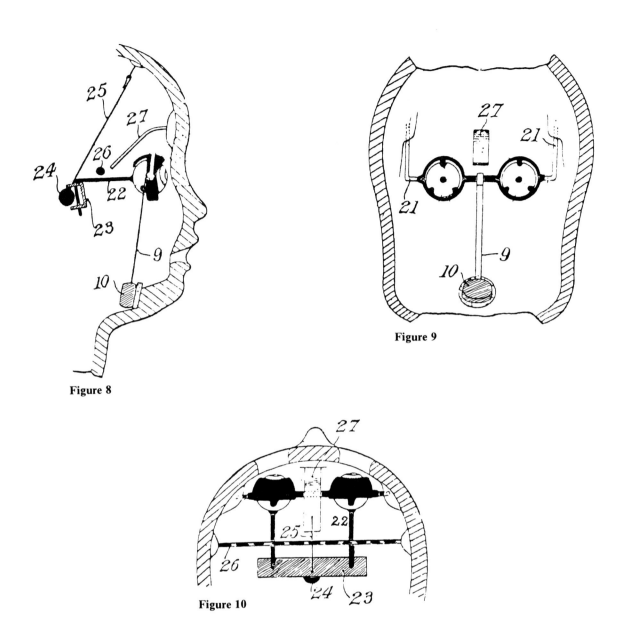

Figure 8

Figure 9

Figure 10

Drawings for patent No. 706,823.

No. 48,193

1st Addition
to Patent
No. 706,823

Gr 20 - Cl 1.

(Initial patent taken December 2, 1930)

Petitioned March 4, 1937 at 2:30 p.m. in Paris
Delivered July 20, 1937 — Published November 3, 1937

Sleeping *bébé*-toy

This addition is a highly complex work adapting hemispheric eyes to the assembly of the previous patent
simply by adding a half-sphere which remade the spheric eye.
The fact that the globe is a half sphere made the patent's author envisage a multitude of mechanical solutions.
We thought it well to reproduce them in totality.

In the initial patent, the eyes were made of glass-enameled globes; their spherical shape allowed them to be easily assembled in the "bridge-lids."

Actually one often replaced these enameled glass globes by a hemispheric shell of transparent, unbreakable material, decorated by a round printed or pastel piece of paper to imitate the iris and a coat of paint to imitate the white.

According to this addition, particular means can allow, without modification, use of the "bridge-lids" characteristic to the original patent.

(Figures 1, 2 and 3 are a first executed form, Figure 4 is a second form, Figures 5 and 6 a third form, Figures 7 and 8 a fourth form, Figures 9 and 10 a sixth form.)

On the drawings the lid-bridge is in each case made as described in the original patent, of two symmetrical pieces, each being formed of a cut metal blade which is stamped and folded to the form of a ring-shaped cage, making at its farthest end, the portion of a sphere forming the lid, on the inside, the lateral fastenings 6; these are connected to the fastenings of the opposite piece by a fork-joint on which is welded the counterweight's support which produces the eye movements when one inclines the *bébé*-toy.

The grudgeon pins 5 are held either in the head cavities or by the bent ends of a metallic clip attached to the interior by appropriate sealing.

According to the present addition, one uses eyes made of a transparent hemispheric shell, such as cellulose acetate, adorned on the inside by a round printed paper, and a coat of white paint. This rould piece can be glued directly on the shell on a transparent rubber patch sealed to the shell.

The different assemblings represented allow the disposition of the eyes, in such a manner in the bridge-lids, that they act as rolling and sleeping eyes, that is, they move laterally as well as up and down.

In the case of Figures 1 through 3, one adds to each half shell, another hemispheric shell of the same diameter in stamped metal or other material, not needing paint, and these shells are glued together to form a spherical globe which one can put in a cage in the same manner as spherical enameled glass eyes.

Each eye is held in its cage by appropriately bent fastenings on the outer edge; one gives the eye sufficient play so that it can turn freely in all directions.

The desired movements are made by a heavy piece 24 with swing 25 suspended to the interior of the head and passing through a hold in a crosspiece 23 that connects two stems with the eyes; the center of the two globes and the stem joints 22 with the crosspiece are placed at the top of a parallelogram which loses its shape according to the oscillations of the swing 25 such that the eyes oscillate laterally or roll.

Under this form, the swing 25 is suspended to the outer end bent to the stem 9a, sealed in the middle of the bridge-lids, and it forms a loop 25a at the place it crosses the crossbar 23 such that it plays the role of a push-rod forcing this crossbar to rise and fall on the horizontal, pivotal axis 5-5, when the *bébé*-toy is inclined backwards or forwards, which brings on the corresponding movements of the eyes through the stems 22.

The attachment of these latter to the respective eyes can be obtained by a wax or other sealing to the shells.

These stems can also be formed in one piece with the shells, by cutting.

Following Figure 4, the eye is made of a shell similar to the one described above, glued together with spherical or hemispheric wood ball, whose diameter corresponds to that of the stem 22 previously embedded in this ball. This eye lodges itself in a cage similar to the one in Figures 1 to 3 and is also held by the fasteners 7.

Instead of completing the shell with a hollow organ or filled with something, to form a spherical eye, one can assemble the shell in the cage and attach an axis 28 according to its vertical diameter, rolling up and down in this cage, as shown in Figures 5 to 10.

In Figures 5 and 6, the eye axes are connected by a transveral metallic thread 29 whose middle section is bent to form a long loop to guide stem 25 which carries the weight 24 and is suspended by a joint to arm 9a sealed in the middle to this bridge; this device, permitting the swing to oscillate sideways, commands the rolling of the eyes, from the fact that the stem 25 crosses a loop 23a in the middle of the crosspiece 23, which connects the two stems 22 locked with the eyes.

To attach each of these latter with the respective eye, in this example, a vertical tube sealed in the shell 8a, and over which axis 28 freely passes has been planned, then we inserted the bent end of the stem 22 in another little tube 28a one against the other. Tube 28a against the rubber patch 8b and the stem 22 against the tube 8f to form a rigid whole with the eye.

Figures 7 and 8 show another manner of attaching stems 22 according to which the end of each is simply embedded in a sealing matter poured into the shell. On the outside of this is glued a round piece 8h of the same diameter which reinforces it and holds it firmly on axis 28 hooked into the slots of this edge.

In the above examples, we planned a single swing 24, 25 to

produce the oscillation of eyes in a vertical as well as rolling manner, but it goes without saying that the original patent's device is equally applicable to the movement mentioned above.

Figures 9 and 10 show that one can also use two heavy masses, one 10 for the bridge-lid oscillations and the grudgeon pins 5, the other 24 for the lateral movements of the eyes in the cage, without using two swings. In this case, piece 10 is mounted on stem 9 sealed to the middle of the bridge-lids, but mass 24 is directly attached on the cross-piece 23 which connects stems 22 rigidly to the eyes; these are still mounted in their cages 1 and 1a on vertical axes 28, such that they move to the right or left depending on the direction mass 24 falls, when on inclines the baby sideways. The weight of this mass 24 adds its action to that of piece 10 to produce the whole oscillation of the bridge-lids and the eyes on the grudgeon pins 5-5.

30 designates a fixed fork on the middle part of the lids, to imitate the lateral movements of stems 22 and the crossbar 23.

Stems 22 and axes 28 can be fixed to the shells by a simple plastic or other sealing.

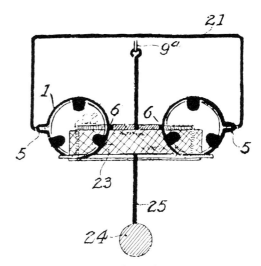

Figure 1

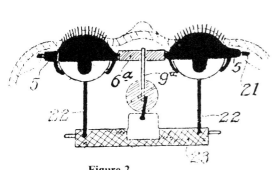

Figure 2

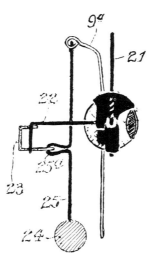

Figure 3

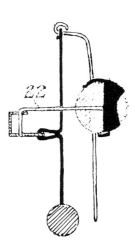

Figure 4

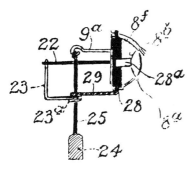

Figure 5

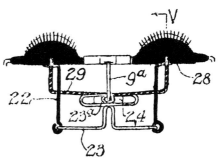

Figure 6

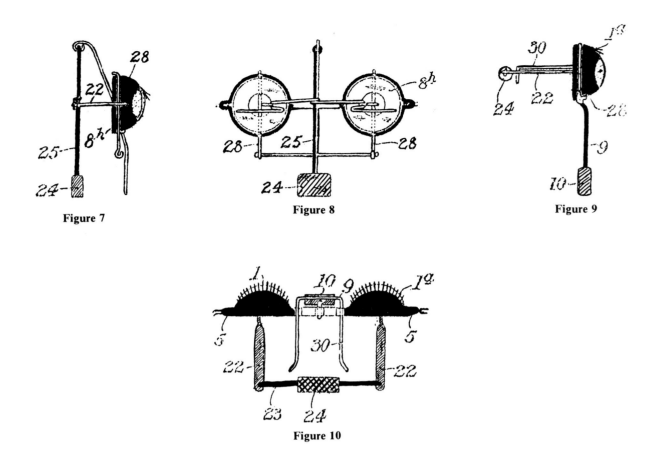

Figure 7

Figure 8

Figure 9

Figure 10

Illustrations for "sleeping *bébé*" patent number 48,193.

No. 798,847

Gr 20 — Cl 1.

Requested February 28, 1935 at 1:38 p.m. in Paris.
Delivered March 11, 1936 — Published May 27, 1936.

Improvements to doll heads

The originality of this patent lies in the fact the attachment of the eyes to the head is median and not lateral.
This patent puts an end to the beautiful glass eye.

This invention is to improve the production of doll heads, and more particularly the assembly of sleeping eyes.

Until now, the bearings, or other supporters, which held the eyes' horizontal axis, or the eyes themselves, are generally attached by seals applied to the internal walls of the head.

In cases where the heads are made of cardboard or other materials apt to lose their shape in humidity or dryness, this results in the spacing between these bearings varying with the weather sometimes causing the eyes to become too tight to turn easily and sometimes so loose they risk falling, especially when children push them with a finger.

According to this invention the eyes' axis is held only by its median part, by supports sealed to the middle portion of the inside wall of the head, such that the extremities of this axis and the eyes themselves are completely independent of the lateral walls of the head and their spacing. They thus invariably maintain their mobility and remain in correct position in a secure manner.

Several ways of carrying out the object of this invention are shown in the following drawings.

In each example, we assumed that the eyes were made with a round piece of transparent material on the inside of which the pupil and iris are painted, and which is then filled with plaster or another plastic material, in which one inserts either an axis or tube where the axis is designed to pass.

According to Figures 1 and 3, axis 3 on which the eyes had been spaced and attached, is mounted on a support made of a metal sheet 4, cut in such a way as to bear two clamps 5 and 6, and two prongs 7 erected parallel whose ends are forked to receive axis 3; the teeth of these forks are preferably turned back over this axis to completely prevent it from coming out. The spacing of prongs 7 is equal to or a bit less than the free interval between the eyes so that these cannot move sideways on their support. The clamps 5, 6 are placed against the middle part of the head and sealed with cement, glue, plaster or other material 8. The eyes are thus kept in place completely independent of the lateral walls of the head. Their ability to rotate is produced normally with a counterweight, axis 3 being mounted in prongs 7 with enough slack to turn freely. 10 shows a stem fixed across the head and limiting the oscillating movements of the counterweight.

To increase the solidity of the attachment on axis 3 a supplementary piece can be added 4a, also sealed to 8 and ending with a kind of yoke that encloses the middle of this axis.

Figures 3 and 4 show a variation of support 4, 5, 6, 7, different from the preceding in that the prongs 7 are pierced with holes to allow the passage of axis 3 instead of being cut like forks. In this case, one must naturally assemble the axis in its support before attaching the eyes to its ends.

In Figures 5 and 6 the support is made by a metal blade 11 which can be single or folded into double, and of which one end forms prong 12 designed to be sealed to the middle part of the head, and whose other end is bent back to form a casing around axis 3, its length being equal to the distance between the eyes.

Figures 7 and 8 show a case where the axis does not revolve and

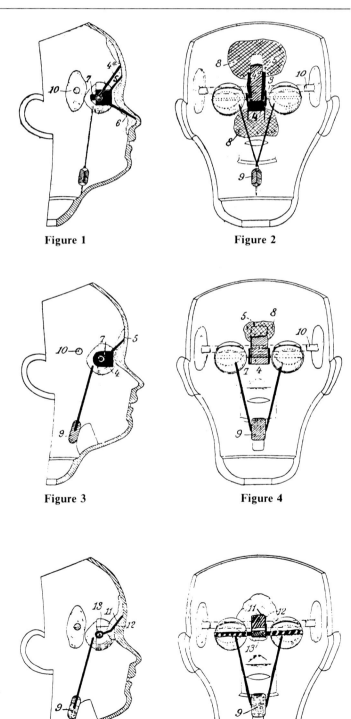

Figure 1   **Figure 2**

Figure 3   **Figure 4**

Figure 5   **Figure 6**

passes freely across tubes 14 fixed in the eyes. In this example, the entire axis and its support are made by a stem 15 bent to form, in the middle an attachment base, and on the ends, 2 prongs bent at a right angle towards the outside, and whose ends are aligned to serve as pivots for the eyes.

Naturally it is possible to conceive of other means of carrying this out with similar characteristics and offering similar advantages. Without diverging from the invention, one could vary the structure of the axis supports, joining them with auxiliary material to increase their solidity, vary their manner of attachment and the assembly details of the axes to their supports and in the eyes, etc.

In particular, should one use glass or enamel spherical oval shaped eyes, instead of eyes made of a round cap painted on the inside or out, it would be difficult to cut across these with the oscillation axis; in this case one could bend the axis so it goes around the back half of each eye to which it would be fixed in an appropriate manner. Despite this modification, the axis could be easily upheld by its median portion as in the preceding cases, this kind of bent axis could be used with eyes formed by a round cap, with or without glass, metal, or other filler.

It should be understood that instead of being sealed, the oscillation axis supports can be fixed to the wall of the head in any other appropriate manner, for example by embedding it in the wall thickness during the molding of the head.

Figures 7 and 8 show that the axis and the support can form one piece; in this example the axis is broken off in the middle. One could also use an imaginary axis, the eyes being thus upheld by two round caps or fixed rings forming bearings arranged between them and supported by the support sealed to the front wall of the head; the eyes would in this case be rigidly united by a stirrup-piece passing behind the round caps and support, this stirrup also being used to hold the counterweight 9.

In this variation, the eyes are free to oscillate around the common axis of the two caps, the imaginary axis which passes through the center of the eyes, and their assembly is still independent of the head's lateral walls.

The whole of the caps or rings forming bearings, can be compared to a hollow, fixed axis.

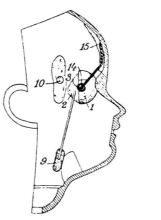

Figure 7   Figure 8

No. 351,422

XX — Articles from Paris and various industries
1. Games, Toys, Theaters, Races.

Petitioned on February 10, 1905.
Delivered on May 6, 1905 — Published on July 7, 1905.

Hooks for fixing of strings

In patents taken out for production procedures we go from very minute detail
(such as this one) to the most elaborate machine.

The present invention aims for a hook used in fixing elastic strings or others, subsistantly made of a metallic string bent or folded in a U shape, with prongs that could wrap around the string to be fixed or that could be flattened more or less tightly against the string.

At present, round smooth metallic string is being used for the manufacturing of these hooks, and the prongs of the hook have to be tightly flattened against the string to obtain a solid hold, so tight that often the string gets cut and thus minimizes or destroys the solidness wanted; this inconvenience arises particularly in fixing elastic strings used in the manufacturing of articulated toys.

The invention is to make this sort of hook with metallic thread that has a starred or toothed-section. Hooks with a grooved surface could also be obtained, and could be fixed on the strings with such a grip that the prongs only have to be slightly brought together to obtain a very solid assembly with the string pinched in between.

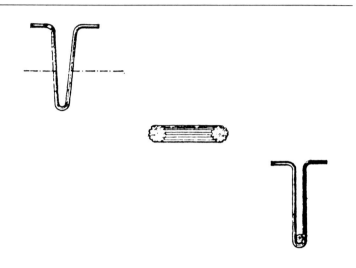

No. 351,423

XX — Articles from Paris and various industries
1. Games, Toys, Theaters, Races.

Petitioned on February 10, 1905.
Delivered on May 6, 1905 — Published on July 17, 1905.

Elastic assembly device for articulated toys

This second patent taken out the same day, at the same time as the previous one,
is for a hook with minute details.

At present an elastic string is used, going through the parts that have to be assembled, with the ends held back and flushing with the external surface by means of metallic hooks flattened upon that string. The length of the string is equal to the total thickness of all the parts through which it passes.

The present device is also made of an elastic string and metallic hooks but it saves considerable elastic string which costs a lot, by using a long hook that deeply passes through at least one of the parts to be assembled.

Hook f could first be fixed on one end of an elastic string a little longer than the one shown, by placing that end way inside the hoop of the hook and by flattening it appropriately; the opposite end of the string is then inserted through leg c, body a and leg b, then hook e is placed on the string, flushing with the external surface of leg b, the hook is flattened upon the string that finally gets cut.

In certain cases a long hook f could be fixed at each end of the string and that way could save twice the amount of elastic string.

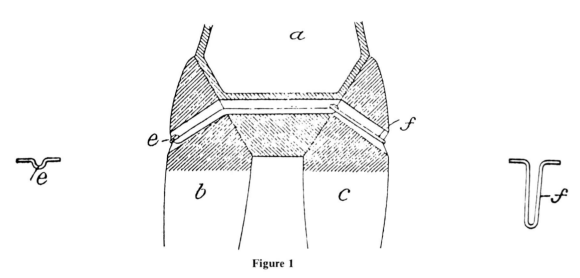

Figure 1

No. 479,798

XX — Articles from Paris and various industries.
1. Games, Toys, Theaters, Races.

Petitioned on September 21, 1915 at 3:46 p.m. in Paris.
Delivered on February 15, 1916 — Published on May 10, 1916.

Improvements in manufacturing dolls' heads and other porcelain objects

This patent reveals a lot about the working of porcelain:
it explains the plaster mold absorbing water from slip
and the stages transforming a dull clay into unglazed porcelain with delicate peachy pink tones.
The patent also shows the advantages of the pouring process over the molding process;
the pouring introduces the contemporary manufacturing of plastic, and the remarkable labor saving it ensures.
This patent also deals with the problem of holes and openings.

In the manufacturing of dolls heads and of other objects made of porcelain obtained through a molding process or so-called "pouring" process based on the fact that a plaster mold's walls absorb water of a china clay mixture poured into that mold and it is often necessary to cut up and manually shape the objects coming out of the mold, because they present a continuous surface similar to the mold. Internal walls are a constant thickness, while they should finally present, for their intended purpose, either openings or continuity solutions, or parts with reduced thickness, or portion of the internal surface with a strictly determined thickness or shape.

For example, in a doll's head that is supposed to have glass eyes, it is appropriate to make, for eye sockets, round holes and openings with a determined shape; for that purpose, openings are manually cut in the molded head made of raw china and clay, and the internal edge of those openings is bevelled; it is also appropriate to thin up certain parts of the lips and teeth by scratching or cutting the corresponding parts of the internal wall. This type of work is relatively long, costly, requires great deftness and could not be done too precisely. The same work is involved in making industrial or artistic porcelain parts that have to present open-work trimming or particular internal shapes.

According to the present invention, the previously mentioned inconvenience is being avoided by placing in the hole of the plaster mold, where openings or reduced thickness should be made, parts of non-absorbing material, e.g. of metal, that have a determined shape and position - either to lean against the corresponding part of the mold, if we are dealing with making an opening in the molded object — or to be located at a point on the mold wall, if we are dealing with limiting or increasing at that point the thickness of the china clay layer that is going to form there.

Without changing anything in the usual pouring operation, molded objects could be produced — presenting, at determined points of the openings reduced thickness or particular internal conforming, with the greatest precision and without needing any last minute retouching, if not very little.

Of course, the parts of non-absorbing material, for example called "counterparts" could be in various shapes, in whatever number, and held in place within the mold by all appropriate means.

a and b designate the two parts of a plaster mold that differs from the normal molds only in the added means of fixing for the counterparts, as described later.

c designates the clay head obtained by pouring clay mixture into the mold, letting part of the water soak in, pouring off the rest of the liquid clay, then, if necessary, starting the same procedure again until the head wall has the desired thickness.

According to the present invention, that wall is neither continuous nor uniformly thick because, before pouring, counterparts d ad e have been placed in the mold. Those counterparts are made of three embossed copper plates firmly assembled one to another by the tight prongs f, preferably cut and embossed from the same sheet as plates d and e, the set forming one part.

Counterparts d have a shape of a spherical segment and make openings and eye sockets; part of their convex surface comes to fit exactly on the corresponding part of the mold's internal surface, so that there would not be any clay deposit in the entire area, and that the molded object takes shape of a level edged gap between the mold wall and the contour of counterparts d, giving the desired reduced thickness to the eyelids and accommodates the apporpirate surfaces for the lodging of glass eyes.

As for counterpart e, equally convex, it is placed behind the upper lip, with the lower part leaning against a protusion a in the mold, corresponding to the gap between the lower lip and the upper teeth, so that there would not be any clay deposit in that gap; above protrusion a', the space allowed between the mold wall and plate e is very small, so that the teeth formed by clay deposit in that gap would be as thin as desired.

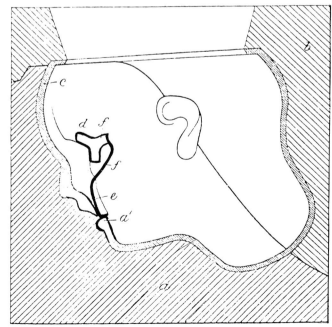

Figure 1

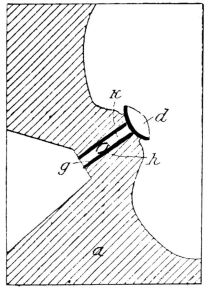

Figure 2

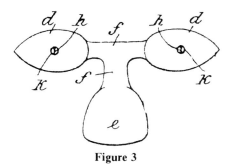

Figure 3

Illustrations for patent No. 479,798 - improvements in manufacturing dolls' heads.

No. 23,399

1st Addition
to the Patent for Invention
No. 479,798

XX — Articles of Paris and diverse industries
1. Games, Toys, Theaters, Races.

(Principal patent dated September 21, 1915)

Requested August 3, 1920 at 9 minutes past 3 o'clock in Paris.
Issued June 15, 1921 — Published November 16, 1921.

Perfecting the manufacture of doll's heads and other porcelain objects

This is a detail almost forgotten in the principal patent, but appearing five years later.

The aim of the present addition is the substitution of the non-absorbent metal "counterpieces" for counterpieces of a more appropriate form, composed of a plastic similar to porcelain-clay, so that the water absorbed by the clay may also be absorbed, at the same time, by the plaster-mold and the "counterpiece."

This "counterpiece," placed in the desired position before the molding, is removed at the same time as the object which is molded and, if left in place, the counterpiece will fall off of its own accord and dry.

The "counterpiece" may be constituted, for example, of a mixture of aluminum clay and vegetable oil, with the addition of water, for moisture and cohesion.

By way of example, the proportions may be as follows:
Aluminum clay 1/2
Vegetable oil 1/4
Water 1/4

These proportions are, however, variable depending on the nature of the plaster/clay used for the molding and on the desired effects.

It should be understood that the method of making and fixing the "counterpiece" may be varied, according to the needs, without greatly deviating from the essential features of this invention.

No. 480,695

XX — Articles of Paris and diverse industries.
1. Games, Toys, Theaters, Races.

Requested January 17, 1916 at 3:30 p.m. in Paris
Issued June 16, 1916 — Published September 7, 1916.

Perfecting the manufacture of dolls' heads and other "papier-mâché" objects.

This is a document which is a little difficult for the amateur to understand but which is of considerable technical interest.
It concerns the molding of the "papier-mâché" in one single piece.
The core is fragmented in such a way as to be easily extracted after the molding process.

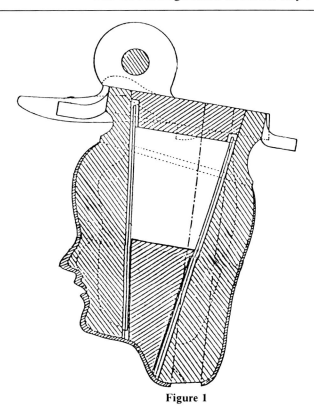

Figure 1

At the present time, the fabrication of dolls' heads and other limbs or detachable pieces of toys or even toys made of plaster (claimed to be "unbreakable"), involves the use of metallic molds. These metal molds, which function either hot or cold, only allow the removal of the mold with regard to the core, in as far as these objects consist of neither counter-relief nor an inner surface of variable thickness.

In order to have counter-relief or these portions of varying thickness within the interior of an object made of one single piece, it is necessary to mold these objects in two parts and then to assemble them with glue, or any other suitable method. As a consequence, this process requires extra labor, considerable ability and rigorous precision on the part of the workman.

Such inconveniences are avoided with the use of the present invention, which involves a core composed of several parts. The lines along which the parts are assembled are at angles more or less closed, which gives the various pieces making up the core, by virtue of their relative displacement, reduced dimensions; this allows the core to pass through the orifice of the mold and, consequently, through the opening of the molded piece tiself; thus this piece may be molded in one single piece, consisting of all counter-relief and the desired variable thicknesses, to the extent of obtaining the reduction in dimensions.

No. 578,765

XX — Articles from Paris and various industries
1.   Games, Toys, Theaters, Races.

Petitioned on March 15, 1924 at 2:41 p.m. in Paris.
Delivered on July 11, 1924 — Published on October 3, 1924.

Improvements on manufacturing dolls and other toys

This patent presents an interesting in-depth study on choice of materials,
their durability and their decorative value.
The aim of the invention is to unite the material to the dough.

The invention aims to bring an improvement to the manufacturing of certain parts of dolls and of other toys through molding. The manufacturing of dolls' heads has long been done, preferably by hot molding of plastic dough of various composition, that hardens when cooling off and drying. As far as dolls' heads are concerned, the drawback is that the dough is not ready for decoration by painting. Way back then, the heads were made of materials that were given appropriate shape by way of embossing with heat, as done in manufacturing masks. Each system has its pros and cons. The head of molded plastic presents a great hardness; it keeps its shape without any stuffing and is made of a rather resistant material, in order to fit certain mechanical parts, such as sleeping eyes that close by an oscillation system. The heads made of embossed materials can take artistic decoration better, and modern dolls with characteristic expression are made of the latter materials.

But on the other hand, the latter materials lack stiffness, and the heads have to be stuffed to keep their shape. Besides they can't hold any mechanism, and can't be fitted with sleeping eyes.

The invention aims to combine in a doll's head all the advantages of both systems mentioned above; it is made of a head molded from plastic, a mask of some material (felt, linen, silk, etc.) will be applied to the head. The adapting is perfect, considering that the same molds could be used for corresponding parts made of dough or material.

First, a head is made from plastic, a mixture of paper, sawdust and glue, poured hot in normal molds, that hardens up by compacting, cooling off and drying up. The same mold serves to emboss an identical head, on the material directly applied to it or, lined with linen, this head is glued to the first one: this application is done better on the mold itself. A head with the outside made of fabric could take different decorations and more sophisticated expressions. The essential shape is, however, in the hard material itself. It keeps its shape without the stuffing, this allows the lodging of mechanical systems such as the sleeping eyes. Besides, it could lodge any other mechanical device such as small record-players, talking devices, voices etc.

Of course the invention is not exclusively limited to dolls' heads; it could be applied to any body part which requires the stiffness without stuffing in order to fit mechanical parts or voices, and the ability to be easily painted for decoration on the outside. The same process could be used in making animals or other toys. The characteristics are the same: combining two parts identically molded, the external one made of material the internal one of solidified plastic.

Numéro 149

Marques

BÉBÉ JUMEAU

BÉBÉ BRU

ÉDEN BÉBÉ

Etc., Etc.

Fabrication Générale

DE

BÉBÉS NUS ET HABILLÉS, RICHES ET ORDINAIRES

COSTUMES PAYS DIVERS

TROUSSEAUX, MALLES GARNIES

SOCIÉTÉ FRANÇAISE

DE

Fabrication de Bébés et Jouets

◆◆◆◆◆◆◆◆◆◆◆

Société Anonyme au Capital de 4.467.000 frs

◆◆◆◆◆◆◆◆◆

SIÈGE SOCIAL

8, Rue Pastourelle, 8

............**PARIS (3ᵉ)**............

Téléphone : ARCHIVES 32-79

┌──── U S I N E S ────┐

160, Rue de Picpus, 160
————PARIS (12ᵉ)————

6, Rue Montempoivre, 6
————PARIS (12ᵉ)————

152, Rue de Paris, 152
MONTREUIL - sous - BOIS

11, Avenue Pasteur, 11
MONTREUIL - sous - BOIS

8, Rue Pastourelle, 8
————PARIS (3ᵉ)————

CHAMPIGNEULLES
(Meurthe - et - Moselle)

In: *Annuaire de la Chambre Syndicale des Fabricants Français de Jeux et Jouets*, 1932.

Bibliography

Books

Broquelet, A.: *Manuel du fabricant de Jouets* — Paris — Bibliothèque Professionnelle 1922.

Calmettes, Pierre: *Les Joujoux* — G. Doin — Paris 1924.

Capia, Robert: *Les Poupées Françaises* — Hachette — Paris 1979.

Cieslik, Jürgen and Marianne: *Les Poupées Anciennes et Puppon Handhich* — 1979-1980.

Claretie, Léo: *Les Jouets de France* — Delagrave — Paris 1920.

Coleman, Dorothy, Elizabeth and Evelyn: *The Collector's Encyclopedia of Dolls* — Robert Hale 1968.

Coleman, Dorothy, Elizabeth and Evelyn: *The Collector's Book of Dolls Clothes* — Robert Hale 1976.

Cooper, Marlowe: *S.F.B.J. French Characters* — Doll Home Library Series - Vol. 1 — 1969.

D'Allemagne, Henry-René: *Histoire des Jouets* — Hachette — Paris 1902.

Du Maroussem, P.: *La Question Ouvrière - Le Jouet Parisien* — Paris — Arthur Rousseau 1894.

Hart, Luella: *Complete French Doll Directory* (1801-1964) — U.S.A. 1965.

Ingram, Denys: *Toys, Dolls, Games* — Paris 1903-1914 — U.K. 1981.

King, Constance Eileen: *The Collector's History of Dolls* — Robert Hale — London 1977.

Porot, Anne-Marie: *Les Poupées caractère de la S.F.B.J.* 1980.

Porot, Jacques: *Poupées articulées* — *Brevets d'invention* 1850-1925 — Paris 1982.

Porot, Jacques: *Les Poupées, ce qu'il y a dedans* — *Etude anatomique et biomécanique* — Paris 1982.

Selfridge, Jim and Madalaine: *Dolls Images of Love* - Volume 1 — U.S.A. 1973.

Theimer, François: *Madame le poupée Bleuette* — Editions Polichinelle — Paris 1982.

White, Gwen: *Toys, Dolls, Automatons Marks and Labels* — Batsford 1975.

Whitton, Margaret: *The Jumeau Doll* — Dover Publications 1980.

Magazines

Avenel, Georges: Jouets Français contre Jouets Allemands — in: Revue des Deux Mondes — Paris May 15, 1915.

Barrington, David and Jo: Doll in Profile — *Toy and Doll* No. 10. — 1981.

Bossi, Georges: Bimbelotiers et Poupeliers — in: *Bulletin de la Société des Amis du Vieux Montreuil* — October 1981.

Douin, Jeanne: La Renaissance de la Poupée Française — *Gazette des Beaux-Arts* — 1914-1916.

Du Maroussem, Pierre: L'évolution du Jouet Parisien — in: *L'Oeuvre Economique* — December 25, 1916.

Fémina — Paris No. 23 — January 1, 1902.

La Revue du Jouet: 1960 "Les plus anciennes maisons Françaises."

L'Art Français Moderne: Les Jouets de France — September 1916.

Archives

Archives du Tribunal de Commerce de Paris.

Department Store Catalogs and Commercial Address Books

Annuaires de la Chambre Syndicale des Fabricants de Jouets, Jeux et Articles de Sports: 191? — 1922 — 1929.

Annuaires du Commerce: 1890 à 1958.

Catalogues:

Au Bon Marché — Paris 1902 — 1913 à 1926 — 1931 — 1933 — 1937 — 1938.

Aux Classes Laborieuses — Paris 1908 — 1913.

Au Coin Musard — Coulommiers — 1913.

Au Printemps — Paris 1907 — 1908 — 1909 — 1920 — 1922 — 1925 — 1928 — 1929 — 1930 — 1935 — 1937 — 1938.

Aux Trois Quartiers — Paris 1906 — 1923 — 1929.

Bazar de l'Hôtel de Ville — Paris 1929 — 1931 — 1933 — 1935 — 1937 — 1938.

Galeries Lafayette — Paris 1912 — 1934 — 1937.

Gerbaulet Frères — Paris 1912.

Grands Magasins de la Place Clichy — Paris 1903.

Grands Magasins des Nouvelles Galeries: A la Ménagère — Paris 1911 — 1912.

Grands Magasins de la Ville de Saint-Denis — Paris 1903 — 1910 — 1911 — 1914.

Louvre — Paris 1913 — 1914 — 1917 — 1921 — 1922 — 1929 — 1934 — 1936 — 1938.

Maison du Petit Saint-Thomas — Paris 1901 — 1902 — 1906.

Old England — Paris 1934.

Pygmalion — Paris 1903 — 1929.

Samaritaine — Paris 1906 — 1909 à 1916 — 1922 — 1924 — 1925 — 1926 — 1927.

Le Jouet Français: organe professionnel des fabricants de jouets, jeux - revue trimestrielle 1949 à 1958 — Paris

Exhibitions

Catalogue de l'Exposition: Jouets Français 1880-1980 — Musée des Arts Décoratifs — Paris November 1982 — February 1983.

Exposition Universelle Internationale — Paris 1900 — Rapport du jury international — Groupe XV, Classe 98 à 100 par Léo Claretie.

Exposition Universelle et Internationale de Liège 1905 — Section française Classe 100 — Rapport par Alexis Chauvin — 1906.

Exposition franco-britannique de Londres 1908 — Section française Groupe XV — Classe 100 — Rapport par J. du Serre Telmon.

Exposition Internationale des Arts Décoratifs et Industriels Modernes — Paris 1925 — Rapport général des Jeux, Jouets, Instruments et appareils de Sports par Paul Léon — Librairie Larousse 1928.

Exposition internationale des Arts et Techniques — Paris 1937 —Rapport général Groupe IX — Classe 48 par Gaston Decamps.

Glossary

Annuaire du Commerce — Annual compilation of producers and businesses, created and regularly updated by Didot-Bottin Printers in Paris since the beginning of the 19th century. It contains a great deal of information on the manufacturers of various periods, including their specialties and addresses.

Anthropometry — The science and technique of human measurements, specifically of anatomical and physiological features; also, the analysis and interpretation of the data so obtained. Such measurements can be made from photographs provided the scale is identical.

bébé — A term designating dolls which represent a young child.

bébés dits nus — Dolls which were sold wearing only a chemise and shoes. The idea originated with Danel.

Bébé Marchant — Refers to a doll with a walking body.

bébé marcheur — A walking doll.

bébé pâte — *Pâte* meaning paste, this term refers to inexpensive doll bodies made of molded composition. Also called "*en pâte.*"

bébé articulé incassable — Unbreakable, articulated baby dolls.

bébé tête mobile — A doll with a removable head, such as that made by Bouchet.

bouche à dents — Refers to dolls which have an open mouth and teeth.

bté SGDG — *Patented san gurantie de gouvernment,* without guarantee of the government.

brevet — Trademark.

carton — In the production of dolls and toy animals, *carton* (cardboard or pasteboard) is used in two ways: first, moistened sheets pressed by hand or machine into a mold, or second, a paste (*carton-pâte*) which may or may not have an additive and which is molded with heat, similar to composition or papier-mâché.

carton-pate — Papier-mache.

carton-moule — pasteboard.

caractère — Used to describe dolls which have faces with a lifelike expression.

Chambre Syndicale des Fabricants des Jouets — A union of French manufacturers with article Francais (French product) as their trademark in 1886.

chemise garnie dentelle — Lace trimmed shirts worn by dolls.

corps du charactere — Refers to the bodies used on the character dolls.

depose — registered

De Vaucanson chain — A type of chain, named for its inventor, which was simply constructed with each link made of a single strand of bent metal. It was used in the mechanism of the S.F.B.J. walking doll originated by Fleischmann.

dormeurs — sleeping eyes

en pâte — Like *bébé pâte*, refers to an inexpensive type of semi-articulated composition doll.

entierement articule — fully-articulated doll bodies.

'hors de serie — A "special model" doll, such as *Bleuette*.

incassable — Translates as "unbreakable" and indicates that the doll was manufactured in a non-fragile material or that the doll body was assembled in a way that made it more durable and more easily repaired. The word was used by French manufacturers during the last third of the 19th century to specifically designate dolls made of separate pieces, strung with elastic bands that, consequently, were shock-resistant and in case of breakage, could be restored to their original form. Some materials used for dolls were originally unbreakable due to their flexibility but became extremely fragile as it ages, gutta-percha for example.

lavables — means "Washable."

loto ball eyes — From the French expression, *yeux en boules de loto*, it means eyes which are round in shape — such as toad eyes or chameleon eyes.

l'union des Fabricants de Jouets — Toy Manufacturers Union which filed *Jouets Francais* as trademark in 1884.

l'union Inter-Syndicale — The Manufacturers Trade Union.

maison — House or firm, as the Maison Jumeau, manufacturing business.

marcheurs — Walking dolls.

marchant — Walking.

marque d'origine — An origin label to authenticate French products.

marque deposée — Registered trademark.

mignonnette-pâte — A small doll with a composition body.

Modelé Extra — An extra model doll.

merchant — In the doll and toy business the merchant might refer to the manufacturer as well as to the middle-man between the manufacturer and the buyer.

open-closed mouth — A doll mouth with parted lips where the opening does not communicate with the interior of the head.

palpebral furrow — Referring to the eyelid.

pâte — translates "paste" and refers to heat-molded cardboard such as was used in the third *Bambino*.

poupard — A baby doll having non-articulated legs and arms either articulated or non-articulated at the shoulder. Generally made of *carton-pâte*.

poupée — Originally, a rigid or semi-articulated figure that represented an older girl or woman. From 1855 to 1900 it referred to a little girl or lady doll. The term was not used commercially after 1900 for bisque dolls, but was used for felt or fabric dolls.

poupon — A term used for a small doll which represented a newborn or young baby with bent limbs. This was a new term in 1928 when it was applied to *Bambino*.

Rhodoid — A material used for dolls and toys which was similar to celluloid but much less flammable. A type of cellulose acetate, it was named after the Rhone factories where it was made.

robe Jumeau — The flowered chemise worn by Jumeau and S.F.B.J. dolls up until 1925.

rotule — In human anatomy, a small, flat movable bone over the knee, visible beneath the skin, the kneecap. In dolls, the manufacturers simulated the kneecap by a light relief on the upper part of the leg. Certain manufacturers used the term *rotule* for what is now known as ball articulation.

sans nettete — Refers to the blurred red "Jumeau" stamp mark found on dolls.

semi-articule bébé — Inexpensive dolls with no wrist joints, usually dressed in ethnic costumes or uniforms.

SGDG — *San gurantie du gouvernment*, without guarantee of the government.

tête — Head.

têteur — A nursing doll.

tout articulé bébé — A doll with a fully-articulated body.

General Index

Molds

Patents Index